GW01605505

NORTHERN HERITAGE

Peter Winter

David Milne

Jonathan Brown

Alan Rushworth

NEWCASTLE UPON TYNE

Published by Northern Heritage Consultancy Ltd.
Princes Building
7 Queen Street
Newcastle upon Tyne

First published 1989

Design: Duncan MacDonald

Reproduction by V & H Reprographics, Newcastle

Printed and bound in Scotland by The Eagle Press plc, Glasgow

ISBN: 1 872346 00 6 Cloth bound edition
1 872346 01 4 Paper bound edition

NEWCASTLE UPON TYNE

Contents.

Acknowledgements.

We are indebted to many people. We must first thank the Newcastle Central Library local studies section where many long hours were spent poring over texts, the staff were always generous with their time and patient with our frequently cryptic enquiries. We must single out Mrs P. Sheldon who has spent many long hours sifting through piles of photographs and prints in the local studies collection on our behalf. Bruce Jackson and the study room staff at Tyne and Wear Archives and Mel Twelves of the Tyne and Wear Museums Service have also helped find illustrations for the book and made them available for our use. Dr Neil Christie of the Dept. of Archaeology at Newcastle University also helped with illustrations in the early chapters. We must also thank Mick Stephenson of Lightlines for taking the front cover shot; Mick Muse for other photographs and advice; and Mr Robinson of Dog Leap Antiques for finding a number of prints for our use.

The project has received generous support over the past year from Alistair Christie, and the staff at NRCDA. Financial support has come from Entrust and British Coal Enterprise - we are grateful to David Tulip and Doreen Matheson for organising this - and also from Harry and May Milne, Brenda Brown and Kev. Margaret McCullagh of MMR Market Research has given us useful advice. Nigel Nwosu-Hope and Mike Pedersen of Public Access Terminals have given us much of their valuable time and experience. Thanks must also go to the staff at the QBDC and Hubert of V & H Reprographics.

Colm O'Brian, Director of the Archaeology Unit for N. E. England, has helped with discussion of problematic points regarding the archaeology of Newcastle. Drafts of the text have also been read over by Susan Lamb, Liz Cundick, A G and G Kerr, Robert Rosslyn, Danny Smith, Elaine McB, and Judith Evans who have helped fine tune the copy.

Lastly a special thanks to Pam Scott for the patience of all the late nights; Alison Kerr and her beer vouchers; Ritchie; Col. Jim Porter for inspiration; Sid James; and, for no apparent reason, Ruth and Chris.

Pictures

Museum of Antiquities p. 9, 10, 12, 15, 17(margin), 24(brooch), 30, 31, (with B. Harbottle) 37. Bibliothèque National Paris p. 57. Bodleian Library p. 22. British Library p. 43. Rachel Burch p. 23. Newcastle Central Library p. 27, 29, 33, 46, 52, 53, 54, 58/59, 61, 62, 66, 71, 75, 76/77, 78, 79, 84, 89, 90, 91, 92, 99 - 107, 109, 111, 113, 116, 118 (margin), 120, 123 - 125, 127, 128, 130, 131 (margin), 134 - 139, 140 (margin), 143, 146, 149, 151, 152, 154, 155, 156, 159 (RVI), 161 (Elswick), 162, 163, 170, 171, 173, 174 (inset) 176, 180 (insets), 189 (St. James). Newcastle City Engineers Department p. 3, 178, 193. Alastair Christie p. 53 Stephen Cope p. 49, 86. Corbridge Roman Museum p. 20(margin), 23(margin). John Coulson p. 11. Dog Leap Antiques p. 114, 158, 159, 161. Dougie p. 189, 190. filmNOVA p 188 (inset). William Henry p. 7, 9, 16, 25, 33(map), 36, 41. Lloyds Bank, Grey Street p. 98. Lord Mayor's Office p. 121. Mick Stephenson of Lightlines - Front cover. Graeme Mitchell p. 14, 38, 45 (inset) 70, 73. Mick Muse p. 140. National Museums of Scotland p. 32. NEI p. 191. North Tyneside Archives p. 172. Photo Mayo p. 129. The Side Gallery p. 169, 174/175(main picture). Tyne and Wear Archives p. 51, 87, 145, 147, 148, 153, 165 - 167, 172. Vickers Defence Systems p. 176-177. The following were reproduced by permission of Tyne and Wear Museum Service: From the collection of the Laing Art Gallery p. 2, 65, 98, 130, 132/133; From the collection of the Joicey Museum p. 93, 96, 131.

Introduction.

"We wonder what blockhead first built Newcastle". Today few would share the opinion of this forgotten nineteenth century writer. The impressive nature of Newcastle's riverside site may be readily appreciated by the modern visitor arriving from the south by rail. As the train slows to cross the King Edward VII Bridge the traveller is greeted by a dramatic view up and down the deep valley carved by the River. Straightaway, the image which perhaps more than any other symbolises Newcastle, the six bridges, leaves a lasting mark on the newcomer's mind. In front lies the city itself, with building piled upon building as it clambers up the steep slope.

At a glance these impressive structures dispel preconceived notions of decay and dereliction, exciting the curiosity of even the most blasé visitor. Foremost among these is the 'new castle' itself, the dark, glowering form of its rectangular keep towering above the Quayside and dominating the northern approaches to the magnificent Central Station, as though still standing guard over the city.

This book explores the story behind this striking panorama - the history of Newcastle from its origins as a Roman bridgehead to the Quayside renaissance of the present day.

It is fitting that the castle and bridges should be so prominent today. These two elements - the river crossing and the need to defend it - are dominant factors in the early history of Newcastle. Nevertheless, as the book reveals, this single image fails to do justice to the rich diversity of the city. It was as a port and a centre of commerce that Newcastle rose to prominence in the Middle Ages.

However, perhaps the grandest of the city's bequests from the past is the classical townscape of Grainger and Dobson. Matching this architectural splendour was Tyneside's contribution to the Industrial Revolution. In shipbuilding, coal mining and railway expansion the region became a world-leader.

The twentieth century has brought mixed fortunes. Two World Wars left deep human scars inflamed by the intervening recession which signalled the end of Tyneside's industrial supremacy. This era too left imposing new landmarks - not only the Tyne Bridge but also the reshaping of Pilgrim Street, and the Co-operative Building on Newgate Street. All this pales by comparison with the massive - and still controversial - phase of redevelopment launched in the 1960's.

It is not simply the aim of the book to dwell on the past, however glorious it may be. Rather it is hoped it may in a small way contribute to the growing sense of pride and confidence in Newcastle and its region. There is much to be proud of in the city of today. Fine buildings crowd the view on every side as baroque exuberance jostles for position amidst classical grandeur. The view down the subtle curve of Grey Street, crowned by the exquisite fifteenth century lantern tower of St. Nicholas cathedral, is surely one of Europe's outstanding architectural vistas. There are still some eyesores, many sadly of recent origin, but projected schemes point the way forward to a bright and pleasant city.

Nevertheless, Newcastle's greatest asset is its people, who remain no less resourceful than their ancestors. The Geordie has had to endure many blows in recent years as recession and unemployment have once again scarred the North-East, so much so that a spirit of optimism might seem out of place to many readers. There is, however, an upsurge of rebuilding underway at last, especially on the Quayside. The future doubtless holds many new challenges but few who are aware of the pinnacles of achievement scaled in the past, despite great obstacles, will believe that revival is impossible. Newcastle has the potential to become once more a powerhouse for the growth of the entire region and take its rightful place amongst the ranks of the greatest European cities.

The Bridgehead.

Setting the Scene

The earliest settlers moved into the Tyne Valley roughly eight thousand years ago, after the last Ice Age had finally retreated. They depended on hunting, fishing and gathering nuts and berries for their livelihood. As a result, coastal sites seem to have been especially favoured by these Mesolithic (Middle-Stone Age) people. River valleys such as the Tyne were used to follow the herds of wild deer and cattle from the lowlands up on to the hills for summer grazing; so even at this early date the area was witness to human activity.

Around 4000 BC a new wave of settlers began to move into the area, the earliest farming communities. Using stone tools they began to scratch a living off the land, clearing vast tracts of the forest that then covered Britain. Progress was not uniform. A worsening climate seems to have brought about a major setback around 1000 BC. Much of the uplands were abandoned leading to increased pressure on the remaining land and greater conflict between communities. The age of the warrior had arrived, cattle raiding and head-hunting were rampant.

Technology slowly but surely improved over this long period. Metal-working was introduced, first bronze then iron. Great building projects were executed, requiring a huge effort in terms of manpower and demonstrating not only a well-organised society but also great skill in carpentry, stoneworking and earth-moving. The earliest farmers concentrated on ritual structures. They built long burial mounds, perhaps indicating an obsession with their ancestors whose presence defined their own right to the land, and enigmatic circular religious enclosures, such as stone circles and henges. The latter may reflect the dominance of a priestly nobility. Later on, in the first millennium BC, many hilltops were crowned by massive stone ramparts protecting the homes and cattle wealth of a Celtic warrior aristocracy.

Towards the end of the first century AD, the area was dominated by the great Celtic tribe, the Brigantes. The heartland of Brigantia lay much further south in the Vale of York but the tribe dominated the whole of Northern England, being surrounded by a cluster of small satellite tribes. The Tyne may have formed the northern edge of their territory as the river is a strong barrier, being difficult to ford below Corbridge.

Settlement on both sides of the Tyne was typically Brigantian, consisting of occasional hillforts and numerous scattered farmsteads. In stark contrast the pattern further north on the Cheviot foothills was very different. There numerous small, but very heavily defended, hillforts were the norm. This was the land of the Votadini, whose ter-

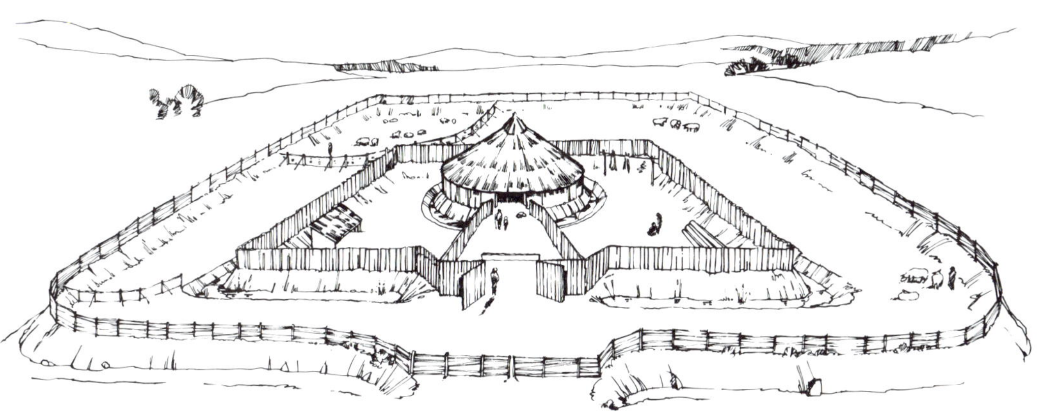

A typical Brigantian farmstead of the time of the Roman Conquest, as reconstructed by William Henry.

Chapter 1

ritory also included the Lothians area around Edinburgh. It may be that the frontier between the two tribes lay in central Northumberland, placing the Tyne Valley firmly in Brigantia.

Most people at this time were peasant farmers, producing food for themselves and a surplus for the Brigantian warrior nobility entrenched in their hillforts. In addition a few craftsmen, such as metal-workers and carpenters, met the other needs of the aristocracy and may have lived alongside them in the hillforts.

For the bulk of the population home would have been a small timber farmstead, consisting of one or more round houses within an enclosure, surrounded by a stout fence of wooden stakes. How many such settlements there were in the area of modern-day Newcastle is difficult to say, but it is very unlikely that such a favourable lowland site, overlooking a major river crossing, was totally unoccupied.

This, then, was the scene around AD 70. A shadow was, however, already looming over this northern Celtic world. Disputes over who should lead the tribal confederation gradually sucked the Brigantian nobility into the arms of their giant neighbour to the south, the mighty and still expanding Roman Empire.

Roman Occupation.

The New Frontiers

In AD 71 the Roman army marched north. Despite vigorous resistance, the Brigantes were overwhelmed within ten years of fierce warfare. The Romans do not seem to have made use of Newcastle's favourable site straight away. Instead, they bridged the Tyne higher up the valley at Corbridge and then pressed onward into Scotland aiming at total conquest of the island. Under the governor Agricola, the Roman armies were victorious in the field, inflicting a crushing defeat on the Caledonian tribes in a final battle at *Mons Graupius*. It seemed that nothing could prevent Roman Scotland becoming a reality.

Roman legionaries in battle pose

It was not to be. Problems on other frontiers, on the Rhine and above all on the Danube, began to drain the province of troops. There was no alternative but to begin the withdrawal from these newly occupied lands. By the year AD 100 the soldiers were back on a line running coast to coast from the Tyne to the Solway. It was still there seventeen years later when a new Emperor came to the throne, Hadrian. Newcastle may be said to owe its foundation to the vision of this ruler.

Hadrian succeeded to the imperial throne in AD 117 after a career spent campaigning on the frontiers in the service of his predecessor Trajan. The drain on the

Hadrian, on a coin discovered in the Tyne at Newcastle.

Empire's resources, both in manpower and taxes, posed by Trajan's wars seems to have had a profound impact on Hadrian. He abandoned the old dream of total world domination, until then a central plank of Roman propaganda. Imperial advance had in any case been slowing down over the previous century. The Empire was already vast, far larger in relation to the communications and technology of the day than any modern state. It could take weeks, even months in winter when sea-borne travel was hazardous, for messages to get from the capital to the more remote provinces. The task of holding it together was immense; capable Emperors had to be workaholics. The world was now known to be a much bigger place than it had seemed only a hundred years earlier. Roman maps had improved and contacts with distant lands, such as China, had been established. Sooner or later a halt would have to be called.

Hadrian grasped the nettle. If a halt had to be called some day why not now? He abandoned hard won but indefensible lands in the East. This was despite the unpopularity of this policy with Trajan's old generals, who saw it as a sign of weakness and were still eager for military glory. He was convinced that the Empire contained all the best territory and so was determined to set up permanent frontiers, marked by great rivers, deserts and mountains. Where no such natural frontiers existed he built walls or wooden palisades, along which were stationed large garrisons.

The greatest of these man-made frontiers was built in Britain and is now known as Hadrian's Wall. In AD 122 Hadrian visited the province and probably spent much time designing the huge project, poring over maps with his generals, inspecting the lie of the land with military surveyors and working out the best route. Everything would have to be planned in meticulous detail. Its eastern terminal was to be located at the lowest point down the river that was narrow enough to allow a bridge to be built. The bridge was named *Pons Aelius* - Aelius' Bridge - in honour of Hadrian, Aelius being his family name. Thus was Newcastle born, a small but important detail in the complex military strategy of a great Empire.

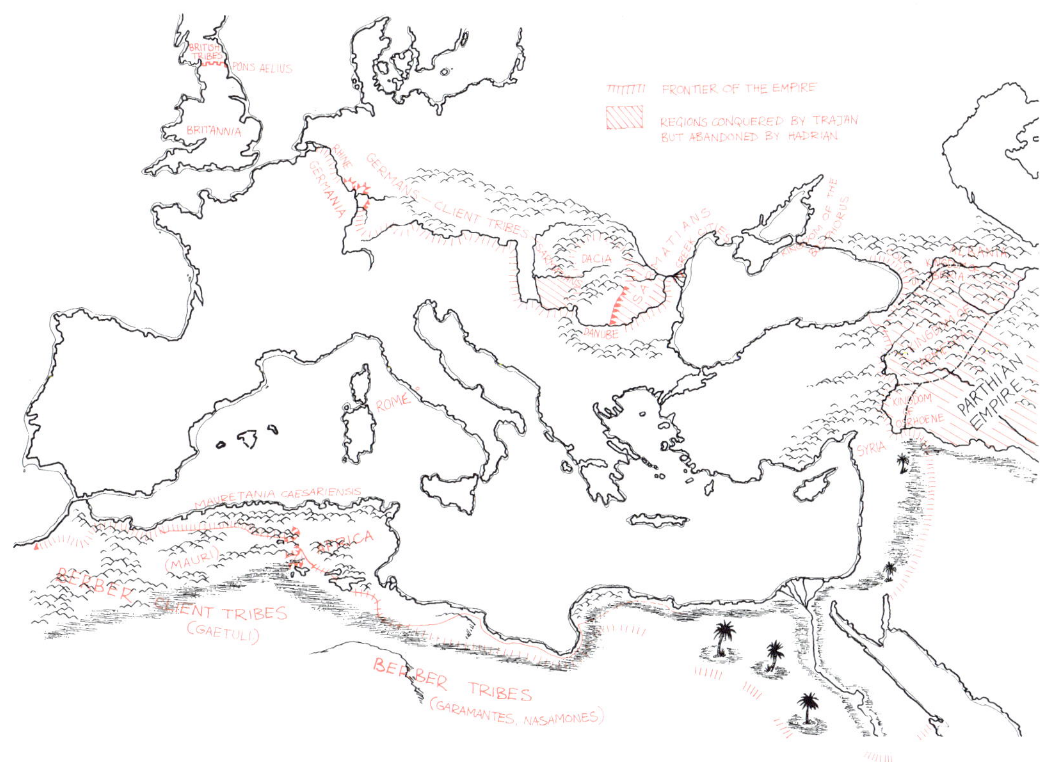

A map of the Roman Empire during the reign of Hadrian showing his new frontiers and the territories he abandoned.

Hadrian's Wall.

This mighty barrier consisted of a stone wall in the east and a turf wall in the west. The stone wall was ten feet wide and probably fifteen feet high. Small fortlets protected gateways at intervals of one Roman mile along its length. Between each of these milecastles, as the fortlets are known, lay two watch-towers, ensuring every stretch of the frontier could be kept under observation. In front of the Wall a deep V-shaped ditch added a further layer of protection. The garrison was housed not actually on the Wall itself but a mile or two behind it, in the pre-existing forts established at intervals along the Stanegate, the road from Carlisle to Corbridge.

It is not known if the Wall was crowned by a parapet and battlements. Other walls or banks of this period do not seem to include such features but the British Wall was an altogether more impressive structure, designed to be a showcase for every frontier. Its width, greater than others of its time, would suggest that it was intended to support a walkway.

The only surviving Roman illustration of the Wall, on a little bowl known as the Rudge Cup, does not show battlements on the Wall itself but clearly does mark them on top of the towers. The most likely solution is that shown in the reconstructed view of *Pons Aelius* on page fourteen, a walkway fronted by a simple chest high parapet. This makes sense, for the Wall was never meant to be a fighting platform; the Roman army fought in the field, not behind battlements. It was first and foremost a barrier, difficult for an enemy to cross - whether it be a small cattle-raiding party or a full size army. Secondly, it was an observation platform, and finally, a boundary marker and customs barrier.

The Rudge Cup.

It is commonly thought that the Wall was built by slaves or the local population press-ganged into service. This is not the case. The bulk of the work was done by the men of the three legions stationed in Britain. Probably only unskilled tasks, such as carting materials, would have been imposed on the local population. They would have had to provide levies of men, beasts and vehicles, a burden greatly resented by the provincials. As the project grew in size, after various changes in plan, other units, such as the British Fleet, had to be drafted in.

The Army

The legions were the battle-winning troops of the Empire. They were all Roman citizens and were mostly drawn from the provinces of the interior: southern Gaul (France), Spain, and Africa; as well as Italy. During peacetime they also worked as engineers on military, and sometimes civilian, construction projects. They did not garrison the Wall; the image of a poor shivering Italian legionary, dreaming of Rome as he strolled the Wall in bleak mid-winter, is a myth.

Instead the Wall was entrusted to the auxiliaries, the troops who provided the Roman army's cavalry and lighter infantry. These men were levied from the less-Romanised provinces and the tribes beyond the frontiers. On their discharge, after twenty-five years service, they were granted Roman citizenship. As a result many of the

Legionaries building a fort, shown on Trajan's column in Rome.

regiments stationed in Britain came originally from Northern Europe. By Hadrian's reign, these units would have been recruiting hardy locals. Right from the start the soldiers manning the Wall would have had a great deal in common with the population on both sides of this frontier.

A vivid impression of what life was like for the Roman soldier in Northern Britain is provided by the wooden writing tablets discovered at the fort of Vindolanda, just south of the Wall. Consisting of letters, receipts and bills, they were written between AD 95-105, a couple of decades before the Wall was built. Conditions were probably not very different for the soldier of *Pons Aelius* one hundred years later.

The Vindolanda Tablets paint a fascinating and sometimes startling picture. One soldier receives an emergency parcel of warm socks and underpants from home, to combat the fierce northern climate. Another acknowledges a gift of fifty oysters, although barley was the most common part of their diet. There are even complaints about the appalling state of the roads!

Changes in Plan

The original plan underwent many modifications, as such large and complex schemes inevitably do. The garrison forts were moved up on to the line of the Wall itself, presumably reflecting grave misgivings within the army regarding the original design. The rapid deployment of troops north of the Wall to counter a hostile force must have been greatly hindered by the need to march a few miles, cross the Tyne and then pass through the narrow milecastle gates.

At the same time as the forts were being built a new barrier was built close behind the Wall. The apparent intention was to keep civilians away from the frontier, preventing a surprise attack by tribesmen conquered little more than a generation earlier. The Anglo-Saxon scholar, the Venerable Bede, mistakenly termed it the Vallum and, although that label should more accurately have been applied to the Wall itself, the name stuck and remains with it to this day.

This curious work consisted of a flat bottomed ditch flanked on either side by earth banks. The only crossing places were gated causeways sited next to the forts, so that access could be closely controlled. This created a no-go area, doubtless cleared of any vegetation which might conceal an assailant, where anyone found could be challenged by the garrison. For traders and herdsmen arriving at the Vallum or the few Wall gateways open to civilians, the experience may have been like a modern border crossing, possibly involving a search and interrogation. Then they would be directed through by the shortest route, perhaps given an escort, or at least issued with a document to prove their right to be in the restricted zone.

In a further attempt to tighten frontier security the Wall was extended in the east, from the Newcastle bridgehead, four Roman miles to Wallsend. It had become apparent that it was too easy to slip across the river between these two points.

These additions increased the cost of the project and may explain why the width of the Wall was reduced, often to as little as six feet, as the builders progressed westwards. Finally, the turf wall of the western sector was rebuilt in stone. This work was begun before the end of Hadrian's reign but was probably left unfinished for more than twenty years, due to changes in frontier policy after Hadrian's death.

Pons Aelius.

The Bridge

The altar of Neptune, set up on the bridge by *legio VI victrix*.

The bridge was an impressive structure, the very first part of the whole Wall system to be built. It formed the basis from which the town could grow over the following centuries. The bridge was doubtless opened with great ceremony - followed by the cutting of the first sod of the Wall itself.

Little is known about the bridge. It was thought to have lain on the same site as the Swing Bridge but recent research has cast doubt on this. During the construction of the Swing Bridge a pier, that was thought to be of Roman origin, was discovered. It is now thought that this is probably medieval. Nevertheless, *Pons Aelius* must have lain close by, to judge from the number of Roman finds dredged up both during and after the construction of the Swing Bridge. Perhaps the medieval bridge-builders demolished it to provide material for their own structure.

We can go some way towards reconstructing the appearance of the bridge by comparing it to its medieval counterpart. The Tyne was wider and shallower in the AD 120's than it is today, so perhaps as many as eleven arches would have been needed to cross the expanse. It is likely that the bridge was built entirely of stone as it was conceived very much as a prestige project.

After the bridge was completed a shrine was set up there by the *legio VI victrix*. The legion had only just arrived from the Continent, where it had previously been based, to reinforce the British army and take part in Hadrian's great scheme. The shrine was no doubt intended to thank the watery gods Neptune and Oceanus for the regiment's safe voyage.

The city area would have been a scene of considerable activity in the early years of the Wall project. Construction camps would have been built, first to house the soldiers working on the bridge and then on the Wall. Supply vessels could have landed troops and equipment in a small harbour at the mouth of the Lort Burn. In those early years the bridge itself would have carried a heavy stream of traffic heading towards the building works.

The Fort

Little was known of the fort in Newcastle until recently. Even its exact location was uncertain. It was thought to lie near Collingwood Street but work by the City Archaeologists from the early 1970's onwards, has finally resolved this point. The fort was on the same site as the Castle and underlies the Black Gate, the keep and High Level Bridge approaches. Indeed, the Castle keep, the hub of medieval royal power in the area, was actually built partly on top of the Roman headquarters building, an example of a good site always coming to the fore.

The excavations have also revealed that the fort was not built under Hadrian at all. Instead, one of his successors in the late second or early third century AD was responsible. Occupation seems to have continued until at least the end of the fourth century, with the fort undergoing many changes in the intervening period.

The administrative buildings lay in a central group comprising the headquarters, the *principia*, with its impressive hall; the commanding officer's house, the *praetorium*; the granaries and stores, *horrea*; and a workshop or hospital. In addition there would be six barracks housing the garrison of roughly four hundred and eighty men.

Roman forts usually have a fairly standard layout, and are commonly described as being playing-card shaped, with square or rectangular ground-plan and rounded corners. The remains uncovered so far have some unusual features so the plan may be irregular, perhaps because of the shape of the site. The headquarters building seems to lack a forecourt whilst the north wall of the fort, overlooking the Side, is skewed to fit the lie of the land. The site may yet have more surprises in store.

Vici

A Frontier Couple. The clothing of the man - long-sleeved tunic, cloak and belt - suggests he may have been a soldier.

Nestling in the shadow of the fort there would have been a small *vicus* or village. It may lie to the west of the fort but no distinct buildings have been found, only bits of flagging belonging to floors or streets. In such a built up area it is too much to hope for substantial remains like those found at Vindolanda or Housesteads. Its cemetery is thought to lie around Clavering Place, near the Orchard Street Postal Sorting Depot, where a number of Roman coffins have been discovered.

Although virtually nothing is known of the *vicus* at Newcastle enough has been learnt from other sites to reconstruct what life would have been like for a citizen of *Pons Aelius*. This bustling village would have housed the soldiers' families and the civilians who provided goods and services for the off duty soldiers. Many of the soldiers may themselves have settled down in the village once they had completed military service. Roman troops were not allowed to make legally recognised marriages until the reign of Severus but there was nothing to prevent a soldier marrying a woman according to local law and custom. Such unions would be recognised when the man was finally demobbed.

The main role of the *vici* was as a market-place serving the troops. Peasants may have come from outlying areas to sell their produce. More important were the merchants, dealing in expensive items or bulk supplies for the regiment, who may have come from the other end of the Empire. Barathes, a trader in military standards who was buried at Corbridge, originally came from the City of Palmyra in the Syrian desert. The majority would have been lesser traders who settled down in one village and built permanent shops.

An occasional sight on the Tyne 1800 years ago? A Roman galley probably transporting barrels of wine. The smile on the face of the steersman suggests he may have been sampling some of the cargo.

The shops typically take the form of long, thin, one or two storey buildings. The plan of these strip-houses, as they are known, is reminiscent of the burgess plots in medieval towns, with their narrow street frontages, with workshops and domestic accommodation above and behind. They were laid out along the roads running away from the fort but lacked the strict grid-iron appearance that would be expected if the settlement had been planned by army surveyors. On the contrary they appear to jostle for position as close as possible to the fort gates - and the soldier's pay packet!

The presence of a small harbour may have given *Pons Aelius* a slightly cosmopolitan feel, though perhaps not so much so as at South Shields, the main port for the eastern Wall forts. The land near the *vicus* was probably used by the villagers to grow some food crops and for the grazing of livestock. The army may also have reserved some land. Cavalry units would have needed pasture and fodder for their horses, but even infantry regiments may well have kept a few oxen or mules to transport supplies to the troops in small outposts.

Some of the villagers, or *vicani*, may have been farmers to judge from the small squarish fields which show up on aerial-photographs and surveys around Housesteads. Whether these were the holdings of peasants who had moved away from their farmsteads into the 'bright lights' of the *vicus* or perhaps veterans who had acquired land to support themselves in their retirement is impossible to say at present.

A view of the Wall looking down Westgate Hill, around AD 200. In the background can be seen the fort and bridge *Pons Aelius*. At the bottom of the slope is the milecastle that was discovered on the site of the Newcastle Arts Centre. The reconstruction was drawn by Graham Mitchell.

The Garrison

By the early third century the *cohors I Cugernorum* was established at Newcastle. This was one of the auxiliary infantry regiments known as cohorts, the second rank troops which performed much of the humdrum day to day duties on the frontier and backed up the legions in battle. The Cugerni, from whom the men of this regiment were recruited, were a German tribe living near the mouth of the Rhine, in present-day Holland. The regiment must have won battle honours under the Emperor Trajan since it bore the title *Ulpia Traiana,* Trajan's Own Cugerni'. Its members were all granted Roman citizenship, a more important reward for their bravery. It had already been in Britain for over one hundred years by the time it was recorded at Newcastle and most of its soldiers would have been recruited locally by this date. The official strength of the unit would be four hundred and eighty men, but the actual size would probably have fluctuated according to the conditions on the frontier and the availability of recruits.

Remains

The inscription recording the arrival of reinforcements from Germany in AD 158. It reads *"In honour of the Emperor Antonius Pius, Father of the Nation, The detachment for the 2nd Augustinian, 6th Victrix and 20th Valeria Victrix legions contributed from the two German provinces, set up this inscription under Julius Verus, the Imperial Governor"*

Nothing remains of the Roman bridge today. All that can be seen of the fort are stone cobbles next to the Castle keep, laid by the City Council to mark the plan of the buildings. Nevertheless, the sites of both fort and bridge can easily be gauged. Standing on the south bank you have only to look for the Castle keep and the Swing Bridge and let your imagination do the rest. Glimpse for a second the long bridge, crowded with the waggons and pack animals, or catch the sounds of the parade-ground drill drifting across from the fort, secure behind its turreted wall.

Sheltering beneath the fort for protection was a small harbour. It was here that most of the supplies needed by the garrison would be off-loaded from the ships and barges which made the difficult journey up the Tyne. It must have taken great courage and considerable skill to navigate past the shifting sand-banks and treacherous currents characteristic of the river before the Improvement Commissioners got to work in the mid-nineteenth century.

Those wishing more tangible remains will have to visit the Museum of Antiquities in the University, which provides a good introduction to the Wall as a whole. The bridge altars can be seen here.

There is also a fine inscription set up some time around AD 158 recording the arrival of troops from the Roman army on the Rhine to reinforce the British legions. Like the altars it was originally placed on the bridge and was dredged up from the Tyne during the last century.

The course of the Wall through the southern half of the city centre is still very uncertain. The Wall in this area was built in two phases. The first was the section heading westward from the bridge. It was perhaps erected late in AD 122, immediately after the construction of the bridge had opened up access to that area for men and materials. The Emperor himself may even have been present. This Wall would have run right down to the water's edge on the north bank of the Tyne, east of the bridge.

The second phase comprised the four mile extension of the Wall to what is now Wallsend, where the fort of *Segedunum* was built. This section probably joined the existing Wall north-west of the bridge. The unnecessary chunk of Wall from the river may well have been demolished at this stage but traces of the flagstone foundations and the ditch might still remain, adding to the confusion.

The reconstructed west gateway of Arbeia at South Shields.

The only sure point is the Westgate Road milecastle. Even the wall-facing in front of the Mining Institute relies mainly on its position on Westgate Road as evidence of its Roman date, otherwise it could just be any old wall. The eastern stretch from Sallyport Tower to Painter Heugh was deduced on the basis of where the defensive ditch was found between 1928-52. More recent excavations, at Silver Street, have failed to find any trace of it along this line, placing a question mark against the whole route. As for the gap between the two lengths, it is anybody's guess. The Westgate Road stretch was probably part of the original broad wall and may have carried on down towards the bridge and the river. Its junction with the later Wallsend extension remains a mystery which only the trowel of the archaeologist will resolve.

For the present, it is difficult to say where the Wall ran, what happened to it during the Roman period, or what effect it had on the layout of the early medieval settlement. This remains one of the largest grey areas in our understanding of Hadrian's Wall.

Other Roman remains in the area can be seen at Benwell, site of the cavalry fort of *Condercum*, where the Temple of Antenociticus and the Vallum crossing can still be seen. Further west at Denton Burn, on the south side of the West Road, lies the first stretch of Wall preserved today. Beyond that lies another length, incorporating a turret.

Elsewhere on Tyneside, the headquarters building of the fort at Wallsend can be seen. This fort has been almost entirely excavated but most of the site has been covered over again. The fort of *Arbeia* at South Shields should not be missed. Continuing work here is bringing to light much new information. A grandstand view of the site can be gained from the splendid reconstructed west gateway. Few sites can better symbolise the impact of the Roman army on Northern Britain.

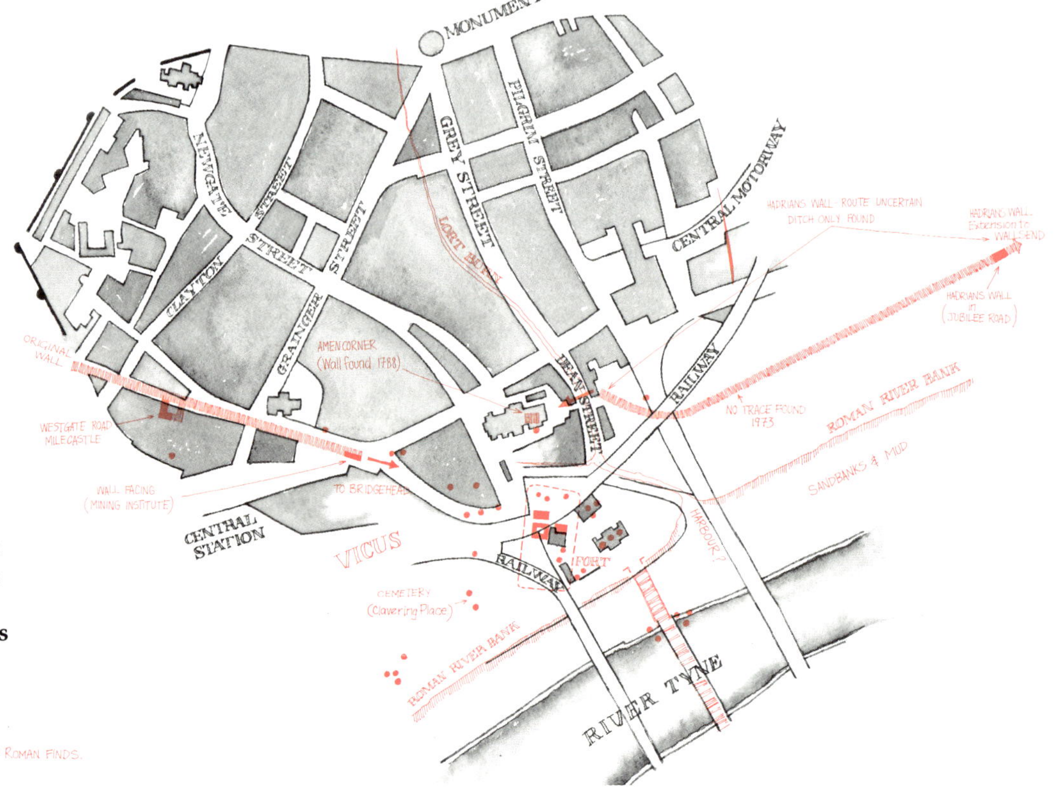

Roman Newcastle, showing the route of Hadrian's Wall through the city. Originally the Wall began near the bridgehead but its course from there to the bottom of Westgate Road is still unknown, as is the first stretch of the later extension to Wallsend. (By William Henry after Clack and Harbottle, 1976, with modifications).

Pax Romana.

The Impact of Rome

What effect would the building of the Wall have had on the Celtic farmers living on either side of it? This is a difficult question to answer since the impact of the Roman Conquest and the construction of the Wall on the local population of Northern Britain is still one of the least studied aspects of this period. Perhaps the best comparison is with a modern motorway. The Wall not only swallowed up a lot of good farmland but also sliced through the countryside severing many traditional routes.

A member of Quinta, a re-enactment group based in South Shields, dressed as a Roman soldier.

The Romans did not enter an empty landscape: on the contrary it was quite densely populated and heavily farmed. Traces of plough furrows have been discovered underneath the Wall. The building of the Wall must have led to a severe loss of agricultural wealth for the nearby communities.

Many peasants would have been evicted from their homes and their farms torn down. The settlement at Milking Gap, near the fort of Housesteads, appears to have been abandoned in the early to mid second century. It lay between the Wall and the Vallum and hence in the military no-go zone. The coincidence of abandonment and Wall construction is very suspicious and points an accusing finger at Roman officialdom. Such activities would have been bitterly resented by the Celtic peasants whose very livelihood they threatened.

This charming figurine of a ploughman and his oxen was found in Co. Durham.

If the Wall did run through Brigantian land it would have divided clans, split estates and separated relatives. With the passage of time some of these effects may have been softened. The Vallum was abandoned by the beginning of the third century, with grazing perhaps allowed right up to the stone wall from then on. Doubtless the Romans were by then more confident of the loyalty of their Brigantian subjects. Elsewhere there was no decline in farming, with many Romano-British farmsteads south of the Wall. Only very rarely does one of these sites develop into a villa, the Romanised farm complex with often luxurious accommodation so common in southern England. The nearest one to Newcastle lies just outside Durham. In short, the area failed to take off and develop the urbanised culture that most other regions of the Empire achieved.

This raises the question of what happened to the Brigantian aristocracy, who would normally have been expected to build themselves villas. They may have been reduced by warfare during the Roman Conquest but the effects of this would only have lasted for a generation or so. It is difficult to see why the Brigantian chieftains did not form the local administration. The Romans did not exclude their conquered subjects from local government. On the contrary, all over the Empire they relied on the provincial nobility to become town councillors and magistrates, to collect the taxes and police their districts. It was their ability to win over the leaders of so many different cultures that had made Roman expansion so successful and their state so long-lasting. The Roman elite may have been arrogant and sometimes brutal but never racist.

The large numbers of troops in the region may have had a damaging impact. The bulk of the army in Britain was stationed in the North. The region did not have the agricultural resources to sustain both the army and the aristocracy. The unfavourable climate of this, the most northerly region occupied by the Romans, saw to that. Although the army would try to support itself locally as far as possible it would not deliberately overstretch a province's resources. The revenue from other provinces could be called upon.

A more subtle effect, one that would have been damaging to the aristocracy alone, is the alternative source of power and patronage represented by the army. Some military officers, like the 'regional centurion' at Carlisle, even appear to have been in charge of whole districts. The Brigantian peasantry may have turned to these officers, especially the long serving N.C.O.'s - the centurions - as a more powerful and reliable source of 'protection' under the new order.

They may even have sought to play their new patrons off against their old chieftains. Given the large number of regiments stationed not just on the Wall but also in the hinterland, this would have severely undermined the power and prestige of the local nobility. With none of their estates at a safe distance from this destabilising influence they were left without a role.

Certainly this mafiosi-like pattern of military patron and peasant client was a feature of the Later Roman Empire; it is recorded on the Syrian frontier in the fourth century. There, peasant villages would approach the commander of the local garrison and in return for an agreed 'consideration' he became their protector. He would station troops in the village to chase away the tax collector and landlord, who were often one and the same man, a member of the local municipal aristocracy known as a *decurion*.

In AD 213 the Emperor Caracala granted Roman citizenship to all free inhabitants of the Empire. He may have done so to increase the number of people liable for the death duty taxes imposed on full citizens. It was a remarkable step, although it is debatable how much difference this made to the life of a peasant farmer on the northern frontier of Britain.

Hadrian's Wall winding its way across the countryside near Housesteads.

Later Roman Frontier.

Another Wall!

Hadrian died in AD 138, with the Wall system virtually complete. Almost immediately the army was pushed forward one hundred miles to occupy a new line from the Forth to the Clyde, complete with a new wall closely modelled on Hadrian's, but built of turf. Hadrian's Wall itself was put into mothballs with perhaps a small caretaker garrison. Little more than twenty years later the army was back. The whole forward venture may have been little more than a propaganda measure designed to win some much-needed military prestige for Hadrian's successor, Antoninus Pius.

Problems seem to have arisen towards the end of his reign. In AD 158 legionaries from Germany were landed at Newcastle, to reinforce the three British legions, as recorded by an inscription set up on the bridge. The Antonine Wall was apparently abandoned then almost immediately reoccupied. The death of Pius in AD 161 removed the Antonine Wall's protector and probably much of the justification for its existence.

The new Emperor, Marcus Aurelius, was faced with threatening situations on other frontiers, and so took the decision to reduce his commitments in Northern Britain. The troops were pulled out of Scotland altogether. Hadrian's Wall was put back into use, with some modifications. A service track, now known as the Military Way, was built behind the Wall, whilst many of the turrets were demolished and milecastle gateways narrowed or blocked altogether. This transformed the Wall from a rigid blueprint imposed by Roman bureaucrats into a more flexible tool, adapted to the actual conditions on the ground.

Hadrian's Wall was to form the frontier for another two hundred and fifty years, until the very end of Roman Britain. Only one further attempt was made to alter this situation by dispensing with the need for a frontier at all.

War

The situation in Northern Britain had deteriorated towards the end of the second century. Rome's enemies in Scotland appear to have become more powerful as a result of the merger of the tribes into two federations, the *Maetae* and the *Caledones*. Perhaps encouraged by the withdrawal of the Romans from southern Scotland, these tribal groups seem to have been in a state of outright war with the Romans by AD 180. The situation was stabilised but all was not well. The British army was mutinous and discipline was not helped by the outbreak of civil war in AD 193, over which army's candidate was to be Emperor. Not surprisingly the largest army, the Danube legions, succeeded, defeating the governor of Britain at Lyons.

Trouble once again threatened in AD 197 but was averted by the new governor, Virius Lupus, who bought the tribes off. He then set to repairing the province's defences, beginning a major programme of building work at the forts along the Wall and in the hinterland. This was continued by his successors during the next ten years. Despite this energetic work the problems of the northern frontier would not go away. The decisive intervention of the Emperor was obviously demanded.

Severus responded, arriving in AD 208 with a large army. He was apparently determined to resolve the British problem once and for all. He clearly had some success. Large forts have been found beside both the Forth and the Tay.However, despite much hard fighting the prize of Scotland was once again to slip from the Romans' grasp. In AD 211 Severus died at York, his work unfinished. This was the last occasion when an

A coin of the emperor Septimius Severus.

Emperor was to pursue the logical solution to the problem of the northern frontier - total conquest of the island.

The building of the bridgehead fort dominating *Pons Aelius*, in the late second or early third century, must be linked with these events. The fort at South Shields underwent major reconstruction during Severus' reign, becoming a supply base containing granaries. It is unclear whether there was any connection between these two building programmes but there are certainly similarities between the two sites, in particular the use of a headquarters building without a forecourt, the sole examples of this type anywhere in the Empire. Until the foundation of Newcastle's fort can be tightly dated it will be impossible to say more precisely what role it played in the northern strategy of Severus or his predecessors.

The campaigns of Severus were followed by a century of peace on the frontier. He had successfully impressed the Caledonians with the might of Rome. As a result the provincial garrison could be gradually reduced. The Wall was still used during these years but the emphasis on frontier control had shifted beyond it. Outpost forts housing large forces were now the key element in the system. The aim seems to have been to anticipate trouble through good intelligence, achieved by long-range patrolling and close supervision of the northern tribes and their meeting places. The Wall was still useful for collecting customs dues and controlling entry into the province. Much of the British garrison was stationed along it whilst the hinterland to the south was almost completely stripped of troops for service abroad.

Diocletian's Junta

If the third century was one of peace in Britain, it was one of chaos in the rest of the Empire as the Imperial frontiers buckled under the repeated hammer blows of barbarian invasion. Towards the end of the century the tide was turned by a series of soldier Emperors of awesome ability. Foremost amongst these was Diocletian, the ruler who was to reshape the Roman World with a series of fundamental reforms. He created a four man military junta, known as the Tetrarchy. His three imperial colleagues were all his men, chosen for their loyalty as well as their ability. Soon the situation in Northern Britain was to require the presence of a member of that junta, Constantius Chlorus.

Conditions in the North had deteriorated in the late third century as a new tribal grouping emerged in central and northern Scotland, the Picts. Constantius made two visits to the province, first to put down a rebellion and then to campaign extensively against the Picts in AD 306.

The face of the later Roman army - a cavalry officer's gilded helmet.

The Last Century.

Barbarian Conspiracy

The Wall probably saw more conflict in the fourth century than the third as pressure mounted not only from the Picts but also the Scots (who confusingly lived in Ireland at this time). North German tribes, most notably the Saxons, were also beginning to raid the east coast of Britain. In AD 343 the Emperor Constans rushed to the aid of the Island in the middle of winter when the hazardous Channel crossing would never normally have been attempted, a clear sign of a desperate emergency.

The most famous assault came with the Barbarian Conspiracy of AD 367. Pict, Scot and Saxon all united to raid the province. They were helped by the *areani*, the Roman scouts and spies north of the Wall, who seem to have betrayed the province's defences. The Emperor Valentinian sent one of his most capable generals, Theodosius, with a small field army to repulse the tribes. Theodosius was equal to the task and restored the province's defences. Historians no longer believe that this invasion caused widespread devastation on the Wall. There were much richer pickings to be had further south. The Picts may simply have sailed round the northern defences, or at most punched a hole in one or two places.

On the whole, Britain was not so hard pressed as other regions and the Wall certainly did not suffer such heavy fighting as on the Rhine and Danube frontiers. The same regiments are found manning the Wall at the end of the fourth century as were there two hundred years earlier at the beginning of the third. Interestingly, the fort at *Pons Aelius* is one of very few which proves to be an exception.

A different regiment, the *cohors I Cornoviorum*, appears at *Pons Aelius*, replacing the *cohors I Cugernorum*. The Cornovii were a British tribe, settled in what is now the English-Welsh Marches, centred on Wroxeter in Shropshire. These soldiers were now at the very bottom of the pile in the new model Roman army forged by Diocletian and continually modified by his successors. They were known as *limitanei* - 'frontier men'. Although they were amongst the lowest paid and least privileged in the army, the men of the cohort at Newcastle were still regular, disciplined Roman soldiers. They could still perform many useful tasks, reconnaissance and intelligence gathering, frontier control and border police, as well as defending their fort for use by campaign armies as a secure base. In these roles their deep roots in the frontier and great local knowledge would be a strong asset.

To the rear, in Yorkshire, County Durham and Cumbria, the old legions were reinforced with new, more mobile units, some of which seem to have been formed by taking detachments from the crack regiments of the imperial field army. The fourth century garrison at South Shields, the *numerus barcarii Tigrisiensium* or 'unit of Tigris boatmen', was one of these better quality regiments. It was apparently a naval force originally drafted from the Tigris River in modern Iraq and Turkey.

All the troops in Northern Britain were under the command of a general known as the *Dux Britanniarum*, or 'Duke of the British provinces'. These could be reinforced by the troops of the field army on the continent in an emergency, as in AD 367.

The End of Empire

Pons Aelius is last recorded in a document of around AD 400, known as the *Notitia Dignitatum*. This records all the administrative and military posts in the Empire. At that date Newcastle's cohort was still in garrison, one of many in Northern Britain. Its men were not good enough to interest the many imperial usurpers the province spawned during its last forty years, so the Cornovian cohort remained to guard its bit of the fron-

Stilicho.

tier, and the bridge across the Tyne. The frontier appeared sound. It had endured for three hundred years and looked as though it might endure for as long again, but terrible events were shaking the western half of the Roman World.

In AD 398, Stilicho, the generalissimo of the Western Empire, came to Britain to repair its defences and campaign yet again against the Picts. He was the last Roman general to do so. Less than ten years later, in the winter of AD 406, the Rhine frontier collapsed under the combined assault of many German tribes. The general of the British army in turn proclaimed himself Emperor and marched off, hoping in vain to seize power on the continent, taking the best troops with him.

In AD 410 the legitimate Emperor, Honorius, in response to their appeals for help, told the Britons he had no more troops to send. The British provinces would, for the time being, have to defend themselves as best they could on their own.

Northern Britain slid into a new era. This may not have been apparent at the time, however. The Romans did not 'leave', with the last one switching the lights off as he went.

For the troops on the Wall the pay would simply have stopped arriving every year. Some soldiers may have turned to farming the land near the *vicus*. A few forts in bleak and unfavourable locations may have been abandoned within a generation. Still naturally thinking of themselves as Roman, without the benefit of hindsight, the more enterprising officers may have organised their men to go freelance and collect their pay from the peasants directly. This would be seen as merely a temporary stop-gap until the legitimate Emperor's field army arrived to bring the province back into the civilised Roman world, perhaps next year...

A page from the *Notitia Dignitatum*, an administrative handbook of the empire around AD 395, showing the chapter of the *Dux Britanniarum*. On the left the title page depicts the more important forts, including South Shields (second row, third from left). *Pons Aelius* and its garrison are listed in the facing text, the first and last occasion that the name is used in a Roman document.

The Dark Ages.

The epitaph of a powerful chieftain dating to AD 500. It reads: *"Brigomaglos, also called Briocus, lies here"* - a rare word from an anonymous age. It was found near the Roman fort of Vindolanda.

The Western half of the Roman Empire collapsed in the fifth century AD and with it the need for the Wall frontier and its forts. The fate of Newcastle as these catastrophic events unfolded is the major remaining grey area in the City's story. Its development in the centuries that followed must be pieced together with help from only the meagre scraps of information provided by literary sources and a small but growing body of archaeological evidence. The turbulent history of the region provides a solid framework into which those pieces may be slotted and the missing ones restored. The result is inevitably speculative. What follows forms a convincing bridge between the Roman frontier settlement, which disappears from view after AD 400, and the Norman borough, which gradually emerges in the late eleventh and early twelfth centuries.

Newcastle will have retained some strategic significance at least as long as the bridge survived. Even if the bridge collapsed before the Norman Conquest, Newcastle would still have been the best crossing point below Corbridge. It may even have been possible to ford the river when the tide was low. Certainly the site was still an important crossing point in the late eleventh century. William the Conqueror expected to be able to cross here when returning from his Scottish campaign in 1072 and Walcher, Bishop of Durham, must have recognised its importance as he met the Northumbrian nobles at Gateshead in 1080.

Raiders and Settlers

Chapter 2

Roman Britain did not immediately succumb to barbarian invasion like so much of the West. The Angles and Saxons from Northern Germany only gradually established themselves over the following two centuries. More immediate threats for the Northern Britons were the raids of the Picts and the Scots.

The Britons managed to reorganise and beat off the Pictish-Scottish menace. Perhaps the remnants of the local army simply diverted local taxation to maintain themselves. Alternatively, the elusive northern nobility may have adapted to the changed circumstances, swapping the trappings of the city council chamber for the the sword of the warrior. The most successful of these warlords gradually evolved into the 'tyrants' or kings and their war-bands who dominated the North when the historical fog began to clear in the sixth century.

Evidence is beginning to emerge at a number of Wall forts for continued occupation well into the post-Roman period. The collapsing defensive wall of Vindolanda was buttressed by dumping earth in front to turn it into a steep rampart, presumably crowned by a palisade or a dry stone wall. Most recently, at Birdoswald, the fort granaries have been found to have long timber halls built over their ruins. These phases

Pictish warriors shown carved on the ninth century memorial stone in Aberlemno Churchyard.

A German Warrior shown on a Rhineland tombstone. His single edged sword, a *scramasax*, was the typical weapon of the Anglo-Saxon invaders.

are infuriatingly difficult to pin a solid date to, because of the lack of coins or fashion-conscious pottery in this period, but they can most credibly be dated to the fifth or even sixth century.

At Newcastle *"Small rough walls, part of a foundation of massive stone blocks of irregular size, a drain and a stone lined tank"* have been reported in the interim notes of the excavation under the railway viaduct which crosses the Castle site. Until the painstaking work of full publication is completed the precise meaning of these structures will remain unclear, but they would suggest continuing use of the fort.

No sooner had the British warlords safely beaten off the Pictish menace than a new, and far more formidable, threat began to emerge; that of the Angles, warlike settlers from northern Germany. In the North East an area roughly corresponding to modern Tyne and Wear and north Durham seems to have been seized first, perhaps as early as AD 500. This was the heartland of the kingdom of Bernicia. The name Bernicia is itself derived from the Celtic Brynaich. It may represent a previous British chiefdom which was taken over by the German tribesmen. Its centres might have been those Wall forts which have produced evidence of continued use. The district was to form the core from which the Northumbrian Angles expanded to become the dominant power in Britain by the early seventh century.

Northumbrian Empire.

Overlords

An early seventh century brooch of a wealthy Anglo-Saxon. It was found at the Roman fort in Benwell.

Under a series of outstanding warrior kings the Bernician Angles overwhelmed their enemies. The first step was the seizure of Dinguaroi, the Celtic kingdom in north Northumberland based around Bamburgh, the fertile Tweed Valley and Millfield Plain. This made the Anglian Bernicia a larger and more powerful unit than its British neighbours. The British kingdoms were hopelessly divided and failed to present a united front in the face of the new threat. One by one they were crushed.

The decisive blow was struck in AD 603, when Aethelfrith 'the Destroyer' expelled the ruler of the neighbouring Angle kingdom of Deria, based in the East Riding of Yorkshire. The kingdom of Northumbria was born. It was a state of unprecedented power in Dark Age Britain, by the standards of the time an empire indeed. All the little chiefdoms and principalities from the Humber and the Mersey north to the Forth and the Clyde had submitted and were gradually absorbed into the kingdom. Aethelfrith's successor, Edwin, extended the kingdom's power yet further. Between AD 617 - 33 Anglesey and the Isle of Man were brought under the sway of the Northumbrians.

Bede numbered Edwin amongst the *Bretwaldas* - the overlords of all Britain. Not for another twelve hundred years was the North to occupy such a dominant position in the Island's affairs.

The seeds of decline, however, were already sown. The area did not have the agricultural wealth to compete with the more fertile Anglo-Saxon kingdoms further south, such as Mercia and Wessex. It simply took more land in the harsher climate of the North to support one warrior. From Edwin's reign onwards Northumbria was involved in a struggle with the Midland kingdom of Mercia. When Edwin was killed in battle against a combined Welsh and Mercian force in AD 633, it seemed that the kingdom might fall apart. The situation was rescued by Oswald, who reunited Northumbria.

Peace with Mercia in AD 679 fixed the Humber and the Mersey firmly as the southern limits of the kingdom. With expansion in that quarter blocked, the Northumbrians turned northwards again. The Picts were to prove no soft option. King Ecgfrith, the last of the Northumbrian Bretwaldas, was killed campaigning against them in AD 685. It was clear that the days of Northern supremacy were over.

A further cause of decline may have been the vast land donations the Northumbrian kings had made to the Church, fatally undermining their own power.

A Royal Estate?

A reconstruction by William Henry of the royal villa of *Ad Murum* in the seventh century. The impressive hall would have housed the king during his brief visits to the estate.

The basic building block of Northumbrian society was the estate. These could be huge. It is thought that the shires of Northumberland preserve the boundaries of some of these early landholdings. Present-day Hexhamshire represents the area granted to the Church by Queen Aethelthryth in the late seventh century. Norhamshire and Islandshire may form the original donation to the monastery at Lindisfarne, though it steadily acquired more and more land. These areas were as large as some local government districts, a sign of in how few hands the wealth of Dark Age Northumbria was concentrated.

At the centre of each estate there would be an administrative villa, little more than a hamlet with a large rectangular hall and various outer buildings for storage. Such villas were the Anglo-Saxon equivalent of eighteenth century country mansions. The traditional food-rents and other dues levied from the widely scattered farms and hamlets around the estate centre would be collected here. These taxes, like the estates themselves, may even have had Celtic origins,

emphasising how little the Anglian conquest changed life for the peasants in the countryside. It is on the unrecorded labour of these men and women that the achievements of king, noble and monk were all ultimately based.

Given the strategic importance of any crossing over the Tyne, one of the major rivers dividing the kingdom, it is likely that the conquering Angle monarchs would have kept the district of *Pons Aelius* in their own hands. The territory of the fort and the vicus may have been taken over as a royal estate. There certainly were royal estates in this area by the seventh century. Bede mentions the illustrious royal villa *Ad Murum* - its name meaning at, or by, the Wall. It was there that Peada - son of Penda, King of Mercia - was baptised before he could marry Aelfleda, daughter of Oswy, King of Northumbria, in AD 653.

The location of *Ad Murum* is uncertain. Bede notes that it was twelve miles from the sea and, as its name implies, close to the Wall. As the crow flies this would put it somewhere in the region of Benwell, since Bede was probably still using the slightly shorter Roman mile. Though it is by no means clear that Bede was using such a direct reckoning. He may have been thinking in terms of an actual track from Tynemouth to *Ad Murum* or the curving course of the Tyne itself so the royal villa may have lain much nearer the centre of Newcastle. The area around the Church of St. Andrews has been favoured as a likely site for an Anglo-Saxon settlement. Pandon and Manors have also traditionally been proposed.

It is clear that other candidates suggested simply on the basis of their Wall names, such as Walbottle, Heddon-on-the-Wall, and Welton, are all much too far west, whilst Wallsend is probably too near the sea.

Whatever its exact position, it is likely that the estate centred on *Ad Murum* included the old Roman fort and the bridge. If the Hexhamshire estate is at all typical, then the *Ad Murum* property would be roughly as large as the City Council district. The size of the estate does not mean that *Ad Murum* itself would have had a large population. A cluster of timber buildings - a hamlet rather than a village - similar to the royal palace excavated at Yeavering in the Cheviots is probably all that should be envisaged. Long distance trade was much reduced after the end of the Roman Empire since Northumbrian kings had no permanent capital which might attract bureaucrats, craftsmen or merchants. As a result there was little to sustain the villages which had attached themselves to Roman forts.

The core of the settlement would be the royal hall, an impressive rectangular building, which would doubtless be covered by ornate woodcarving. The other buildings would be smaller versions of the main hall, providing storage and additional accommodation for servants and officials. There might also be a private chapel for the royal family, though this would look little different to the other buildings, as, like them, it would be towerless and built of timber.

During his brief visits the king would feast and sleep in the royal hall, alongside his retainers; he would also dispense justice, deliberate with his council of advisors, and take part in lavish court ceremonies here. He would then move on to another great estate to consume its surplus. This continual movement of the royal household was not only a good way of collecting taxes, without the help of a large bureaucracy, but also enabled the king to make direct contact with his warrior nobilty. Government was far more personal than it is today and the thegns (nobles of lower rank) were loyal to a man rather than a state.

By the late seventh and early eighth century the estates were increasingly passing into new hands: the monasteries of the Northumbrian Church.

(Opposite). A page from the Lindisfarne Gospels, a masterpiece of Northumbrian civilisation unmatched in Europe.

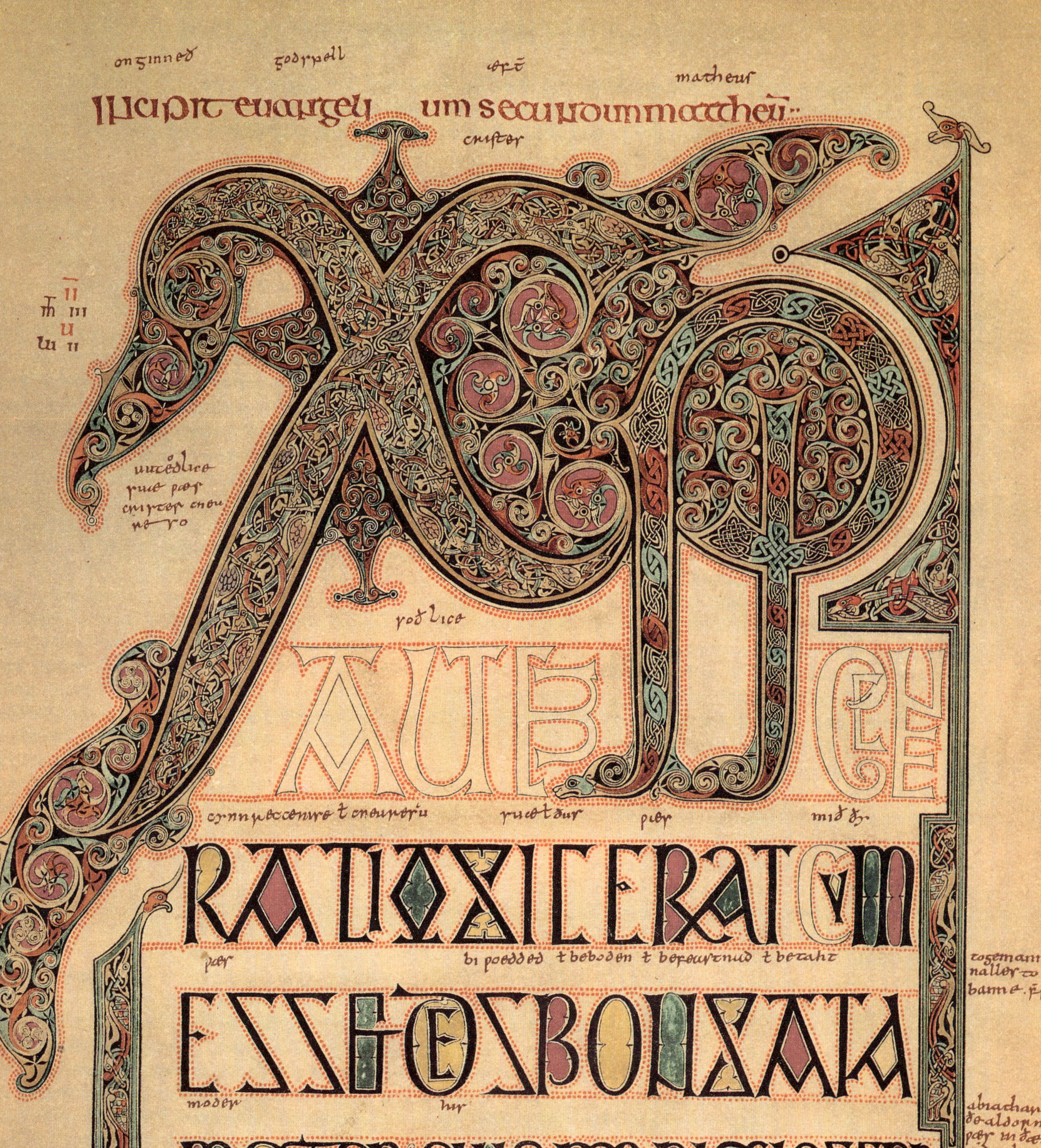

The Power and the Glory.

The Church

The Northumbrian Church was based around half a dozen great monasteries. Initially there were no parish churches. There was only a single bishop for the whole kingdom. The Church's history figures largely in any account of the period. The Church touched the lives of the privileged few: the religious community, the king and the nobility - not the ordinary peasant on the farm. Only when a renowned holy man visited their estate would the peasants benefit. The most notable was St. Cuthbert whose fervent preaching had a profound impact as he pushed into the remotest parts of Northumbria.

Gradually the Church became better organised and more bishops were appointed. These looked after the many less important monasteries and the new churches and cemeteries being founded by Northumbrian landowners on their estates.

The greatest monasteries such as Lindisfarne and Jarrow Monkwearmouth, together probably held more land than the king himself, giving their abbots and bishops immense political power.

The Golden Age of Bede

Lindisfarne produced the magnificent *Lindisfarne, Durham* and *Echternach Gospels* and provided the inspiration for centres outside Northumbria, which in turn were responsible for such works as the *Book of Kells*.

Jarrow was distinguished by achievement in another sphere, the study of history. There, Bede (AD 673-735) wrote *The Ecclesiastical History of the English*, a book which stands out as one of the great works of medieval scholarship. The shrewdness displayed by the scribe in handling his various sources and matching different chronologies still provokes admiration today. Despite their religious bias, there is much concerning other aspects of Northumbrian life to be found in these works. It is still very much through his eyes that we see the world of his generation, to the extent that it is often termed simply the *Age of Bede*.

This creative explosion probably involved no more than a few hundred monks at a very small number of monasteries. The flame was small and brief, nevertheless it burnt with a brilliance so intense that it sent a shaft of light across Europe. English missionaries, armed with beautiful copies of the Gospels produced in Northumbrian monasteries, plunged into the depths of heathen Germany, bringing the area into the fold of Western Christendom.

The Church of St. Pauls at Jarrow, with the ruins of the Norman monastery in the foreground. It was at this site that Bede wrote his renowned history of England.

The Lesser Houses

Not all monasteries had equally importance. The big six had daughter houses. Lindisfarne especially had a large brood. In addition there were many other less prestigious sites founded by great nobles or members of the ruling dynasty to serve as pleasant tax-havens. Life there was far removed from the stern discipline of Benedictine Jarrow and Monkwearmouth or the artistic achievement of Lindisfarne.

Such monastic houses are easily ignored, obscured by the brilliance of the great Northumbrian houses. They may receive a solitary brief reference by Bede or another chronicler but many fail to achieve even this meagre immortality. Instead, the only reminder of its existence may be a tall intricately carved cross in the corner of a churchyard or perhaps just an interesting placename, such as Monkchester.

Just as the supremacy of the Northumbrian kingdom was short-lived so the Golden Age of its monasteries, which may have contributed to the royal decline, was itself to last for little more than the generation of Bede himself. The causes are not difficult to find. The large number of monasteries diluting the religious fervour, and the lax discipline of many was noted with anxiety by Bede himself. The dominance of these by powerful noble families and the increasing involvement of the bishops and abbots in the politics of state were also corrosive forces.

The combined monastic house of Jarrow and Monkwearmouth stood alone in following the disciplined rule of St. Benedict. Only there was the abbot of the monastery not succeeded by a family relative. Not only its church but also some of the residential buildings were built of mortared stone, with coloured glass in the windows *"in the Roman manner"*, as was commented at the time.

The power of the Church in Northumbrian Society was unaffected, but the glory of its achievements in the late seventh and early eighth centuries would soon only be found in the books which it left behind.

Lindisfarne, site of St. Cuthbert's monastery, abandoned following devastating Viking raids and re-established by the bishop of Durham. The visible remains are of Norman origin.

Monkchester.

The Fort of the Monks?

The top the Rothbury cross shaft. The superb carving depicts the figure of Christ.

The pre-Norman name of Newcastle, as recorded by twelfth century chroniclers such as Simeon of Durham, was *Munecacaestre* (Monkchester - the Fort of the Monks). The name may indicate that a monastery was founded near the ruins of the Roman fort - the *caestre* or chester - in the late seventh or early eighth centuries. Many were established in the heady days after the conversion of the Northumbrian monarchy to Christianity and especially after the adoption of the Roman Catholic rite following the Synod of Whitby in AD 664.

Four hundred years later the name was sufficient to convince Aldwin and his two companions that there ought to be a monastery at Monkchester. It was the first place the Evesham monks headed for, in 1074, on their determined mission to re-establish English monasticism in the North - before their new Norman overlords did. They found no traces of one.

Aldwin and his companions may have been essentially correct. Just because there was no evidence of a monastery when they arrived does not mean there had never been one. A small timber-built site would have vanished a lot more easily than the stone ruins of Jarrow, where the monks next went. Jarrow had been one of the most important religious centres in Western Europe. Monkchester would have been a monastery of much lesser rank, perhaps founded to provide a royal minister or relative with a comfortable retirement home, free from the tedious burdens placed on ordinary civil estates - like paying taxes.

The evidence is slender. Bede does not refer to Monkchester at all, let alone record the existence of a monastery there. No fragments of sculpted stonework, such as fine carved crosses, have been found in the city. Such sculptures are useful clues as to the presence of a religious house since only the Church had both sufficient wealth and the inclination to employ skilled stone-carvers.

This does not rule out the possibility of a religious house at Newcastle. Bede mentions the Gateshead monastery only once and no Anglian carving has ever been discovered within the borough to pin down its location. This shows just how easily that site could have escaped all record. More evidence comes from Rothbury. Its splendid Anglian cross, one of the finest pieces of Northumbrian carving, suggests the presence of a monastery here. Yet no historian or early charter mentions a monastic centre at Rothbury. Fragments of the cross have survived because Rothbury never grew to be more than a small rural market town. Much the same is true of the beautiful slender cross shaft in the churchyard at Bewcastle. How much more easily could a similar site in the intensively used centre of Newcastle have been entirely obliterated?

The Cemetery

Firmer ground is reached in the eighth century. Recent excavations north and west of the Castle keep have revealed a large Christian cemetery, with a total of over four hundred burials. This began in the eighth century and was in use until the twelfth. It was located within the walls of the old Roman fort. This use of Roman sites as cemeteries occurs elsewhere in the North, at Corbridge and Binchester, perhaps because the surrounding wall made a neat enclosure for the burial ground. The cemetery provides the clearest indication of a major settlement at Newcastle since the fifth century. It also shows the site was continuously inhabited from the eighth century up to the Norman Conquest, when it is mentioned by historians again. This may have been a burial ground created to hold the mortal remains of monks settled beside the old fort.

There is another, equally attractive, explanation for its foundation. This period sees the origins of the local parish church, as both the king and his nobles began setting up chapels and Christian cemeteries on their estates, where their subject peasants could be baptised and buried. The policy was copied by the local gentry. The process was already underway by the early eighth century when Bede mentions several instances. This work laid the foundations of the parish churches of today. It brought Christianity out of the secluded monasteries and firmly established it in the wider community.

The eighth century church of Escomb in County Durham, one of the best preserved Anglo-Saxon churches in the country.

Whatever its origin, whether royal, noble or monastic, it seems likely that the cemetery would have been attached to a small church lying nearby, perhaps just up St Nicholas Street where the present cathedral now stands. A small rectangular building is most likely, consisting of no more than a hall or nave, where the worshippers might hear a service, and perhaps a little square chancel at the east end, where the priest would perform his duties. It might have been embellished by a carving. The Anglo-Saxon church at Escomb, near Bishop Auckland, gives the best impression of what such an early chapel would have looked like.

A New Region.

This ivory panel from the lid of the Franks Casket made in eighth century Northumbria gives a good impression of Anglian nobles in full war gear attacking a settlement.

It was the nobility who were to gain most from the growing weakness of the Northumbrian monarchy and the decline of monasticism. Such men, called ealdormen and high-reeves in Northumbria, were becoming the new power in the land all over Western Europe. Steadily, as the eighth century wore on, posts which had once been royal appointments became theirs by traditional right and were passed on in turn to their sons. In this process lie the seeds of the feudal system, whereby military service was performed in return for the tenure of land.

As their authority increased these lords became kingmakers. Northumbria slid into anarchy as rival groups toppled first one royal candidate and then another. This endless feuding ensured that the kingdom would be extremely vulnerable in the event of an external attack. In the ninth century just such a threat emerged - The Vikings.

These splendid Norse chess pieces, modelled on Viking Warriors, were found on the Isle of Lewis.

The Danish and Norse invasions of the later ninth and tenth centuries irrevocably shattered the cultural unity of Northumbria and extinguished its monarchy. The dominance of new settlers - Danes in Yorkshire, Norse in Cumbria and Lancashire - split the kingdom into the familiar areas of today.

This allowed the new kingdom of the Scots - formed by the union of the Scots and the Picts - to push their border with Northumbria south to the Tweed in the tenth century.

The area between the Tweed and the Tees and east of the Pennines was not marked by widespread immigration. It retained its Anglian character and institutions, welcoming refugees from the hard-pressed districts of the West. Following the demise of the royal dynasty, the mantle of defending this rump of the old kingdom was assumed by two new leaders, the bishops of the Community of St. Cuthbert and the Ealdormen of Bamburgh.

New Lords

The Community of St. Cuthbert was formed from the remnants of the monastery and bishopric of Lindisfarne. In AD 875 they fled from the path of Halfdan's Viking raiders. For seven years they wandered through western Northumbria and Cumbria, bearing the Community's most precious relic, the body of St. Cuthbert - the ultimate symbol of Northumbrian identity.

In AD 883, after forging an alliance with Guthred, the Danish King of York, the Community was able to settle down at Chester-le-Street. It moved to the splendid natural fortress of Durham in AD 995. As heir to all the religious institutions of the North East it had immense power and wealth. It amassed new estates in what was to become County Durham - notably the lands formerly held by the devastated Jarrow-Monkwearmouth monastery - to add to the Community's already sizeable holdings. These in turn provided the bishop with a source of patronage and considerable military might. When the Norman conquerors turned their attention to the northern border in the eleventh and twelfth centuries they were to find in the Community of St. Cuthbert all the material they needed to create the Prince bishops of Durham.

North of the Tyne lay the base of the region's other powerbroker, the Ealdorman of Bamburgh. His noble clan had doubtless risen to prominence during the kingdom's decline in the eighth and ninth centuries. Bamburgh - the original base of the noble house - had once been a major citadel of the Northumbrian royalty. The fortress was presumably entrusted to the care of an official known as an ealdorman during the eighth or ninth century, that post gradually becoming hereditary. Other lands which were firmly in their hands - such as Warkworth and Corbridge - had also been royal estates. This suggests that when the Viking storm swept over the North, overthrowing the monarchy, the Ealdormen of Bamburgh - like the Community of St. Cuthbert - were able to profit from the calamity. They swallowed up not merely Bamburgh itself but all the former royal property. Later chroniclers include Monkchester amongst the Bamburgh domains.

These estates provided the House of Bamburgh with the resources to defend the region. Their importance did not simply consist of strong fortifications. Nothing is known of any defences at either Corbridge or Newcastle, for example, during this period. What was more important for the earl was to ensure that these locations were under the control of his men, who could be relied upon to block the river crossings, if need be.

The ealdormen submitted to the distant authority of the West Saxon *"King of all the English"*. In doing so, they preserved the region's virtual independence but gained Saxon help in defending Northumbria's borders.

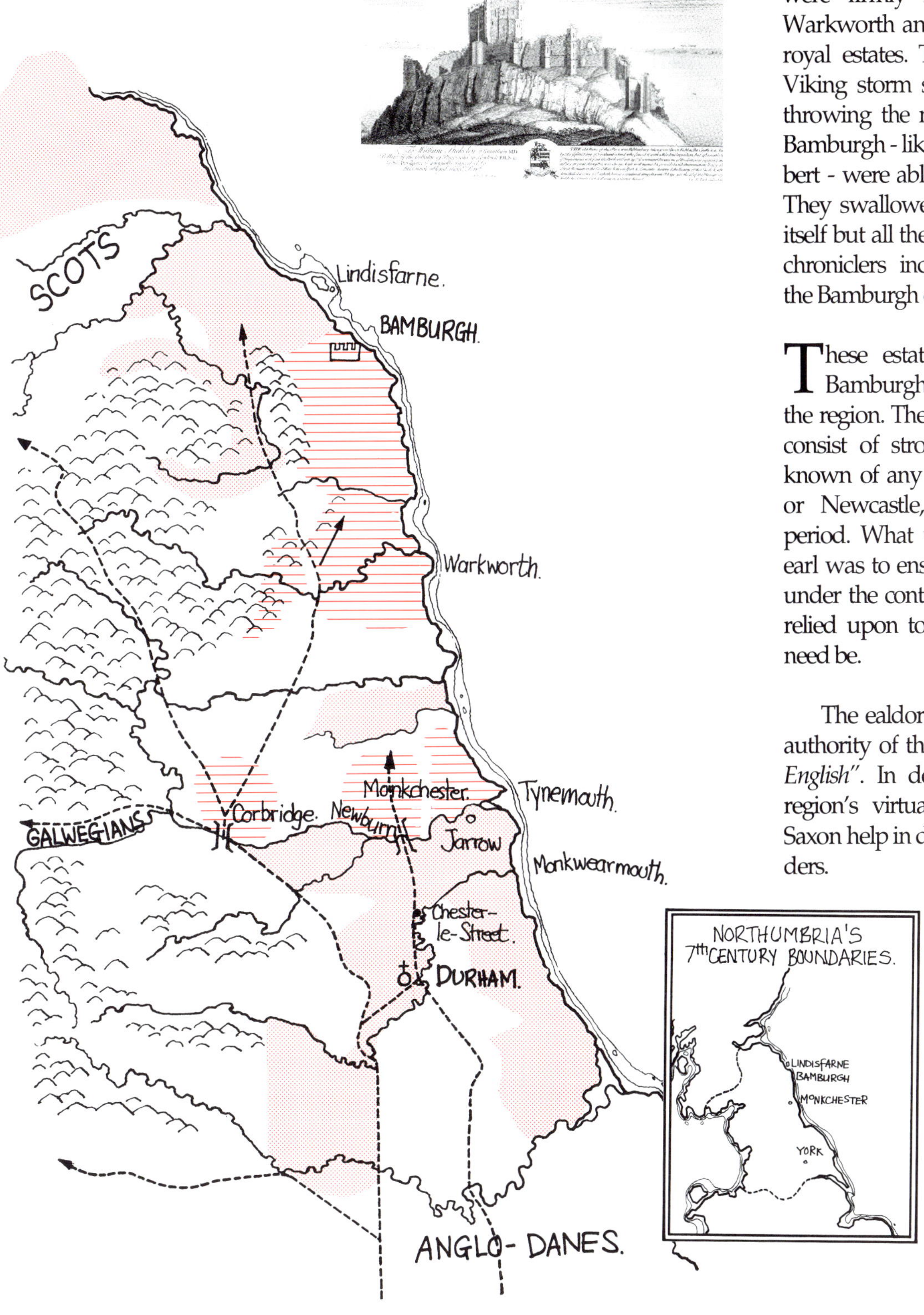

The new Northumbria - showing the estates of the House of Bamburgh and the Community of St. Cuthbert. Inset - the earl's ancient stronghold of Bamburgh

ESTATES OF THE DURHAM BISHOPRIC.

ESTATES OF THE EARLS OF NORTHUMBERLAND.

Birth of a Town.

Regional Hub

Monkchester lay at the heart of this new region. Both Chester-le-Street and Durham lay on the former Roman road leading southward from Newcastle. Traffic along this eastern road, which would eventually become the modern A1, would doubtless have increased as a result of the settlement of the Community there. It is perhaps from this time that it begins to overtake the inland Dere Street route, followed by the modern A68, as the principal regional artery. In turn, the Tyne crossing at Newcastle would gradually have become more prominent than the one at Corbridge.

Monkchester, therefore, lay at the river crossing on the direct route between Bamburgh and Durham. This crucial strategic position, where their spheres of influence met, was a major factor in the settlement's growth.

No ninth or tenth century chronicler records the impact of these political upheavals on Newcastle. The Domesday Book's silence regarding the town is as complete as it is for the rest of the North East. On the other hand, historians writing after the Norman Conquest do provide a few clues. Recent archaeological discoveries also shed the first light on the site's role as a centre of trade and commerce. Similarly, the earliest medieval town charters can be used to deduce the organisation and plan of the pre-Norman borough.

The excavation of the Castle cemetery suggests there was a marked increase in economic activity in Newcastle from the ninth century onwards. The numbers of coins found, though not large in real terms, are still significant in a region where so few have been discovered at all. For example five ninth century *stycas*, copper coins minted only in Northumbria, were unearthed, as was a silver penny of King Aethelred the Unready, which belonged to the years AD 979-91. The latter and one of the *stycas* - minted under King Aethelred of Northumbria between AD 835-45 - can be seen in the exhibition in the Castle keep.

This suggests that Newcastle may have begun to develop as an alternative trading centre to York during the ninth century. York was still pre-eminent, the largest town, most thriving port and the only mint in the North. Nevertheless, it is easy to see why these years might have witnessed a growth in other trading ports in the North East, and at Newcastle in particular.

Initially Newcastle may have been only one of a number of small ports on the Tyne and the Wear. Coinage from both Jarrow and Monkwearmouth shows these may have been every bit as important in commercial terms until the late ninth century. They had the steady market provided by their important twin monastic house to sustain a harbour and the attention of a few merchants.

At Monkchester there may also have been a monastery but a much less prestigious or politically powerful one. It is likely that the attraction there was based on a combination of assets. These may have included the existence of an important estate centre and perhaps the continued survival of the Tyne bridge. The same combination of royal villa, monastery, market centre and river crossing can be found further up the Tyne at Corbridge.

Market Forces?

The Viking invasions brought monasticism along the Tyne to a dramatic close. Halfdan's Danes wintered on the river in AD 876, as did Ragnald's Norsemen in AD 914. The undefended monasteries, as the richest concentrations of portable wealth in the kingdom, were both easy and appealing targets. No one could withstand Halfdan's men. Flight was the only option.

Ironically, amidst all this chaos, Monkchester's growth may actually have received a major boost from the Danish invasions. Alone of the ports and markets on the lower Tyne, Monkchester may have been able to profit from the massive upheaval and the elimination of its rivals. The destruction of Jarrow and Monkwearmouth at a stroke wiped out the customers served by these two harbours. No longer was all the surplus wealth of southern Tyneside channelled through the control of the most disciplined monastery in the North. The buildings could be rebuilt but not the religious communities. The spiritual zeal fuelling northern monasticism had long gone and was not to revive for another two hundred years.

No doubt Monkchester suffered cruelly during these years as well. Halfdan established a base at the mouth of the Team Valley. They cannot have been pleasant neighbours. Newcastle's monks would have left by the time the tenth century opened.

Despite the uncertainty caused by Viking raids, trade and urban life were at last beginning to expand everywhere during the ninth and tenth centuries as the Western European economy gradually took off. Indeed, the Vikings may have played a positive role in this. Not only were they great traders themselves but also, wherever they raided, the most effective response of the defenders was to build fortified towns. In England these were known as *burhs*. They provided new market-places, fostering craftsmen and merchants. At the same time the rural population was beginning to increase, bringing outlying land back into cultivation.

It was inevitable that the surviving ports of the North would participate in this explosive growth. The entrepreneurial flair of York's new Viking merchants more than compensated for the damage done by the invasions of Halfdan and Ragnald. This was of little comfort to the Ealdorman or his thegns. Relations with the rulers in York were often openly hostile. This was especially the case between AD 921-54 when the House of Bamburgh backed the West Saxon monarchy against the Norse kings of York. The frequent movement of armies to and fro across Yorkshire, moreover, may have disrupted the trade routes to York.

A Noble Patron

The North East needed a port and a market where foreign ships could bring their wares directly. Monkchester was apparently under the Bamburgh dynasty's control. The evidence for this is scant but clear. Virtually the whole northern bank of the Tyne, from Corbridge down to the river mouth, seems to have been in the grip of the Earl. This is implied by the striking inability of the Community of St. Cuthbert to expand its vast Durham holdings northwards, suggesting their path was blocked by the lands of an equally powerful landowner. Only the House of Bamburgh fits that description. There is more concrete evidence as well. Waltheof, earl between 1072-75, granted the Church of St. Oswin at Tynemouth to the newly refounded monastery of Jarrow. Newburn, too, is mentioned as a residence of the Earl.

Simeon of Durham specifically states that Monkchester was under the jurisdiction of the earl, though he also lays claim to it on behalf of the bishop of Durham. That piece of ecclesiastical imperialism may be ignored. If it had ever belonged to the bishop we can be sure Monkchester would figure far larger than it does in the early-medieval sources - mainly the work of monks and clerics.

Monkchester must have been yet another of the earl's Tyne estate centres. The New Castle built by the Conqueror's son, Robert Curthose, was to serve as a secure fortress for the new Norman Earl, Robert de Mowbray. After the earldom was eliminated in 1095, the New Castle - like Bamburgh - became a royal castle. It appears that the king simply took over those lands which the earls had formerly held, and then ruled them as his personal domain. The remainder of the land was granted to his barons.

Monkchester, therefore, had a powerful protector to guide and shield it through the troubled centuries which followed the death of the Northumbrian monarchy and the Danish invasions.

A reconstruction of Monkchester in the tenth-eleventh century. The cemetery in the foreground lies on the site of the old Roman fort (now covered by the Castle). The curving track up the hill represents the birth of the most important road in medieval Newcastle. The nearer church is the predecessor of St. Nicholas whilst that at the top of the slope is the forerunner of St. Andrews. Between the cemetery and the near church run the ruinous fragments of Hadrians Wall. Drawn by William Henry

The Pre-Norman Town

A late-eleventh century grave-cover discovered during the excavations of the cemetery beneath the Castle.

The cemetery continued in use throughout these years, only finally being abandoned in the late twelfth century, long after the Norman Castle had occupied much of the site. Coin hoards are still found on the site from this period, in contrast to the monastic sites of Jarrow and Monkwearmouth. In its last hundred years or so some of the graves were marked by signs of greater distinction. One grave was covered by a stone slab with a head carved into the shape of a rounded cross, in a style suggesting the late eleventh century. Originally a millstone, it was first intended to stand it upright as a tombstone but it became damaged, perhaps during reshaping, and so was laid on top of the grave in typical medieval fashion. A second grave-cover may be somewhat later. It seems reasonable to see in both of these the last resting places of important burgesses of Newcastle.

The existence of the graveyard would tend to confirm the impression gained by looking at the layout of the Norman borough that its origins lie well before the Norman Conquest. The Market Street complex almost certainly evolved over a long period of time rather than being created by the Normans. The main throughfares of the medieval town conspicuously avoid the Castle, suggesting they were in place before it was built. This is particularly telling in the case of Westgate which could so easily have been aligned on the western gateway of the Castle.

Similarly the borough customs recorded in a charter of Henry II but relating to the reign of Henry I (1100-35) are too complex to have grown up in what would at most be fifty-five years since the building of the New Castle. They appear to be based on a mixture of Anglo-Saxon and Danish customary law. There are also a few innovations to take account of new Norman laws. This combination implies that the community had grown up over a long period, attracting merchants of differing origin.

The Normans

Despite the vagueness of the chroniclers we can be reasonably confident that Monkchester was the main crossing point over the lower Tyne on the eve of the Norman Conquest. It was here that William made for with his army when returning from Scotland in 1072. He doubtless expected an easy crossing but *"it so happened that the river was in flood as to be nowhere fordable, nor was a crossing open by means of the bridge which is seen there"*, as a twelfth century monk at Tynemouth recorded with masterly ambiguity. Every other ford or bridge must have been similarly out of action for William made no attempt to detour upstream. The flood of 1072 may have been as severe as the Great Flood of 1771, destroying every bridge on the Tyne. In 1080 Walcher, bishop of Durham and Earl of Northumbria, chose Gateshead to meet his rebellious subjects, who dwelt north of the river. His fatal choice was made because that spot was the most convenient venue south of the Tyne for both parties, convenient because of the bridge between Gateshead and Monkchester.

The Norman Conquest of the North was to be long and hard-fought. During the course of this struggle the town was to acquire its other great symbol and its name: the New Castle.

The Norman Conquest.

The Conqueror

Contrary to popular belief, the Conquest of England was not accomplished on a hillside near Hastings on a single day in 1066. This is one of the great myths created by history focused on London and the deeds of kings and their courts. In fact the conquest of the North was to take fourteen years, far longer than in the South. It was to be longer still before the region was securely attached to the remainder of the English kingdom and the threat from the Scottish kingdom finally removed. Today this appears to be a crucial event in northern history but the Northumbrians of the eleventh century probably regarded William as just another southern king trying to enforce his rule over them.

The northerners' mode of resistance was guerrilla warfare, using the wild terrain; the hills, moors, marshes and woodland, to good effect. The Northumbrian nobles would wait until the bulk of the Norman army had retired south and then emerge to launch lightning attacks on undefended settlements or small parties, often surprising senior royal officials whilst feasting or catching Normans away from the security of their castles. The Normans retaliated with tactics still employed by modern governments in such conflicts. By rapid forced marches they might hope to catch the enemy massed in the open, when the Northumbrians dared to besiege Norman strong points. In the last resort, William was prepared to mount savage campaigns of attrition, aimed directly at the civilian population, in order to destroy the economic base of the Northern nobility.

William initially tried to follow the policy of his Anglo-Saxon predecessors by ruling indirectly through traditional leaders of northern society, the earls of Northumbria and York and the bishops of Durham and York. This was backed up by the threat of a royal expedition. The eventual collapse of this strategy, partly through a poor choice of officials and partly because William apparently attempted to levy unprecedented levels of taxation from the northerners, was to have a profound impact on Northern society. The old Northern Anglo-Danish nobility was effectively destroyed and replaced by a new warrior aristocracy of barons and mounted knights.

A Norman Knight of the late eleventh-early twelfth century, drawn by Graham Mitchell.

Chapter 3

1069

It was not until January 1069 that a Norman force penetrated north of the Tees. Seven hundred men under the command of the newly appointed Earl of Northumbria, Robert de Commines, pressed north to avenge the murder of William's first Earl, Copsig. He had been killed at Newburn whilst trying to collect taxes from the Northumbrians. Commines' force was in its turn wiped out, ambushed at night within the ramparts of Durham. The revolt spread, engulfing Yorkshire where the garrison at York itself was overrun. The situation was perilous for William who had no garrison north of the Humber. His problems grew worse. In the autumn a Danish fleet arrived to contest his claim to the English throne.

He rose to the challenge. Once again he appeared before his enemies expected, continually harassing the Danes to prevent them establishing a secure base for the winter. Unable to return home because of the winter storms, or build their own stout timber defences, the Danes were forced to accept his terms.

With his most dangerous foe disposed of, William's hands were now free to deal with the unruly northerners. That winter William avenged the disasters of 1069 personally, and in characteristic fashion. He first ravaged Yorkshire, destroying opposition in the most dangerous focus of revolt. When the Domesday Book was compiled, sixteen years later, much of the county was described as *"waste"*, reflecting the continued effects of William's work. Then he pushed north, as far as the Tyne, sacking the ancient church at Jarrow and pillaging the Tyne Valley as far west as Hexham, before returning south in January 1070.

William was only to make one further appearance in the region. In 1072 he entered Scotland with a large army, determined to punish Malcolm III (known as Canmore - big headed) for raiding the North. Malcolm managed to avoid a decisive battle with the superior Norman host but was forced to submit at Abernethy, recognising William as his overlord.

William retraced his steps, marching south via Monkchester. He was unable to ford the Tyne because it was in flood, a fact which would suggest that the old Roman bridge had been washed away some time previously. Short of provisions he was able to find assistance at the monastery of Tynemouth, until he could proceed southward.

Before leaving the region for the last time he built a castle at Durham to protect his recently appointed bishop, Walcher of Lorraine. Its great earthen mound remains to this day - a reminder of the boundless energy of the first Norman king of England.

Revolt and Retribution

William's achievements are less impressive than they first appear. He had not been able to win over the nobles. The peasants of Northumbria had not suffered as severely from the Norman's *"harrying"* as those of Yorkshire - having had more warning and time to flee into hiding with their livestock. As a result further revolts broke out, in 1075 and 1080.

This last uprising culminated in the murder of Walcher, Bishop of Durham and Earl of Northumbria. The Northumbrians were enraged by Walcher's murder of one of their leaders, Ligulf, and by his failure to repel yet another raid by Malcolm's Scots. In an attempt to calm the situation Walcher, accompanied by his bodyguard of one hundred knights, agreed to leave the safety of Durham Castle and meet the Northumbrian nobles at a public assembly in Gateshead. He was walking into a trap.

After much argument the bishop and his advisers retired to a nearby church. Then the Northumbrians struck. They massacred Walcher's retainers and set light to the church, killing the bishop as he tried to escape.

The murder of Walcher, the last royal official north of the Tees, proved to be the final straw for William. In retaliation he sent his half brother Odo, bishop of Bayeux, to put down the revolt.

Odo was a thorough worker. He laid waste the countryside, spreading slaughter and devastation from the Tees to the Tweed. With their estates burnt to the ground, the Northumbrian nobles were too weak to continue their resistance. Their traditional leaders had been killed or had fled to Scotland. It was the last of the native revolts.

This 'solution' only made the task of defending the North from Scottish attack more difficult. As a result Robert Curthose, William's eldest son, was dispatched that same year in a bid to try to achieve a decisive victory over the Scots. Like his father Robert was unsuccessful but he made up for this by building a 'new castle' at Monkchester, on the north bank of the Tyne opposite the spot where Bishop Walcher had been murdered.

When Henry I (William's youngest son) died in 1135, the task of securing the North was complete. Thereafter, despite over twenty years of Scottish control from 1136-1157, Northumbria remained part of the English kingdom. The building of the 'new castle' was one of the first and most crucial steps in that process of consolidation.

The "New Castle".

Robert's Castle

When Robert Curthose first built his castle on the Tyne it was one of only very few Norman strongholds in this troubled region. Lying between the bishop's castle at Durham and the ancient fortress seat of the earls (and kings) of Northumbria at Bamburgh, Newcastle provided the king's officer with a base secure from Scottish attacks and native revolts. In the longer term it served as much to overawe the unruly Nor-

The tombstone effigy of Robert Curtose in Gloucester Cathedral.

A dramatic reconstruction by William Henry of the first New Castle built in 1080.

thern barons as to ward off Scottish attacks. By ensuring the loyalty of the Northern lords the Castle could hold the northern frontier of the kingdom secure. This was the very essence of the feudal system. The king needed powerful barons with strong castles and wide estates in order to provide the knights he needed to defend his kingdom, but he had to be even stronger to keep them under control so he kept the greatest estates and the strongest castles himself.

This momentous step laid the foundations of modern Newcastle. The Castle provided a major spur to future growth, marking out the site as the centre of royal power in the region. It replaced the administrative estate centres of the Anglo-Saxon earls whose focus in southern Northumberland lay around Corbridge. Under the Castle's protection, the town grew steadily.

The original Castle was built of earth and timber. The site was a natural fortress, in the shape of a roughly triangular ridge. Deep ravines, carved by the Lort Burn (where Dean Street now runs) and its tributary (down the Side), protected the Castle on the north and east sides. To the south there was a sheer drop down to the river. Only on the west side was the approach easy and level. This Robert cut off by digging a deep ditch.

The clay dug out of the ditch was spread across the triangular site and heaped along the edges to form defensive banks. These ramparts would have been crowned by stout timber palisades. A small stone tower seems to have been incorporated into the bank at this stage. Its foundations can still be seen today, preserved between two of the piers of the railway viaduct which slices through the Castle.

A Motte or not?

It has generally been supposed that the Castle must have had a large earthen mound or motte to serve as a wartime strong point and a final refuge. The main enclosure would have formed a bailey, where most of the buildings were housed and the everyday life of the Castle took place. Such motte and bailey castles were typical of the Norman occupation but efforts to find the motte at Newcastle have so far been unsuccessful.

The first candidate is the Mount, a large mound which lay near the south-west corner of the site. Its location, at once dominating the weak western approaches and perching above the steep drop to the river, is a plausible one for a motte. The Mount was removed in 1811, when Castle Street was being laid out to provide better access to the Moot Hall. The conditions attached to the sale of land associated with this redevelopment, deal the Mount's candidature a heavy blow. They state *"The Bank [ie. the Mount] is supposed to consist chiefly of ashes, and may probably be disposed of for manure, and be removed at very little expense."* This description, if it is accurate, suggests the Mount was nothing more than one of the huge middens which spread over the western part of the Castle after the fourteenth century. By then the military role of this once proud fortification had virtually ceased and it was being used as the urban tip.

The other candidate, the site of the Half Moon Battery, is equally unlikely. During the building of the Moot Hall traces of an earlier wall were found. This indicated that the area was part of an earlier Angevin circuit rather than a motte. The Half Moon itself was perhaps a thirteenth century addition, approximately contemporary with the Black Gate. It was certainly in existence by the sixteenth century when it appears on a sketch.

In any case, more and more work on early castles is showing that there was nothing unusual in such a Norman stronghold consisting simply of a banked and ditched enclosure, a form known as a ringwork. Sometimes a motte might be added later, while others gain a less stoutly defended outer enclosure, or bailey. Occasionally this process was taken to its logical conclusion by filling in and raising the whole central platform of the ringwork, converting it into a huge motte.

Newcastle's earthwork defences clearly never underwent such a radical transformation, though they may have acquired an outer bailey. As regards the motte, it might be said that the jury is still out but the weight of current evidence would suggest that a verdict of 'not present' might be expected.

Henry's Stone Castle

The Castle presumably continued to rely on the strength of its natural defences. In 1095 it experienced its first siege when the Earl of Northumbria, Robert de Mowbray, revolted. Despite its strong site it was unable to resist the weight of William Rufus' royal army, and was forced to surrender. From then on the Castle was to be kept firmly in the king's hands. It was too important for the security of the northern frontier to be treated so recklessly again. The earldom was abolished and a new official, the Sheriff of Northumberland and Warden of the New-castle, was appointed. Thereafter little is known of the Castle until it was rebuilt in stone from 1167 onwards, at the orders of Henry II.

Henry was the first king of a new dynasty, the Angevins - so named because they were originally counts of Anjou, another French province - but better known to their contemporaries as 'the Devil's Brood'. Four rulers, Henry II, his wife Eleanor of

This early thirteenth century manuscript illustration shows the *Devil's Brood*, Henry II, his sons Richard and John and grandson Henry III. Each holds a model of the monastery they favoured.

Aquitaine and their sons, Richard I and John - all larger than life characters - were to dominate the story of much of Western Europe for sixty years. They were to leave their mark on the skyline of Newcastle, still present after over eight hundred years.

Between 1168-1178 Henry II rebuilt the Castle in stone at a total cost of £1,144. It was one of a whole series of fortifications built by this energetic monarch, who was determined to re-establish royal authority after the anarchy of the civil war which had preceded his reign.

Henry's Castle consisted firstly of a surrounding curtain wall built on top of the Norman earthen bank. The circuit was equipped with rectangular towers and two main gateways, one to the north and one to the west. The towers scarcely project beyond the line of the circuit wall, and thus could not provide covering fire to deal with attackers who managed to reach the base of the wall. This weakness would be corrected in castles built only a decade later, reflecting the rapid developments in siege warfare at this time. As knights returned to the West from the Crusades they brought with them knowledge and experience of the more sophisticated fortifications of the Byzantine Empire and the Muslim states of the eastern Mediterranean. There the military heritage of the Later Roman Empire had been maintained and developed, giving rise to powerful defences which made a profound impression on the Crusaders.

The most important element of the Angevin Castle was the keep, the massive rectangular tower. Built between 1172-77 this was the work of Maurice 'the Engineer', one of the last and perhaps the greatest exponents of such rectangular strongholds. It was Maurice who, in the next decade, was to design and build the largest and most powerful of Henry's mighty keeps, that at Dover Castle.

The keep has changed in appearance over the centuries. The current battlements were erected in the nineteenth century. The original ones would not have projected outwards. The present entrance, past the custodian's office, is also a modern addition. The original route carried on climbing the

steps, turning left and through the massive wooden doors into the Great Hall. This would have had a pitched roof supported by massive oak timbers, instead of the present vaulted ceiling which supports a flat roof. The holes in the stonework where the timbers would once have rested can still be seen. The fireplaces in the hall and room below are also modern. Presumably the twelfth century hall would have been warmed by braziers and perhaps a central hearth of stone slabs.

Despite these alterations the keep still gives a good overall impression of what one of Henry II's great tower strongholds would have looked like. Its towering mass is still breathtaking, affording one of the best views of the city. The Norman stone carving in the chapel is a complete contrast, a masterpiece of exquisite craftsmanship in a small chamber.

The Angevin building programme was resumed under John, Henry's youngest son. The defences were now complete but the Castle still lacked comfortable modern quarters. John erected a large, single-storey hall against the eastern wall of the Castle, overlooking the Lort Burn. It would doubtless have been sumptuously decorated as would befit the residence of the king when he was in this region. The main hall probably measured sixty-six by forty-four feet. It was there that the king or his officers would have feasted, and also where royal justice would have been dispensed by the Sheriff of Northumberland. At the south end of the hall lay the king's own private chamber or solar, whilst the kitchens were at the north end, with huge fireplaces capable of meeting the occasional needs of the royal household.

The hall stood until 1810, when it was demolished to make way for the present Moot Hall. Sadly few good illustrations survive.

The interior of the Castle would probably have been full of ancillary buildings; stables, storehouses and sheds, all necessary to meet the needs of the administrative and military headquarters of Northumberland.

The Castle keep and Moot Hall in 1834.

The Black Gate of today, now home to the library of the Society of Antiquaries. The inset - drawn by Graham Mitchell - shows how much it has changed since 1250.

The Black Gate.

The Black Gate in the eighteenth century after its conversion into tenements. It was named after Patrick Black, a seventeenth century resident.

Between 1247 and 1250 the Black Gate was added by Henry III. Costing more than £500, this was one of most sophisticated pieces of military engineering of its day. It enabled defenders on the main curtain wall to cover the approaches to the gate. It also contained a cunning series of obstacles to attackers who managed to force their way in.

Imagine the task facing the commander of a Scottish army besieging the Castle. Firstly, his troops might have to force their way through the temporary timber outer works protecting the main gateway. Then they would be confronted by a ditch, a raised drawbridge, and a hail of arrows and stones from the defenders.

Even if his forces could surmount this obstacle, perhaps using grappling hooks to pull the drawbridge down or filling the ditch and burning or battering a way in, there was still a portcullis and two stout wooden gates to be battered through in turn.

Here at last, as he entered an open courtyard, the attacker might breath a sigh of relief, a fatal mistake. This small area was one of the most fiendish elements of the whole design. Yet another drawbridge faced the besieging troops and behind that a passageway leading to the final gateway into the North Bailey of the Castle. This small open courtyard area would thus become a deathtrap with missiles pouring down from all around.

At this point retreat might seem the best option but the Castle garrison could sally forth from two doors on either side of the passageway through the gate-tower, cutting off many of the attacking troops from their companions outside. Clearly, to stand any chance, the besieging forces had to take the tower-gateway before they could proceed further, a daunting task indeed.

So the construction of the Black Gate converted the gateway from being a source of weakness to being a major strong-point on the outer defences of the Castle. Once again this part of the fortress is similar to its counterpart at Dover, the Constable Tower, bearing out the comparable roles these two Castles played as royal sentinels standing guard at either end of the kingdom.

Decay and Renewal.

In 1300 the Castle was still a formidable fortress equipped with a virtually impregnable gatehouse. The curtain wall had not kept pace with the latest innovations in siege warfare but the strong natural defences compensated for this. Furthermore, the Black Gate provided cover for the northern end of the circuit. The Half Moon may have been added at some point during the thirteenth century to strengthen the south-eastern angle and dominate the bridge immediately below.

Thereafter the Castle begins to enter a long period of decline. The decisive factor was the construction of the town walls. It had originally been intended to incorporate the Castle in the line of the walls so it could serve as a citadel. This meant excluding the western Quayside districts and the Carmelite Friary from the walled town, provoking an understandable public outcry in 1311. As a result, the Wall was diverted southward to enclose the district. The Castle was now isolated within the town, unable to play any role in its defence in the event of an attack. Its decay was slow but steady.

Dung Heaps

The Sheriff continued to dispense justice in the Moot Hall, where the County Assizes were held; but for the townsfolk the Castle's main function was as a rubbish tip. The ditches were particularly tempting for this purpose and the Sheriff always had to struggle to prevent furtive dumping.

Continual efforts were made to maintain the Castle during the fourteenth century, but in the early fifteenth century the drawbridge was abandoned. Two walls were built between the abutment and the gatehouse and the space between filled. This indicates that even the royal government and its officers no longer believed the Castle would have to withstand serious assault. In 1460 the ditches seem to have been made the site of the official town refuse tip. By 1589 the Castle was described as *"old and ruinous"*.

From now on the dungheaps grew apace. Filling the ditch, they began to tower over the western curtain wall. By 1621, when yet another inquiry into the state of the Castle was held, it was reported that the Dunghill *"had increased to such bigness that it was in length 98 yards, the depth of it was 10 yards and the breadth of it 32 yards; which being such a prodigious weight upon the wall of the westside of the Castle...that a great part of it is entirely thrown down."*

The Civil War meant a brief military revival with the addition of *"diverse curious fortifications"*. The rubbish was cleared away by the mayor, John Marley. A pointed artillery bastion was built just to the south-east of the Black Gate, which was itself refurbished with a new pit being built inside it as a further obstacle, whilst cannon were placed on the keep and the Half Moon Battery.

Between the second half of the seventeenth century and the mid-eighteenth century the Castle was surrounded by tightly packed houses. The Black Gate was itself turned into a house. The top storeys with the large mullioned windows reflect this remodelling. It was let as a dozen small tenements, *"approached by intricate dark passages and step ladders."* As for the keep, the Newcastle historian John Brand observed on its parapets an artificial garden complete with apple trees and rose bushes. The occupier regarded the now roofless interior as a pit within his garden!

Revival

In 1809 the town corporation took over the Castle. This marks the beginning of a period of revival. The buildings around were cleared away and the present battlements erected. Guns were mounted on the keep for holiday celebrations. This led to tragedy in 1812 when a cartridge exploded hurling the gunner over the parapet.

In 1811, sadly, King John's hall was demolished to make way for the present Moot Hall, but at least the city benefited from the building of a splendid classical building in return. The construction of the High Level Bridge and the railway viaducts leading to Central Station in the 1840's brought further demolition. The Bailey Gate was lost now. This was to be the last destruction. The keep, south curtain wall and Black Gate have survived intact.

The Black Gate now houses the library of the Society of Antiquaries. The Society leased the keep in 1848 for a museum and a meeting place. It is very much as a result of their efforts that the castle survives in such good condition. They formed an active pressure group during the nineteenth century when continual development might have obliterated the castle entirely, as happened in so many major cities. The city still has its 'new castle'.

The Defence of the North.

The Border

Following the Roman departure the border shifted back and forth. The Northumbrian kingdom had stretched from the Humber to Edinburgh. The line slowly moved southward with the Scottish advance which had been taking place during the latter days of the Saxon kingdom. The new Norman-Angevin monarchy firmly established the claim of the English kingdom to the Northern Counties and the border became more or less fixed to its present position between the Solway and the Tweed.

The border was in any case fairly artificial, dividing two culturally similar regions. Both Northumberland and South East Scotland had formed part of the same Anglian kingdom and were English, in the original sense of the word. Furthermore, many of the Northern barons held land in both countries. The devastating power of Norman armoured cavalry had deeply impressed the Scottish monarchy, with the result that King David I invited large numbers of Norman lords to settle, in what has been called the Norman invasion of Scotland.

David was at ease with Normans, having spent a long period in exile at the Anglo-Norman court. Above all, he was anxious to modernise his state. He needed Norman manpower to help conquer the wild regions of Galloway and the Western Isles. He and his descendents replaced those regions' old tribal societies with the new feudal system, a system geared around the maintenance of that essential symbol of the Middle Ages - the mounted knight.

It is often imagined that the Border Wars were a single continuum of unending strife. This is far from the truth. Although there was some fierce fighting in the late eleventh and twelfth centuries the warfare of Stephen's and Henry II's reigns did not have the same intensity and bitterness as was sparked off at the end of the thirteenth century by Edward I. There were, for example, no more castles in Northumberland than in any other part of England at the end of the thirteenth century.

The conflicts of the earlier centuries were each of relatively short duration, whereupon a formal treaty would be signed, and by and large kept to, putting a stop to cross border raiding. The Norman kings were too busy consolidating their position against the barons whilst the Angevin kings were trying to maintain an Empire in France.

Anarchy

Following the death of Henry I, the North was once again shaken by political upheaval. Civil war broke out between Matilda, the daughter of Henry, and her cousin Stephen, Count of Blois, over who should succeed to the throne. Matilda had been assuming the support of the Northern earls, who had been made to swear an oath of allegiance to her by her father. Failing to get it she turned to her uncle, King David of Scotland. He invaded Northern England, overrunning Northumberland and Durham. It seemed that Scottish rule might extend to the Humber, but not so. Near Northallerton the Scots met a combined army of Yorkshire barons and the most potent force in Europe - the English peasant archer. They were wiped out in the hard fought struggle which followed, known as the Battle of the Standard.

In the midst of a long civil war Stephen was not able to follow up this victory to drive out the Scots completely. He needed peace more than he needed Newcastle and the northern counties, so he sought a truce.

David was granted Cumbria whilst his son, Henry, was made Earl of Northumberland. The royal castles of Bamburgh and Newcastle were strictly excluded from Scottish rule under the terms of the treaty but David is recorded holding court at Newcastle. Evidently Stephen was in no position to quibble when the Scots interpreted the treaty differently!

Scottish Rule

King David of Scotland, the father of Scottish feudalism, drawn from an 1159 charter.

The town was thus in Scottish hands and remained so from 1139 to 1157. During this period David may have built St. Andrews church and the Benedictine nunnery.

This image of Scottish power was illusory. After David's death his grandson, Malcolm IV, was unable to stand up to Stephen's successor, Henry II. Henry was a towering figure even amongst the capable English monarchs of the eleventh and twelfth centuries. He had no difficulty in moving the border back to the Tweed-Solway line. Meeting the Scottish king, at Chester in 1157, Henry's threat of war was alone sufficient to bring Malcolm IV to heel.

Henry had the support of the Northern barons as well as the resources of an empire stretching south to the Pyrenees to back up his intimidation. Malcolm's desertion was prudent as most of Europe stood in awe of Henry's military flair but neither he, nor his successor William, were reconciled to the loss of Northumbria and Cumbria.

In 1173, while Henry was fighting not only most of his own sons but also the King of France, William 'the Lion' invaded England. It was to become a common ploy for the Scots to attack after encouragement from their French ally. Newcastle was threatened, but the Castle's new stone defences proved their worth, despite being incomplete. After this preliminary foray he returned in greater strength in the next year. His army is said to have numbered eighty thousand men. This time Newcastle was not besieged.

After being repulsed at Prudhoe Castle, William besieged Alnwick. Whilst an English army was making slow progress from the South, the Sheriff of Yorkshire, together with four hundred horsemen, advanced ahead to reconnoitre the area. A heavy fog settled and he became lost. When it lifted he found himself on the edge of the Scottish camp. His group swooped in and captured William. He was held at Newcastle, which was not considered strong enough, so he was taken, finally, to Rouen. When released, at the cost of the five strongest castles in Scotland - including Edinburgh - under the Treaty of Falaise, he was attacked by a mob in Newcastle as he returned home, such was the antipathy of the locals towards their Scottish neighbours.

This was the last occasion that a Scottish king seriously threatened to detach the northern counties from England. In 1237, at the Treaty of York, Alexander III finally abandoned his forefathers' claim to Northumbria and Cumbria. The value of the determined work of the three Norman kings had been proved by their Angevin successors. Newcastle was to be an English borough, not a Scottish burgh.

The Fledgling Borough.

Ancient Rights

The Norman town, or borough, was initially governed as part of the royal demesne - that part of the conquered kingdom which the king retained in his own hands, rather than granting to his barons as feudal tenancies. He ruled through a sheriff in much the same way as a lord would rule his manor. This system was too restrictive to appeal to the burgesses of the young urban community and the struggle for greater independence began early.

The earliest known document relating to the rights of the town is a charter dating from the reign of Henry II but which allegedly refers to the time of Henry I. These customs appear to be based on a mixture of Anglo-Saxon and Danish customary law, with some peculiar local variations. They allowed the burgesses their own courts and jurisdiction over merchant shipping. The laws also exempt the burgesses from *merchet*, a fee paid by a tenant to his Lord on the marriage of his daughter; *heriot*, a type of death duty paid to the Lord; *blodwite*, a fine paid when a crime involving bloodshed was committed; and *strengesdint*, a fine for offences involving striking someone with a stick.

Perhaps the most important privilege was the so-called burgage tenure whereby *"a burgess can give or sell his land as he wishes, and go where he will, freely and quietly unless his claim to the land is challenged"*. These rights were hereditary and were also acquired by any *villein* (peasant) who managed to reside within the borough for a year and a day. The charter also confirms the crucial economic exclusivity of the medieval borough, such as the restriction of the right to sell merchandise to the burgesses alone: *"No merchant unless he be a burgess may buy [outside] the town either wool or leather or other merchandise."*

There are a few innovations to take account of new Norman laws, leaving the burgesses exempt from the burden of trial by combat. This combination of Norman, Danish and Anglo-Saxon laws implies that the community had grown up over a long period, attracting merchants of differing origin. So even by the mid-twelfth century - and probably much earlier - the borough possessed a distinct legal identity, defining and protecting an economic role very different from that of the villages of the surrounding countryside.

New Freedoms

Towards the end of the period Newcastle took another major step towards independence, when it was allowed to pay its taxes in the form of a fee farm. In this context the term farm has nothing to do with livestock or crops. Instead it denotes a system whereby instead of collecting his taxes directly, through his own officials, the king 'farmed' the taxes out to a contractor, or tax farmer, who paid him a lump sum and then collected the tax at his leisure. Here instead of being put out to tender the farm was placed in the hands of the burgesses and their representatives. The fee farm was thus a collective tax for the whole town and ensured that the king's inspectors would not interfere in the town's affairs.

The fee farm also benefited the king since it provided a greater degree of protection against rising inflation than the multitude of flat rate tolls which preceded it. The sum owed could be periodically revised by negotiation with the borough, as successive charters of King John record, the fee farm increased step by step until it reached £100 in 1213. Some of the measures taken to find the required amount may be gauged from a charter of Edward III, in 1357, which confirms the right of the burgesses to dig coal and quarry the Town Moor to pay the fee farm.

Just as the vital urban institutions and borough freedoms were emerging during this crucial formative period, so this progress was being physically translated into the familiar layout of much of the city we know today.

Early Foundations

It is doubtful that the street-plan of Newcastle was formally laid out by the Normans. They frequently did establish small fortified towns beside their new castles but these tended to display far more order and regularity than is evident at Newcastle. There is some evidence to suggest that the Normans may have attempted to replan the town by creating a fortified nucleus next to the Castle.

The medieval street leading out of the west gate of the Castle was named Baylygate meaning 'the bailey street'. Its location just west of the Castle, and its name, may imply it lay within an enclosed area, which was either fortified or intended to be fortified. This may have been designed to establish a new main throughfare aligned on the western gateway of the Castle and linking up with the Westgate street. It appears that this failed to develop as a major throughfare probably because there was already an existing borough with too much economic vitality to be altered by the whim of a Norman official.

It was the bridge, rather than the Castle, which was the key to the early street pattern. The existence of a bridge or, at least, the ease with which one could be built, must have been a crucial factor in convincing Robert to site his Castle there in 1080. It is likely that the Roman bridge was rebuilt or an entirely new one constructed soon after the Castle.

There were two routes leading off the bridge and up into the town centre. Both were in existence by the end of this period and probably a great deal earlier.

Edward III's charter of 1357.

One climbed eastward up All Hallows Bank, today Akenside Hill, to reach Pilgrim Street and All Hallows (All Saints) Church. An early description and drawing of All Saints reveals late Norman work preserved in the west doorway suggesting it was already standing by the late twelfth century. Pilgrim Street is first mentioned in 1230 but was probably in use by the time All Hallows was built. Indeed, it was the sole throughfare in the town to be denoted 'street' and as such it may have used an earlier metalled track.

The second route from the bridge, the Side, climbed westward, following the channel carved by the Lort Burn and then one of its small tributaries. It skirted around the Castle and led towards the borough's principal church, St. Nicholas, which is traditionally dated to 1091 and was definitely in use by Henry I's reign. Moreover the existence of a large Christian cemetery, from the eighth century onwards, on the nearby Castle site, could well imply the church was of far greater antiquity than previously thought.

By far the most impressive of the medieval churches, St. Nicholas, became a cathedral in 1882. Much of the present exterior belongs to the fifteenth century, whilst the interior is largely fourteenth century. The original building was severely damaged by the great fire which razed the town in 1248. The familiar crown spire, a gift from the merchant Robert Rhodes, was added in 1470. Six of the eight shields on the font are dedicated to the Rhodes family.

Other additions over the years have included a new library and vestry, in 1730, and extensive alterations and renovation by John Dobson. He painstakingly restored the remains of the North Transept window in 1824, and was responsible for the installation

of heating and major underpinning of the tower. The tower has seventeen bells, three of which date from 1400.

Late in the 1700's the well meaning desire of local subscribers to turn the church into a *"sort of cathedral"* resulted in the loss and mutilation of the old choir stalls, pews and other artefacts.

A poem in Bourne, attributed to Ben Jonson, concerns the church:

My Altitude High, my Body four Square,
My foot in the Grave, my Head in the Air,
My Eyes in my sides, five Tongues in my Womb
Thirteen Heads upon my Body, four Images alone;
I can direct you where the Wind doth Stay,
And I tine God's Precepts twice a-Day.
I am Seen where I am not, I am heard where I is not,
Tell me now what I am, and see that you miss not.

The Cathedral is the second least visited in Britain, after Bradford.

All Saints

The old Gothic church held a congregation of up to two thousand, and was a favourite of local legend Roger Thornton, who was in fact buried there and endowed the church with the massive Thornton family memorial brass (now kept in St. Nicholas). In the winter of 1785 parts of the structure began to crack, and it was decided that the cost would be so great that the church was not really worth repairing. The last service was held on July 9th 1786. The new church, designed by David Stephenson, was consecrated in November 1789, although it did not receive its ninety-four feet spire for another seven years, and cost £27,000 to build. It is a good indication of the prosperity of the Quayside area at the time that the cash was raised largely by levies on landlords and tenants, and by public subscription.

Sadly, the fortunes of the church ebbed with those of the Quayside. By the late 1800's money for repairs, which had previously been forthcoming, was in short supply, and appeals had to be launched. All Saints was deconsecrated in 1961.

The church has recently been given a new lease of life, being bought by the Council in 1970, who have since renovated it and given it over to Town Teacher Ltd.

St. Andrews

There was a stone church at St. Andrews by the mid-twelfth century, its chancel arch is certainly Norman work. Even this may only represent a rebuilding of an earlier smaller chapel since many scholars have suggested St. Andrews also had pre-Norman origins. Part of its tower is twelfth century and contains stones from the Roman Wall.

It was so badly damaged in the 1644 siege that *"Ther was no child baptd. in this parish for one years tim after the town was taken, nor was sarmon in this church for one years tim."* It contains the tombs of John Wesley's step-daughter, Jane Smith; Bessie Surtees' father, Aubone; local architect William Newton and officers from Fenham Barracks.

The Norman chancel arch in St. Andrews.

St. Johns

Twelfth century architectural fragments would suggest the presence of a Norman stone church here, though the present St. Johns dates largely from the fourteenth and fifteenth century. In a window in the north side is the oldest known representation of the City Arms. Robert Rhodes provided the money to build the tower and has a coat of arms here. There is an exceptional Jacobean pulpit, dating to 1610.

The foundation of the Benedictine nunnery of St. Bartholemew has also been placed during the rule of King David and his son Earl Henry. An earlier date of 1086 is hinted at by one historian, John Forden. The nunnery took up the largest area of any religious establishment within the borough, which might support an early date since it would be easier to acquire such a large block before the area was built up. It may be that David simply endowed it with estates to provide a secure income. Little is known of the buildings of the nunnery. It was connected to the market streets by Nuns Lane, at the north end of which lay the main gatehouse into the precinct.

North of St. Nicholas stretches the long, curving Market Street complex, which today consists of the Cloth Market, Groat Market, Bigg Market and Newgate Street. This probably evolved over a period of time, rather than being founded in one go. It seems to consist of two separate centres which gradually expanded until they met near the bend in Newgate Street, opposite

Nuns Lane, where the medieval street was at its narrowest. The markets may have grown up as two entirely separate units, each outside a different church, St. Andrews' to the north and St. Nicholas' to the south.

The original southern market would have been aligned roughly north-south and the northern one east-west. As they gained in popularity, more stalls and then houses were added on the ends, gradually extending the markets northwards and westwards until the two linked up.

In the western part of the town the Hospital of St. Mary the Virgin was also in existence by the mid-twelfth century. Together with St. Johns this would imply that the Westgate street was also a major thoroughfare by this time.

Hence the three major arteries of the medieval borough, Westgate, Market Street and Pilgrim Street were already formed by the end of the Norman period. It is likely that the network of minor routes, or chares, was also well-developed by that time, likewise the characteristic burgage plots running backwards in long narrow strips, with their frontages on the major streets. Little remains of this medieval minor street plan today but the buildings in the Cloth Market preserve the layout of some of the former burgage strips.

The creation of the Quayside was an achievement of the following centuries, except perhaps around Sandhill, the triangular piece of ground just east of the bridgehead. The first tentative steps of reclamation may have begun during the latter part of this period. It was probably already the site of a harbour at the mouth of the Lort Burn, and this, together with its proximity to the bridge, would have made it a logical place to start. The earliest public building in this area, the chapel and hospital of St. Thomas the Martyr at the bridge end, is first mentioned in 1248. The fact it is dedicated to St. Thomas Becket, victim of one of Henry II's famous rages, would suggest it was erected in the late twelfth century.

Not only did the familiar street plan begin to take shape during the Norman period but also what were long to be the core industries of Tyneside's economy became well-established. Commercial shipbuilding and extensive coal mining were certainly underway by the twelfth century at the latest. This strong base ensured that Newcastle was one of the wealthiest ports in the country by the beginning of the thirteenth century. It was also the centre of royal administration in Northumberland and was about to gain another important victory in the struggle for self-government.

The Middle Ages.

King John's Death

John was the last king who was as much at home in France as he was in England. His turbulent reign saw the loss of most of the continental empire built up by his father, Henry II, an area comprising nearly half of the French kingdom. His death, in 1216, opens a period of history in which we can no longer talk of Norman or Saxon, only of Englishmen. English unity was slowly beginning to emerge, helped by the loss of the French territories. The barons might indeed still speak French but the bulk of their lands, and hence their loyalties, now lay in England.

Shortly before John's death he granted Newcastle a mayor, marking the end of Norman feudalism and the beginning of self-rule in the town. Indeed, Newcastle had much to thank this supposedly cruel king for, since he was a generous patron of the town, granting it many new rights. We know little of that first Mayor, Sir Peter Scott, the chief magistrate who also held the Lordship of Eshott in Northumberland.

This independence set the stage for Newcastle to become a regional centre of considerable importance. But it was as a *"bulwarke against the Scots"* that the town began its rise through the medieval period.

The Border Wars.

Chapter 4

On the whole the thirteenth century was generally a very peaceful time along the border, later to be looked upon as something of a 'Golden Age'. The two kingdoms were virtually moving towards union under a single monarchy. There followed a series of unlikely events that were to shape British history for the next three hundred years. In 1286 Alexander III, King of Scotland, stumbled over a cliff face and was killed. It was possibly the most tragic trip in British history. Both his sons and his first wife had already died. His successor, Margaret the Maid, was an infant in Norway.

For two years Scotland was ruled by a council. It was agreed that Edward I's son (later to become Edward II, a truly disastrous king) would marry Margaret. Any heir would have been undisputed king of both England and Scotland and advanced history by three hundred years. Of course, things might not have worked out well even if the marriage had gone ahead but it remains one of history's great might have beens. It was not to be. In a further tragic event Margaret was drowned in a shipwreck on her way to Scotland.

Edward I was invited to choose a successor out of twelve claimants. These, in the main part opportunists, were whittled down to two serious contenders. The decision was announced in the Great Hall of Berwick Castle in 1292. The choice of the politically weak John Balliol over Robert Bruce set the scene for future conflict. Balliol paid homage to Edward in Newcastle in the same year.

A fragile peace existed until 1296 when English shipping was burnt in Berwick harbour. Balliol had found it impossible to appease both Edward's interference and the demands of the Scottish nobility. He was summoned to appear before Edward in Newcastle but failed to turn up. Edward invaded to complete what he thought would be the final crushing of the Scots. So started three hundred years of border warfare.

Despite inflicting what seemed to be decisive victories over the Scots, Edward was unable to stamp out their resistance. He was already an old man and time was running out. In 1307 he died, once again campaigning to achieve that elusive final victory. His son was to prove unequal to the task he inherited.

In 1309 Edward II assembled the English forces in Newcastle. He was too interested in his handsome lover, Piers Gaveston, to pay proper attention to his army. They became restless waiting and eventually revolted. Edward escaped to Tynemouth, Piers lost his head. In 1314 Edward returned and met the Scottish forces at Bannockburn. *"The finest army England had ever put in the field was destroyed in two days....it had been easier to take a kingdom from the son than a yard from the father."* (George MacDonald Fraser). And so it continued, as England the empire builder found it impossible to share this Island with another country.

The prolonged warfare had a profound impact on northern society. For Newcastle itself the effect of Scottish raids and sieges was to some extent eased by the benefits provided by the frequent presence of the royal court. There was also the steady market provided by the professional troops which had replaced the feudal levies of earlier conflicts. Newcastle continued to grow in importance, apparently unimpaired by the surrounding turmoil. In 1400 it gained the status of a separate county, only the third town in England to do so.

The Battle of Neville's Cross in 1346, as shown in Froissart's chronicles. The battle was fought outside Durham but the French artist mistakenly drew Newcastle. This is possibly the earliest representation of the town, but cannot claim to be at all accurate. It is unlikely that the artist ever saw the town and either drew from a traveller's description or he simply drew an idealised view of a medieval walled town.

The Walls

Mindful of the ever-present threat of Scottish invasion the burgesses set about the construction of the town's walls. The borough was allowed to levy a special tax, known as *murage* - from the Latin murus, meaning wall. The first grant was in 1265 so building must have begun soon after. The work proceeded steadily but slowly and grants of *murage* continued for the next hundred years. Some of these grants may have been to fund repairs, but construction was probably not completed until the mid-fourteenth century, if not later.

Work began on the north side of the town and progressed down to the river, with teams working on both the east and west flanks simultaneously. For many of the townsfolk the wall may have been a mixed blessing as it sliced through their property, separating house from garden. Only the most powerful institutions were able to secure posterns through the wall to their lands immediately outside. The Dominicans gained one in 1280, which can still be seen today. Ten years later it was the turn of the Hospital of St. Mary the Virgin - an indication of the builders' progress.

The original plan was to include the Castle as a strong point in the line of the defences but this aroused considerable protest - especially amongst those burgesses whose properties would be left outside the walls. In 1311 the route was changed to meet their demands and the wall ran down from Neville Tower south to the river. A similar change of plan occurred on the east side. The formal incorporation within the borough of Pandon, in 1299, resulted in the diversion of the walls eastward to include the new quarter. These last minute alterations account for the awkward bends in the circuit.

The onset of the Scottish wars found the walls still far from complete. As an emergency measure the town was hastily enclosed by an outer ditch, known as the King's Dyke. This was already underway by 1312, when the astute Dominicans were granted a wooden drawbridge over the ditch, and finished before 1317. The ditch was over eleven metres wide and four and a half deep in front of Heber and Morden Towers. In places it is even said to have been flooded. Certainly the defences were strong enough to repel a Scottish army in 1341.

Building work absorbed much of the town's surplus wealth over a long period. The fact that it was pressed to completion when other English towns abandoned the task shows the burgesses regarded the Scottish threat as very real. It was money well

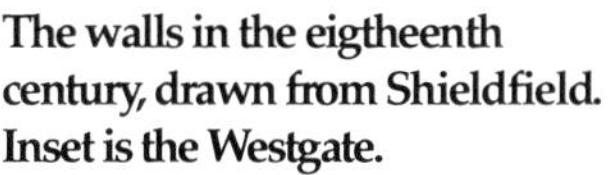

The walls in the eigtheenth century, drawn from Shieldfield. Inset is the Westgate.

spent. In Henry VIII's day John Leland described the circuit as being stronger and more magnificent than *"all of the walls of the cities of England and most of the cities of Europe"*. There is certainly an element of exaggeration in that statement but Newcastle's defences would certainly have held their own amongst English town walls.

Just over two miles long, the walls were between seven and ten feet thick and up to twenty-five feet high. The circuit was studded with seventeen D-shaped towers, situated within bowshot of each other, whilst turrets rose from the wall-walk. It was pierced by six main gates and at least four lesser gates and narrow posterns. The only access to the parapets was via stairs within the towers and gatehouses. Any assailant who managed to raise his ladder on what little space there was between the ditch and wall, was then exposed to fire from the towers. With no steps he was then unable to get down the other side, without taking the risk of jumping over twenty feet. Wooden shutters were fitted in the spaces in the battlements. Defenders could raise the shutters to fire, then lower them, closing the gap and preventing the attackers from using their arrows to any effect.

They were regularly repaired and upgraded over the years, notably by Sir Arthur Hazelrigg, Parliamentary Governor in 1648, and again during the Jacobite rebellions of 1715 - when all but one of the gates were built up - and 1745. They were also put into a state of defence during the Napoleonic wars. This was despite the fact that long sections, notably along the riverside areas, had been demolished between 1763 and 1798 to make way for the expanding Quayside. Such attempts were more for psychological comfort than for any real effect.

Successive government reports underlined the vulnerability of the walls in the time of gunpowder and more effective artillery. Far from being an impregnable fortress Newcastle was hopelessly exposed, being surrounded by higher ground on all sides, enabling the enemy to wreak havoc in the crowded town. This fundamental fault could only be rectified at immense cost by building a vast circuit with artillery forts on the higher positions.

Despite this the walls were only ever breached in battle once, in 1644, when they succumbed to gunpowder - something which was not anticipated when the burgesses laid the foundations some three centuries earlier!

The Walls Today

Substantial lengths of the circuit have survived nineteenth century redevelopment to adorn the modern city. The council has justifiably devoted considerable effort to the excavation and landscaping of these stretches which symbolise the special character of the city - a modern commercial centre with ancient roots.

The best preserved sections lie to the north-west, running from the site of the Newgate, around St. Andrews Church, between Stowell Street and the Gallowgate bus station, and on past Blackfriars. At Heber Tower the wall turns and heads south-east towards Westgate Road where it comes to an end, though its route can still be followed by walking along Pink Lane.

The condition of these walls is remarkable. They survive to the level of the wall-walk. Their arrow loops and original battlements can still be seen in places. Even the postern to let the Dominican friars pass through to their gardens outside remains, though now blocked up. It is not difficult to imagine the friars filing through, carrying the fruits of their labours.

The four towers are each crowned by a ring of projecting stone corbels. In wartime these would have supported an overhanging wooden platform and screen, known as a hoarding. The defenders could clamber into the hoarding and pour missiles and stones down on to attackers who managed to reach the base of the wall. Outside, to the west, the ditch has been excavated and grassed over between Morden and Heber Tower. It is now possible to gain a good impression of just what a powerful contribution this made to the defences.

The second length on the west side has recently become more accessible with the demolition of buildings along Forth Street. The stretch now stands proud and unmistakeable, just east of the Orchard Street Postal Sorting Depot. A new path laid by the City Council runs alongside and follows the wall

The Walls today. Heber Tower, with the 1804 House of Recovery in the background.

down the precipitous slope to the Close. The open area just east of the wall, now occupied by parking for Royal Mail vehicles, is the site of the Carmelite Friary grounds which, like those of the Blackfriars, lay just inside the medieval circuit.

On the east side survival has been much patchier. Only three towers remain - Plummer Tower overlooking the Central Motorway, the Corner Tower which still has a short length of wall and a projecting turret attached, and Wallknoll or Sallyport Tower. The latter has a narrow gateway to allow defenders to sally forth and disrupt enemy siege operations. Unfortunately, both the motorway and City Road carve routes through this area, making it difficult to appreciate the layout of the medieval town here.

These remnants do not rise to a lofty height. They may even seem puny when compared to the defences of powerful castles. Nevertheless, Newcastle's walls were among the strongest of English town circuits with little of the jerry building that is found elsewhere. They repaid the effort lavished upon them, serving the borough well throughout the border conflict of the later Middle Ages.

The town walls between Newgate and Westgate in the 1780's.

The Reivers

In the countryside the well organised Scottish raids, especially after Bannockburn, created widespread devastation. As English fortunes began to revive under Edward III, it was the Scots' turn to suffer. It was the small scale cattle raiding and kidnapping which was perhaps the most damaging factor - continuing year in year out, no matter what official truces were signed. A vicious cycle of counter raids and feuds was set up, of kidnapping for ransom or simply revenge. The effects were most severe in the districts nearest the border - Tynedale, Redesdale, Glendale and Teviotdale. There the raids compounded the poverty of these upland valley communities.

The result was a gradual breakdown of law and order. Royal authority was on the wane on both sides of the border and only the most powerful lords - the Percies and the Nevilles - could keep order. As the temporary crisis became a permanent way of life, northern society painfully adapted. Most strikingly, gentlemen began adding to their lightly defended hall-houses the forbidding towers which are such a common feature of the Northumbrian landscape today.

Raiding was not the only ill fortune that the countryside had to bear in the fourteenth and fifteenth centuries. Cattle and sheep diseases, pestilence and a gradual worsening of climate all depressed the agrarian economy. Land was turned over from arable to pasture, some never to be ploughed again. The corrugated pattern of medieval ridge and furrow ploughing abandoned then can be seen today on the slopes of the Breamish Valley near Wooler, for example.

The effects of both warfare and environmental changes should not be overstated. Good agricultural land was still cultivated, but there was a shift towards livestock in the uplands. As a result rents may have declined in value, a problem for the lord, if not the peasant. The prosperity of the thirteenth century had clearly come to an end.

The New Nobility

If the decline in rents may have improved the lot of the Northern peasantry, the wars by contrast led to the impoverishment of the old Norman nobility, the Umfravilles, de Vescis and Roos. Many of these families held land on both sides of the border. They were in an impossible position. Whichever side they chose, and not all were loyal to the English crown, they lost some lands once the dream of a single Kingdom was shattered on the field of Bannockburn.

The Scots Inn on Newgate Street. This town mansion was used by the visiting Scottish court in times of peace.

The result was the emergence of a new northern nobility, the Percies, who originally had held no estates in Northumberland whatsoever. The first Percy property in the region was centred on Alnwick, acquired from the de Vesci family. It provided a staging post between their main estates in Yorkshire and new lands they had been granted by Edward I in Scotland as a reward for faithful service in the Scottish wars. They steadily expanded their power base in the North, despite losing their new Scottish manors.

Not having the same divided loyalties as the old aristocracy the Percies could pursue warfare with greater vigour and earn royal favour. They soon began to monopolise the royal posts instituted by the English monarchy to defend the frontier, especially the Wardenship of the Eastern Marches. The income from the salary and perks provided by these posts in turn enabled the Percies to maintain the large retinues which became essential for border defence. Once established, the English kings found it was extremely difficult to dispense with their services, even when they became *"over-mighty subjects"* as in Henry IV's reign, when Hotspur rebelled.

Towards the end of the fourteenth century the North was controlled by three of these powerful families: The House of Lancaster; the Nevilles, based around Raby; and the Percies. Invariably they squabbled amongst themselves, but when they joined forces they were kingmakers. The Percies and Nevilles helped overthrow Richard II and put Henry Bolingbroke, of the House of Lancaster, on the throne as Henry IV. Rivalry between the Percies and Nevilles was a major factor in the countdown to the Wars of the Roses in the late fifteenth century. It says something of their power that both families survived these Wars.

The Medieval Town.

Rural Life

At this time England was essentially rural, with few people living in towns. Even by 1400 only about four thousand people lived in Newcastle, about the size of modern day Amble in Northumberland. The town itself had a rural atmosphere with many townsfolk still working the land.

A daily scene would have been the driving of cattle from within the town's walls on to common-owned pasture on the Town Moor, Castle Leazes and Nun's Moor, areas which the townsfolk guarded jealously for grazing - and still do. The Town Moor was still extensively used in this way in the 1600's where we have records of the council employing a variety of people; the Grassman acted as a Moor policeman, whilst the Neateherd oversaw four servants who performed the task of collecting the cattle. The men went through the streets at four in the morning sounding trumpets to notify the townsfolk to bring their cows to the gates. The men then went to the Moor, tended the animals and returned them before sundown. This was carried on for centuries, a legacy of a more rural age. It took the advent of the railways before the system disintegrated. As late as 1895, a third of Newcastle's milk was produced within the city, in one of the seventy odd byres which housed over six hundred cows.

The medieval Town Moor was a mixture of open ground and dense oak woodland. The trees were gradually cleared away and often supplied the timber for an infant shipbuilding industry growing along the river. The land was leased to the town in a charter drawn up during the reign of King John and reaffirmed under Henry III.

Despite this rural atmosphere towns still differed fundamentally from their surrounding countryside in that they existed primarily for the purpose of commerce and manufacturing which generated increasing wealth.

The town consisted of four parishes within the walls, surrounded by the villages of Heaton, Elswick, Benwell, Kenton and Pandon. Pandon was an industrial area, centre of the unpleasant tanning and fulling industries.

The Quayside

Upstream, the shipbuilding industry was beginning to take shape. One of the first relevant documents relates to the building of a galley, part of a twenty-ship order from the king, distributed amongst the country's most important towns and ports. The galley was constructed at the mouth of the Lort Burn and finished in 1296 at a cost of £205.

By 1334 Newcastle was the fourth wealthiest town in England. One of the key factors in this

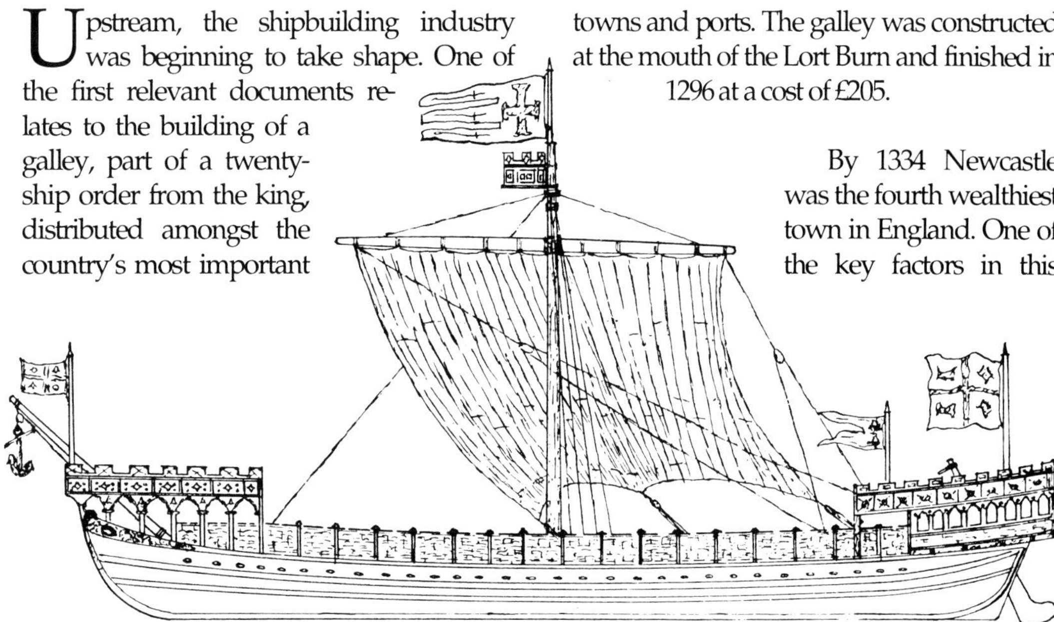

A reconstruction of the 1296 galley. It was 135ft long and probably built from trees cut down on the Town Moor.

rapid growth was the reclamation of the Sandhill and the Quayside from the river. Before 1200 the Quayside was nothing more than mud and sandbanks. Soon afterwards the process of reclaiming the area began as clay jetties, faced with stone, were built out into the river. Ships and boats could then load and unload their wares with greater ease, fuelling Newcastle's development into a major port.

By 1300 the spaces between these original jetties had been filled by dumped material. Houses, warehouses and workshops were built now. The drawback of flooding did not stop the area expanding to become the focal point of the town, linked to the increasingly vibrant port, laying the basis of the Quayside as we know it today.

This immense feat is perhaps the single most important contribution to the modern city's medieval facilities. Few visitors to today's Quayside realise that, when they walk around admiring the fine buildings, eight hundred years earlier there would have been nothing but sandbanks and the occasional jetty.

The Quayside wall had *"on top a walk... and at the bottom of it a great many gates, called Water Gates....These were ordered to be locked up every night, except one or two to stand open, for the masters and seamen to go to and fro their ships. This was done to prevent servants casting ashes and other rubbish into the river"*.

Gradually during this period there was a steady flow of merchants and the wealthy into the Quay area; the Sandhill, the Side, and the Close. Many remained up in the centre, around the Cloth Market and along Pilgrim and Newgate Streets - near to the most important buildings, such as the mother church of St. Nicholas, and the Castle. It is only lately, centuries later, that the wheel has turned full circle and we can witness the return of the wealthy to the heart of the city as new luxury flats are planned and built along the waterfront.

There were fewer boundaries between rich and poor areas than there are today. The prosperous tended to live along street frontages, whilst artisans and craftsmen lived behind them, around the 'stairs' going up to the Close and at the back end of the newly built chares.

The word chare is almost peculiar to Newcastle. It is thought to derive from the Saxon 'cerre', meaning turning or bending. The chares were a cluster of narrow alleyways at a right angle to the Quay. Originally there were over twenty, running from Sandhill to Pandon burn, but many were destroyed by the 1854 fire or swept away during Victorian slum clearances. One of the few remaining is Broad Chare, so named because this was the only one where two carts were able to pass. Their names changed regularly, and many have been forgotten. Bourne bafflingly noted that Dark Chare's original name, *"had it been worth remembering, would, in all probability, have been lost by now"*.

This was the place to be, close to work and the busy port. The buildings had to be squeezed in between the walls at either end of the Quay, such was the demand to live in this prosperous area. The district, as a whole, was described as *"the most crowded part of the kingdom"*, buildings were packed together and each had overhanging storeys larger than the next. It would have felt like walking through a tunnel as the top storeys extended nearly touching each other with very little skylight reaching the ground.

For most of the population there was congestion and streets clogged with rubbish and excrement. Conditions, however, were gradually improving, and were perhaps not as bad as those brought about by the overcrowding caused by the Industrial Revolution in the nineteenth century. The house of a shopkeeper or craftsmen might have a shop or workrooms on the ground floor, a first floor hall, larder, kitchen and bedrooms, with further bedchambers on the third storey.

Town Life.

Guilds

In 1216 King John allowed the formation of guilds in the town. Guilds gave tradesmen the right to form strict cartels that protected their markets, controlled all trade in the town and regulated the standards to which their members conformed. The influence of the guild extended beyond that of a trading cartel; they shared tools, jointly purchased raw materials, and sought to oversee the spiritual and social welfare of members.

In all there were twelve such guilds, known as Mysteries, from the French 'metier' - to trade, and a further fifteen lesser guilds. The Merchant Adventurers were the original society of free merchants whose formation John permitted. In 1480 we find evidence that they approved rules for better self management, holding court and meeting at the Maison Dieu.

Once a year, on Corpus Christi day, each member appeared in the guild's apparel to take part in a performance of a Miracle play. All the guilds performed Miracle plays, based on stories from the testaments. Each guild performed the same play every year. They toured the town in rotation, playing at several different sites. The Merchant Adventurers performed a play titled 'Hogmagog', though unfortunately no copies exist. The only surviving copy of any of the plays, 'Noah's Ark', performed by the Shipwrights' Guild, is contained in John Brand's history of the town.

The Corpus Christi performances were one of the most spectacular days in the medieval calendar, part of the pageantry we always link with the period. Each of the guilds vied with each other to be the most colourful and produce the best play. The plays themselves, though having a religious content, were, by all accounts, vulgar, foul-mouthed and sensational, the leads often performing completely naked.

The Corpus Christi procession, painted as a roof mural for the Laing Art Gallery in 1934 by Louisa Hodgson.

Markets

Newcastle's growing wealth allowed the merchants to start building the foundations of the town that we might recognise today. These early developments included the expansion of Pilgrim Street and Market Street. If the street plan was beginning to take on a familiar form, retailing in this blossoming centre was still very different. There were few permanent shops as we would know them today. Instead people bought and sold goods in the many periodic and specialised markets. This is reflected by the modern names to the Market Street complex which comprised the Bigg (barley), Flesh, Meat, and

Cloth Markets. Others included Cale Cross, where cale, a type of cabbage soup was sold, the Milk Market down by the river, and White Cross Market, at the top of the town, where livestock was sold.

Perishable foodstuffs were brought in from surrounding areas and only meat and grain came from greater distances. The main markets were held on Saturday:

"There is such a concourse of people out of this county in the streits every Saterday to all sorts of corne and flesh, buy all sorts of provision for house and family, receive money of maisters of cole for cole work, that every Saterdays Market is like a faire."

Burns and Bridges

Expansion in the town was restricted by a number of features that no longer confront today's planners. Streams, now covered over, crossed the area. The Lort Burn split the central part of the town, its steep banks not allowing building to the east; whilst Pandon Burn isolated the industrial village of Pandon from Newcastle. Bridges were built across them to improve access. Two were built across the Lort Burn, on the present day sites of High and Low Bridge Streets. Stocksbridge was added to link Pandon Village to the Quayside.

In addition, the presence of several large religious houses, with their substantial grounds, was to hinder growth until the Dissolution in the mid-sixteenth century.

Barras Bridge.

Nether Dene Bridge which carried the road across the Lort Burn between Pilgrim Street and St. Nicholas' churchyard. The bridge, which was demolished in 1788, gave its name to the present day Low Bridge Street.

Religion.

Friars

One of the most striking characteristics of the town was the existence of a number of imposing friaries. Religious establishments - priories, friaries and nunneries - occupied what seems to modern eyes an extraordinarily large proportion of the late medieval town. In Newcastle alone there were five friaries, a nunnery and many hospitals. Newcastle was certainly not abnormal in this respect. Such major provision not only reflects the undoubted importance of religious belief in the medieval world but also the crucial role of the Church as a social and political, as well as spiritual, force. Moreover it was clear that the rapid growth of urban life, not just in England but all over Europe, demanded a new religious movement.

The lack of a large cathedral, with all the ecclesiastical services which it would have brought, made their presence even more important. Newcastle was essentially a thirteenth century new town, a medieval Milton Keynes, built after the great Norman cathedral building days.

The earlier monastic orders had sited their establishments away from towns, preferring secluded locations such as Rievaulx or Fountains in the wilds of the Yorkshire Dales, or Brinkburn in the depths of Coquetdale. The friars were everything that the early orders were not. The Cistercians or Benedictines sought remote locations providing near total exclusion from earthly pleasures, in order to ease spiritual contemplation. The friars, on the other hand, plunged deep into that earthly world, healing the sick, preaching in the market place and consoling the bereaved.

The evangelical friars struck a chord with mid to late medieval Europe, especially in the crowded towns and cities. The friars subsidised themselves by begging rather than relying on the incomes the huge estates bequeathed to the monastic orders. As a result they were later able to tap deep into the rich vein of medieval piety, benefiting from the increasing wealth of the merchants, craftsmen and burgesses in a way the long established orders could not. Medieval man thought he was not long for this earth and spent much of his time contemplating the transient nature of his existence. He considered the day of redemption was near and sought to smooth his path through purgatory with vast gifts to the Church.

As might be expected, the contrast between the old and new orders gave rise to conflict between the monks and the friars. Not only did the austere life and charitable activities of the friars contrast well with the isolated, but by now enormously wealthy, monasteries, but there was also a financial source of discord. The friars were accused of stealing the bread from the mouths of the parish priest by taking over the latter's function. They were in general more learned and understanding than the priests and their popularity increased. This was a source of great concern, especially to the Augustinian monasteries, which had earlier taken on the management of the parish churches' revenue. Disputes between them were usually sorted out at a local level, often restricting the friars to healing or medicinal roles.

The Benedictine nunnery was the oldest religious house in the town and occupied the largest area, covering what is now the Grainger Market, Binns Department Store and much of Eldon Square shopping centre. It may have been established as early as 1086 but more likely was founded in the mid-twelfth century to provide a home for devout daughters of the gentry. Little is known of the buildings but Nuns Lane formed the original approach to the main gateway which stood where the lane opens on to Nun Street.

The Greyfriars, or Franciscans, arrived in the town in 1274. The order was founded by St. Francis of Assisi and was perhaps the most austere and best known of the orders because of this. They were possibly established in the town by the Carliol family. The site, together with St. Bartholomew's, was bought by Robert Anderson, one of the wealthiest men in the town. He constructed the magnificent Newe House which dominated the town's landscape for the next three hundred years.

Blackfriars, or Dominicans, were known in the town as shod friars because, unlike the barefooted Greyfriars, they wore shoes. The order was founded in 1216 by St. Dominic and their first house in England was built in Oxford in 1221. They had settled in Newcastle by 1239.

Austin Friary was established in the town in 1290. It was kept as the seat of the King's Council in the North when, on rare occasions, it did not sit at York. It cannot have been put to great use as it was recorded, in a survey of 1595, as being in bad repair. The site was renamed the King's Manor. Later the Holy Jesus Hospital was built on the ruins, one of the friary's towers can still be seen incorporated into the old hospital.

The Trinitarians, founded by William de Acton in 1360, wore a white robe with a red and blue cross. One third of their income went to ransom crusaders taken captive by the infidel, one third went to the poor and the rest was used to maintain the order. Shortly before the Dissolution, John Felle, a member of the house, was convicted of *"incontinence"* with two women.

Whitefriars or Carmelites. There is nothing to see of the Whitefriar's house but, like Blackfriars, the friary has been excavated by the City Archaeologist, and as a result is better understood. The Whitefriars had not always occupied this site. Before them the Friars of the Sack had a house here. The first mention of the Sack friars comes in 1266 when an area of land called *"Cunstable-galgothe"* was granted to them. The order was swept away by the internal feuding which characterised the medieval Catholic Church, ordered not to recruit new members by the Council of Lyon in 1274. In 1300, when Edward I gave them a pittance, there were only three monks left in the order. When the Carmelites took over the site in 1307 there was a solitary friar left from the old order who was supported by the Carmelites.

The Carmelites themselves had arrived in the town in 1262 and settled around Pandon Burn on land given to them by John de Byker. A new section of the wall was built through this friary and as compensation they were offered the Westgate site together with fourteen marks. This site stretched from the Westgate down to the river but was in turn split by another section of the wall which was built through the garden. In compensation the friars were given one pound of pepper corn. When the friary was dissolved in 1539 the declaration of surrender was signed by the prior and nine friars, probably their complete number.

Blackfriars

Of the five friaries that once existed within the town walls, only at Blackfriars are there now substantial remains. The friars are first mentioned in 1239 when they received gifts of cloth from Henry III. The order had a powerful patron in the shape of Sir Peter Scott, mayor between 1245-51, who may, if the tradition is at all trustworthy, have provided the land and money for the present friary.

In 1280 the king, having already allowed the friars to construct some form of aqueduct from *"a well without this court"*, granted them a licence to make a narrow gate through the town walls which bisected their garden. The bricked up gate can still be seen near Heber Tower. Later they were allowed to build a narrow wooden bridge across the King's Dyke, providing they would remove it during times of trouble.

The friary soon became the regular residence of Royalty visiting the area. These visits were accompanied by gifts of alms from the king to all the members of the religious houses for each day the king stayed in the town, alms which amounted to vast sums of money. Edward II and Queen Isabella stayed there, and Edward Balliol paid homage to Edward III here.

After the Dissolution, the friary was bought by the corporation in 1544, who promptly demolished the church, the sacristy and part of the chapter house. In 1552 it was leased to nine of the town's mysteries: The Bakers and Brewers; Butchers; Cordwainers; Fullers and Dyers; Saddlers; Skinners and Glovers; Smiths; and Tanners and Tailors. The new tenants carried out some degree of rebuilding, restoration and conversion during their occupation, which was to last for the next four hundred years.

Bourne complains of the dirtiness of the place, and Brand tells us *"their want of cleanliness is the more to be wondered at as they still enjoy abundance of fine water"*. Many of the buildings not used by the trades soon fell into disrepair. Brand describes the chapel: *"the whole pile has still a monastic appearance....Once the recess of a respectable order of religious, who were the patrons and possessors of the learning of virtues, it is now tenanted by ignorant old women: some of it is converted to stabling, and its out offices are appropriated to the feeding of hogs."*

By the 1950's the whole area was neglected and dilapidated. The buildings only survive today through the efforts of Alderman Peter Renwick in the 1960's, and now those buildings that survive and the surrounding area have been carefully restored and landscaped. In keeping with their past they are now used by local craftsmen and women. The refectory also houses a coffee shop. The new development was opened in April 1980 by the Queen Mother, and had cost some £600,000 - £300,000 from the City Council, and the rest from Tyne and Wear Development Corporation, The Department of the Environment, and the English Tourist Board. Restoration work began in August 1975, and concluded in 1981, with the excavation of the church site completed in 1985 and the landscaping in the following year.

The original buildings were typical of their type, arranged around a cloister - an open square with a covered walkway along each side. On the north side was the church, of which only the ground plan can be seen. To the east lay the principal room. The ground floor formed the chapter house with a dormitory above. To the south was the refectory and to the west the guest-hall.

A reconstruction, by Graham Mitchell, of how Blackfriars would have looked in the Middle Ages.

Healthcare

The religious orders in the town were also responsible for healthcare provision. The appalling living conditions - squalid, insanitary housing and poor diet - were the main cause of poor health and high death rates in towns such as Newcastle, although the low level of medical knowledge did not help matters.

Leprosy was the most feared of illnesses in the Middle Ages, since it was widely believed to be far more contagious than is in fact the case. The location of Newcastle's leprosarium of St. Mary Magdelene, near Barras Bridge, well outside the medieval built up area, is typical of such hospitals. Once diagnosed by a panel of clergy, or a jury, lepers were outcast *"dead to the world but alive to god"*. Land at Spital Tongues was given to the sufferers so they could become self-sufficient and need not mix with the town's population. Spital itself means a hospital for contagious diseases. By Henry VIII's time the disease was fortunately so rare that the hospital was accepting other patients. In any case it must have paled by comparison with the repeated plagues of the later centuries which may have halved the English population.

The earliest mention of a physician in the town comes in 1352 when a William de Burntof treated the Earl of Cornwall, one of the King's entourage. In 1442 a new Guild, the Barbers and Surgeons, was incorporated. They moved to permanent buildings at Manors in 1648 where they kept a specialist herb garden for medicines. It is debateable whether such surgeons were a greater threat to their patients than the ailments they claimed to cure. This was certainly true of the quacks used by the poor majority of the townsfolk. All practitioners used leeches to bleed their victims, often to the point of death, whilst apothecaries supplied herbal remedies which were sometimes effective but more often bizarre.

Nursing care was provided by various bodies. The town had about a dozen hospitals, chapels and almshouses, by the end of the Middle Ages. Furthermore, their endeavours would have been supplemented by the charitable work of the friaries. Of the three major hospitals St. Mary the Virgin, on Westgate, was the earliest recorded, having existed since Norman times. The leper hospital of St. Mary Magdelene, would have also originated in the twelfth or thirteenth centuries when the scourge of leprosy was at its height. It is mentioned in a Papal Bull, or decree, of around this time. A late addition was the Maison Dieu, otherwise known as St. Catherine's Hospital, founded in the early

The Hospital of St. Mary Magdeline shortly before its demolition. The Hospital was home to the medieval Town's *leprosarium*. It lay well beyond the walls, between what is now St Mary's Place and Vine Lane opposite the Haymarket Metro Station.

fifteenth century by Roger Thornton. He established it down on the Sandhill next to the site of the later Guildhall.

It appears all manner of bodies were helping the sick, but this is a misleading impression, since none of these institutions was dedicated solely to this task. This is obvious in the case of the friaries, but medieval hospitals equally had many different roles. They provided assistance, like almshouses, for the poor and also accommodation for travellers, especially pilgrims. Indeed the name hospital has no medical connotation, being derived form the Latin word, *hospitalitas* - hospitality. Moreover, as in most late medieval foundations, the poor housed in the Maison Dieu were expected to pray for the soul of their wealthy patron. This function as a permanent and pious memorial was a vital consideration for men like Roger Thornton, in the plague-ridden and death-obsessed Middle Ages. However, given the very limited medical knowledge available to medieval man, prayer was perhaps in any case one of the more useful tasks that either patient or health-carer could perform.

Manors and Villages.

Adam's Camera

Life would have been different for the peasants in the villages surrounding the medieval town. These have all been swallowed up by the modern suburbs but one trace of these rural communities can be seen in Heaton Park: the Camera of Adam of Jesmond, popularly known as King John's Palace ('Camera' is a Latin word meaning a room, hall or enclosed space). It was built by Adam of Jesemuthe, a powerful local figure in the mid-thirteenth century, who was appointed Sheriff of Northumberland in 1262.

The picturesque little ruin comprises the remnants of a two storey hall-house. Such hall-houses were the standard dwelling of the northern gentry and lesser nobility in the thirteenth century. Only one end of the camera survives today, complete with an angle turret. Originally it would have consisted of a long two storey building with little turrets at each corner and battlements around the roof. Arranged around this main hall building would have been all the out buildings associated with the manor such as workshops, byres, stables, and barns. Here, the produce from the manorial fields, pigsties, beehives and dovecots would have been stored and processed, providing a more varied diet, at least for the lord and his immediate family. There was also the obligatory brewhouse supplying the vast quantities of ale which medieval households consumed.

Today such ruins, like the visible tip of an iceberg, symbolise the highly developed system of the organisation of land and labour, of which they formed a part. This system of manors covered medieval rural England. It was geared to the maintenance of armoured cavalry, knights who would be at the disposal of the king.

and its Lord

The focus of the lord's activity would have been on the first floor. The main room was the hall, the communal eating and sleeping area. The lord would have eaten here in the company of his retainers. He would have been seated on a raised platform (a 'dais') at one end of the hall together with his wife, family and guests. His retainers would have occupied long trestle tables arranged at right angles to the high table. They would also have slept in the same room on thin straw filled mattresses which could be rolled up and stowed out of the way during the day. This lack of privacy is, to modern eyes, one of the most incomprehensible features of medieval life. Originally the lord and his family would have slept in the same room. Although their power was great, medieval lords had to be seen by their households to command their respect and obedience, which was based partly on shared experiences.

By the thirteenth century the nobility were beginning to have had enough of this idea - their tastes were becoming more sophisticated and they demanded more comfort and privacy. So by this time halls usually had a private room opening off the high table end to which the lord and his immediate family could retreat after the meal. This room would be much more splendidly adorned with carpets, wall hangings and cushions.

A reconstruction by Graham Mitchell of a feast in progress at Adam's Camera.

A fair impression of the original scale and appearance of the hall-house can be gained by visiting Aydon Castle near Corbridge.

Town Government.

Mayors

By 1300 the town was being governed, although not always smoothly, by a mayor and four bailiffs. One such Mayor was John of Kenton, elected four times during the 1300's. He was accused by a group of the town's freemen of being a profiteer, opportunist, and even of being corrupt; accusations that would appear to have some basis. His re-election in 1341 caused uproar. A group of burgesses elected a rival candidate and seized the town gates. Riots followed between supporters of the two candidates which were so severe that the king was forced to resume control of the town as in feudal times.

This royal involvement meant that the lesser burgesses were able to make a case to the king for a greater say in the running of the town and were able to secure a new charter in 1342. From this date formal elections could take place, although the electorate was still formed from a minority of the town's population. The Corporation, or council, comprised twenty-four members.

Elections

The system of elections was complex to say the least. The twelve guilds elected twenty-four delegates, known as the 'former electors', who elected four to the council: the old mayor, and three who were already aldermen. This group in turn elected seven aldermen and one person, who had to have been a sheriff, to make an initial twelve, or 'first electors'. If seven aldermen could not be found then eight sheriffs were elected; if eight sheriffs could not be found then they had to choose from the ranks of the burgesses. The twelve mysteries then sent twelve delegates, and the twelve 'first electors' elected six from this group to join them, making eighteen. The fifteen by-trades then chose a delegate each, these fifteen chose twelve freemen, six of these chosen by the original eighteen. Thus twenty-four councillors were eventually elected. They then went on to elect a new mayor and aldermen from their own number.

Why a system was adopted that was so open to pressure, when the old system had been removed because of evident corruption, is puzzling. There appears to be no evidence of royal collusion to keep the status quo, but then there very rarely is.

Towns guarded their hard won rights jealously and it would have caused problems for Newcastle's ruling elite if they had been seen to be in league with the king. Indirect elections were a common feature of medieval urban government. Universal suffrage would have been looked on with horror (at least by those in power).

The election was held yearly at the Spital, amongst vast feasts and *"merry making"*, if an event in 1733 was representative. A butcher, already drunk, seized a bottle of what he thought was wine. The vinegar he drank led him into such a state that he was fined 3s 4d by his company for *"unmanly behaviour"*. The elections on the Spital were discontinued in 1760.

The next major change to the town's government came in 1400 when it was made into an independent county separate from Northumberland - apart from the Castle and its surrounding land which remained under the king's control. This really gives us some indication of the town's importance as few were awarded this status. Henry IV's decision is thought to owe much to the influence of Roger Thornton. It was also an attempt to remove a potential power base from the Percies.

Roger Thornton

Though comparatively unknown, Roger Thornton is Newcastle's own Dick Whittington. He arrived in the town a poor man and became its wealthiest citizen, with the ability to influence kings. A popular medieval verse described Thornton's entry into the town:

> *"At the Westgate cam' Thornton in,*
> *with hap, a halfpenny, and a lambs skin."*

The poem is an allegory. Hap, a word still used in Scotland, simply means 'good fortune', that is, even if Thornton had only owned a halfpenny and a lamb's skin he would still have been successful. The chronicler Stone notes that *"Thornton was at the first very poor, and, as the people report, a pedlar."*

We first find mention of Thornton's name in 1394, in a document that shows him to be part owner of a ship. Four years later he had risen to become one of the town's bailiffs, and was then sent to represent Newcastle in Henry IV's parliament. He soon found favour with the recently crowned king and secured a new charter for the town, *"to be called the County of the Town of*

A rare print of the Maison Dieu drawn during its demolition in 1823.

Newcastle for ever". Only London, Bristol and York had been given this privilege. In honour of his effort, Thornton was made the first mayor of the county town. He was to become mayor on no fewer than eight occasions and represented Newcastle in three parliaments.

Thornton drew his wealth from silver mines in Weardale and from trade. He used his money to become a benefactor, founding the Maison Dieu, in 1412. He may also have built the 'Town House'. Thornton died in 1430, *"The richest merchant that ever was dwelling in Newcastle"*.

He commissioned a brass after his wife died in 1411, part of an altar tomb destroyed when All-Hallows was demolished. The brass depicts ninety-two figures in all, including all fourteen of his children, and various Saints and Angels. Thornton and his wife are depicted in full size. The brass, reputedly one of the biggest in England, is now kept in St. Nicholas Cathedral.

Medieval Tyne Bridge.

The longest standing of any of the Tyne bridges was the one built during the reign of Henry III in 1250, after the fire which razed Newcastle in 1248 had destroyed its predecessor. The present Swing Bridge lies on the same site. It is generally assumed that this medieval bridge was built on the foundations of *Pons Aelius*. This may well be the case but the evidence for this has recently been discredited. It is now argued that the wooden pile supports - discovered during the last century when the Swing Bridge was being constructed - belonged to the medieval and not the Roman bridge.

The bridge was an important part of the town's defences as it guarded the southern approaches. Guard towers were included at either end to keep out plague ridden travellers and rebellious armies. The keeper of the bridge at first was a cleric but this job was later given to a layman of Newcastle.

A huge flood destroyed a large section of the bridge in 1339 and it became evident that regular funds would be needed to maintain it. Taxes on local property partly paid for the upkeep, as did special donations from the royal coffers. The Prince bishops of Durham were granted possession of the southern third of the bridge in 1417 after a lengthy dispute with the town council over access to the southern banks and port rights. The town's rights to the river, from its mouth

The medieval bridge drawn in 1700.

to high above the town, had been granted by King John in a Charter. The monopoly rights to all merchandise were to come later, in a charter of Henry VIII. Despite these royal privileges both the bishops of Durham and the Prior of Tynemouth constantly challenged Newcastle's domination of the river. In 1267 the town's merchants had gone out and destroyed wharves at Tynemouth and parliament ordered more wharves to be destroyed in 1292. After the dissolution this threat from the priory ceased.

The blue stone, now kept in the Castle keep, marked the boundary on the bridge between Durham and the town. One of the more dubious fund-raising methods was provided by the bishops. They offered indulgences, between ten and thirty days off your purgatory, in return for money and labour.

The bridge was a miniature town with shops and houses running its full length and was one of the busiest parts of Newcastle. One of the greatest spectacles of its five hundred year history was the royal procession of Henry VII's daughter on her way to marry James IV of Scotland. The entourage was headed by the Prior of Tynemouth and the Earl of Northumberland and coming off the bridge Margaret was met by townsfolk, *"in so grett nombre that it was a playsur for to se. At even, th'erle of Northumberland, made to mony lords, knights and others, a goodely baunket, which lasted to mydnyght, for cause of the games, daunces, sports and songs, with force of ypocsas, succres and metts of many delicyouses maners."*

Ten years later, the unfortunate Margaret's return journey passed virtually unnoticed. Her husband had been killed at Flodden Field fighting the army of her brother, Henry VIII.

The aftermath of the 1771 flood, which destroyed the central part of the old medieval bridge.

The Great Flood

Being the main road to the south of the town, the bridge became gradually weakened by an ever increasing load of traffic. It had only been designed to carry medieval carts. The old bridge could not cope with the great storm of the 16th of November 1771. Brand describes the flood in detail:

> *"On the Saturday night preceding the 17th of November, 1771, a great land flood, occasioned by heavy rains in the west, happened in the river Tyne, causing it to overflow its banks and every where making its progress with the most dreadful devastation. At Newcastle upon Tyne, the water began to rise about eleven o'clock at night, and continued increasing in height till seven the next morning: about three o'clock, the arches of this bridge were filled up, and between three and four, two of them on the south side were driven down, as was the North arch, adjoining to the toll shop, burying the houses erected thereon, together with several of their inhabitants."*

Every bridge along the Tyne apart from one at Corbridge was destroyed. Around thirty people were killed. Perhaps the most fortunate of the night was a baby who was picked up by a boat alive and well in a cradle. A dog and a cat were found inside a whole house floating down the river. The storm also caused flooding on the Sandhill and totally destroyed the Customs Shed on the Quay. Along the length of the river the banks were littered with ruined keels and ships.

The council provided a ferry service from the Sandgate until the bridge was patched up with a wooden structure. The council eventually replaced the five hundred year old bridge with a sturdier stone one completed in 1781.

Reform and Revolt.

The Dissolution

Chapter 5

Henry VIII's severance of English life from the Church in Rome transformed Newcastle. The first religious houses in England began to be closed in 1536. To begin with only the smaller houses closed, but it would be only four years before all the town's imposing friaries had gone, stripped of their wealth, and turned over to the crown.

Many saw this as an opportunity to make their fortunes, although the king was the chief beneficiary of the extensive land holdings and treasures that the Church had built up over the centuries. The vast wealth of eight thousand religious houses in England and Wales was to provide him with a secure financial base for years to come. He leased much of the land to the lesser gentry, using his rights of patronage to secure their support against any insurrection which might unfold from these unpopular measures. Great swathes of land became available and many of the town's merchants were able to become landed and moved away.

The five Newcastle friaries were dissolved during 1539 and the nunnery a year later. Between them they had less than sixty brethren at the time of their closure, the Trinitarian House being home to a solitary member. The monks and nuns were pensioned off, whilst the friars received gratuities to enable them to find new professions. Many were to turn to the priesthood.

The years that followed saw the greatest social and physical upheaval since the Norman conquest. The social fabric was torn up and rewoven in only a few years when such change had previously taken centuries. The friaries, which had been responsible for education, health and religious well-being, and which had taken up vast amounts of land in the town, were gone within the space of a year. There are no modern comparisons. What followed was indeed a reformation.

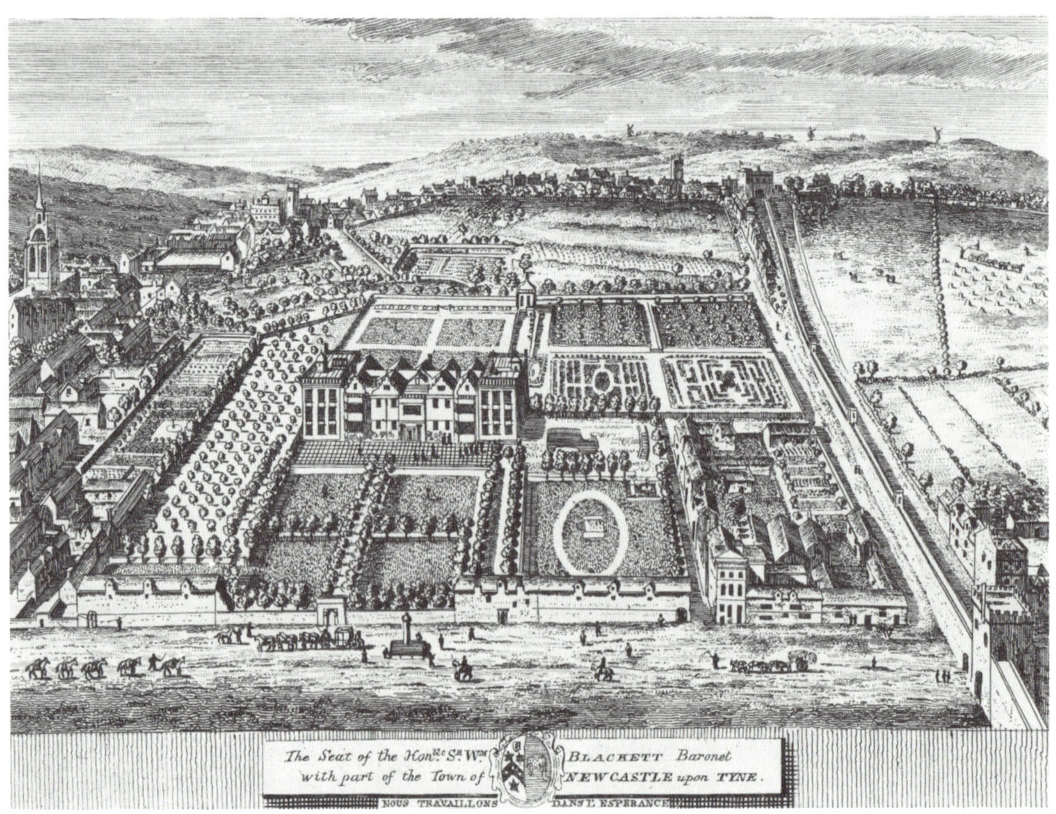

The Grey Friars and adjoining Nuns Moor was purchased by Robert Anderson in 1580. He built himself a *"a princeley house"* which he called *Newe House*.

The removal of the religious houses opened up a massive block to new building in the town. Given this, much of the land within the walls remained untouched green belt until the seventeenth century. There was now too much land available - and in the wrong place. The Quayside was rapidly becoming the centre of activity whilst the land vacated by the friaries was higher up in the top of the town.

It would also be some time before the wealth from the dissolved friaries would trickle down from the merchants into new building projects. When regeneration finally got underway in the seventeenth century it was rudely and violently cut short, by plague in 1636 and then by civil war.

The post Dissolution history of the Carmelite site is typical of the fate of the religious houses, and of the acres of land in which they stood. The site, together with the Trinitarian house, was granted to Sir Richard Gresham, a London alderman, and Richard Billingford. There follows a gap in the historical record until 1647 when they were sold by Ralph Delaval the elder, from London, and Ralph Delaval the younger, of Seaton Delaval, to Robert Jennison, the vicar of Newcastle, for £300.

The sixteenth and seventeenth centuries saw stagnation in this part of the town and many of the buildings were either in decay or leased out to less wealthy porters and labourers.

In the early eighteenth century the land was split up. In 1720, part was bought to build a Unitarian church and a square of houses. In 1746 the best section was sold to Dr. Adam Askew, a wealthy landowner, to build Clavering House and Clavering Place. During the 1840's more land was used to build Hanover Square.

The area declined in fortune from then on and no longer attracted the wealthy middle-classes. It gradually became commercialised as new warehouses were built. The process was complete by the 1960's with the expansion of the Federation Brewery.

The site of the Austin Friary was used by the mayor and burgesses for the Holy Jesus Hospital in 1681. A tower from the friary was incorporated into the north-west corner of the building and can still be seen today. The hospital was built for the care of the town's freemen and their families. The residents, thirty-nine of them in 1736, were appointed by the corporation and must not have been able to raise, or been entitled to, any more than £15 a year. They received a small annual allowance (£4 in 1681, which was raised to £6, then £13) and a measure of coal at Christmas. The indentures state that the inmates should be called Master,

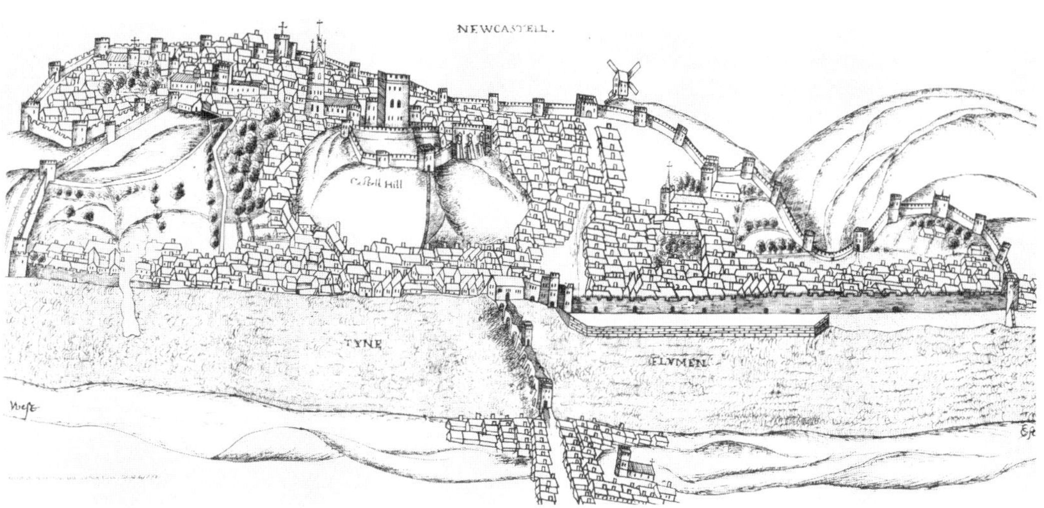

The earliest accurate view of the Town - depicted in the Cotton Manuscript of about 1590.

Brethren, or Sister of the Hospital of Holy Jesus.

By 1937 the building had been declared unfit, and the institution was resited in Spital Tongues. The building itself was left to go to ruin. Proposals to turn it into a museum were eventually taken up thanks to a bequest from John George Joicey in 1968, and work was completed in 1971. Help came from the Ministry of Housing, Public Buildings and Works, the Council and the Laing Art Gallery. The museum now houses a social history of Newcastle.

The Plague

The town's growth was hampered from time to time by visitations of the plague. It came in 1589, taking over seventeen hundred souls, then returned in 1636 for its most brutal visit. It entered North Shields in 1635, reaching Newcastle the following year. When plagues approached anybody who could, would leave the town for the relative safety of rural areas. All that was left behind was a skeleton population of poor and artisan classes, servants and labourers.

The plague stayed for thirty-six grisly weeks. Death came suddenly, often in only a few hours. Symptoms began with sweating, a *"grete stynking"*, followed, hardly surprisingly, by a sense of deep foreboding, high fever, a violent headache, dizziness, abdominal pains, and black spots. *"Fumigations of pitch, resin and frankincense appear to have been used on this melancholy occasion, and to cleanse the apartments of those who had died of it, to prevent the spreading of the infection."*

Colonel John Fenwick recorded that Newcastle was in a state of near collapse, *"almost desolate, thy streets growne greene with grasse, thy treasurie wasted, thy trading departed, as thou never yet recovered it."* Over five thousand died. This must have been an alarming blow for a town whose population ranged from only ten to eighteen thousand between 1500 and 1700.

The End of the Wars

Newcastle was beginning to lose its military importance as a *"bulwarke against the Scots"*. Although the town was used in 1547 by the Duke of Somerset during the Pinkie campaign the border was slowly becoming more settled. Even the walls began to be neglected. The end to centuries of border conflict was in sight.

Newcastle's existence until then had owed much to its military role. This was where the English army would muster before a campaign. The regular visit of the mighty English army of many thousands, to a town whose population had hovered around five thousand for most of the wars, had provided a steady stimulus to growth over the preceding centuries. The king and his court, together with the cream of English nobility and their hangers on, would provide the town's merchants with a generous market - all needed housing, feeding and provisions for a campaign. Even in peace time there would have been continual maintenance of the town's defences, which no doubt provided steady work for craftsmen and labourers. This was a worrying time in Newcastle as the town moved into a recession. A new role had to be found...

Industry.

The merchants moved into an industry which had previously been the domain of the Church, coal. Many of the mining areas were owned by the Church, who had never allowed the industry to develop to its full potential. This is where the importance of the Dissolution lay for Newcastle. It brought a massive stimulus to the coal industry, taking it out of the hands of the Church into the hands of the Merchant Adventurers - the new nobility.

This expansion in the coal industry provided the spark for the growth of other industries along the water-front. Many had been there for centuries, but they never had the conditions that now existed, access to abundant coal reserves for power, and an increasingly wealthy merchant class.

It is sometimes easy to forget that Newcastle was not only dominant in the coal industry but that forty per cent of the nation's glass was produced around Tyneside. Other flourishing industries included the production of lime as fertiliser, the *"great plenty of salmond"*, iron smelting and various trades related to shipping. Gray, Newcastle's first historian, tells us of salt pans in County Durham, *"which makes whits salt out of salt water, boyled with coale"*, which was exported through Newcastle. Another contemporary, Sir William Brereton, records pans at Shields in 1635 *"wherin is more salt works than in any part of England that I know"*. The town was also renowned for the production of grindstones from the quarries at Kenton. A popular phrase of the time was: *"A Scot, a rat and a Newcastle grindstone, you may find the world over"*.

Coal

From Roman times coal has been a staple commodity of the North East people, providing employment and prosperity. Coal would have been used in the forts along the Wall. Horsley, the eighteenth century author of 'Britannia Romana' states:*"that there was a colliery not far from that place [Condercum, the Roman fort at Benwell]....to have been wrought by the Romans."* Mining began to increase in importance under the Norman kings. By the fourteenth century coal was beginning to be sold outside the area, mainly to London.

The first area to be exploited was high above Newcastle along the Tyne Valley. By 1256 coal mining was so extensive in Tynedale that it was said to be dangerous to travel along the road from Newcastle to Corbridge at night, for fear of falling into one of the open pits. Here coal was near to the surface and easily mined. The earliest miners used the open cast system, simply digging large bell pits, extracting the coal and moving onto the next coal field. As you travel east towards the coast the coal seams are deeper and less accessible. As the early pits became depleted so the industry slowly drifted east towards the town. To make this possible new techniques were pioneered to sink ever deeper pits. This made Newcastle not only the biggest producer of coal, but also a world technological leader.

Pits had to be close to the Tyne because of the high costs of land transport. On reaching the river the coal was transferred to small keel boats. At first these sailed down the river to Newcastle where the coal was transferred to collier boats. By the 1300's these colliers had grown too large to navigate the river, so they docked at Shields.

The earliest written records on the coal industry come from the start of the fourteenth century and give a fascinating insight into the early coal trade. The oldest surviving document concerns a Thomas Migg, who shipped a consignment of coal from Newcastle to London on board the *Welfare* in 1305.

In 1652 Ralph Gardiner was imprisoned for brewing in Shields - against the Brewers and Bakers monopoly. Not able to gain legal redress he escaped and eventually made his way to London to present his case. He petitioned parliament, on behalf of himself and shipwrights, for freedom of navigation of the river. His cause was looked upon sympathetically in the radical *barebones* parliament. A bill was proposed that would have ended the town's monopoly. The day it was to be considered parliament gave up its powers to Cromwell and the case collapsed.

England's Grievance Discovered was written by Gardiner after this defeat. It contains much valuable information about the town, including this map and the witches and branks prints on page ninety-four.

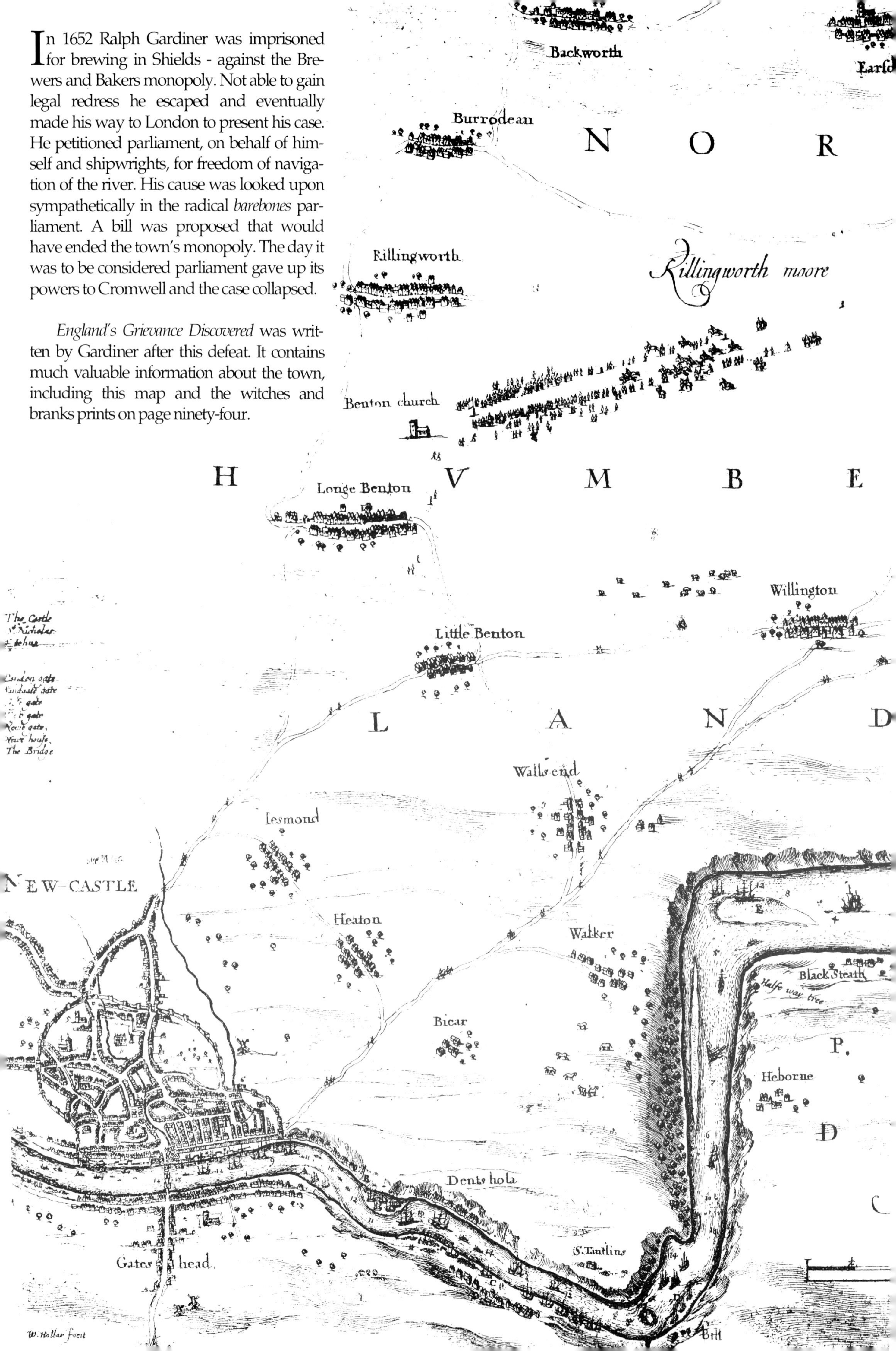

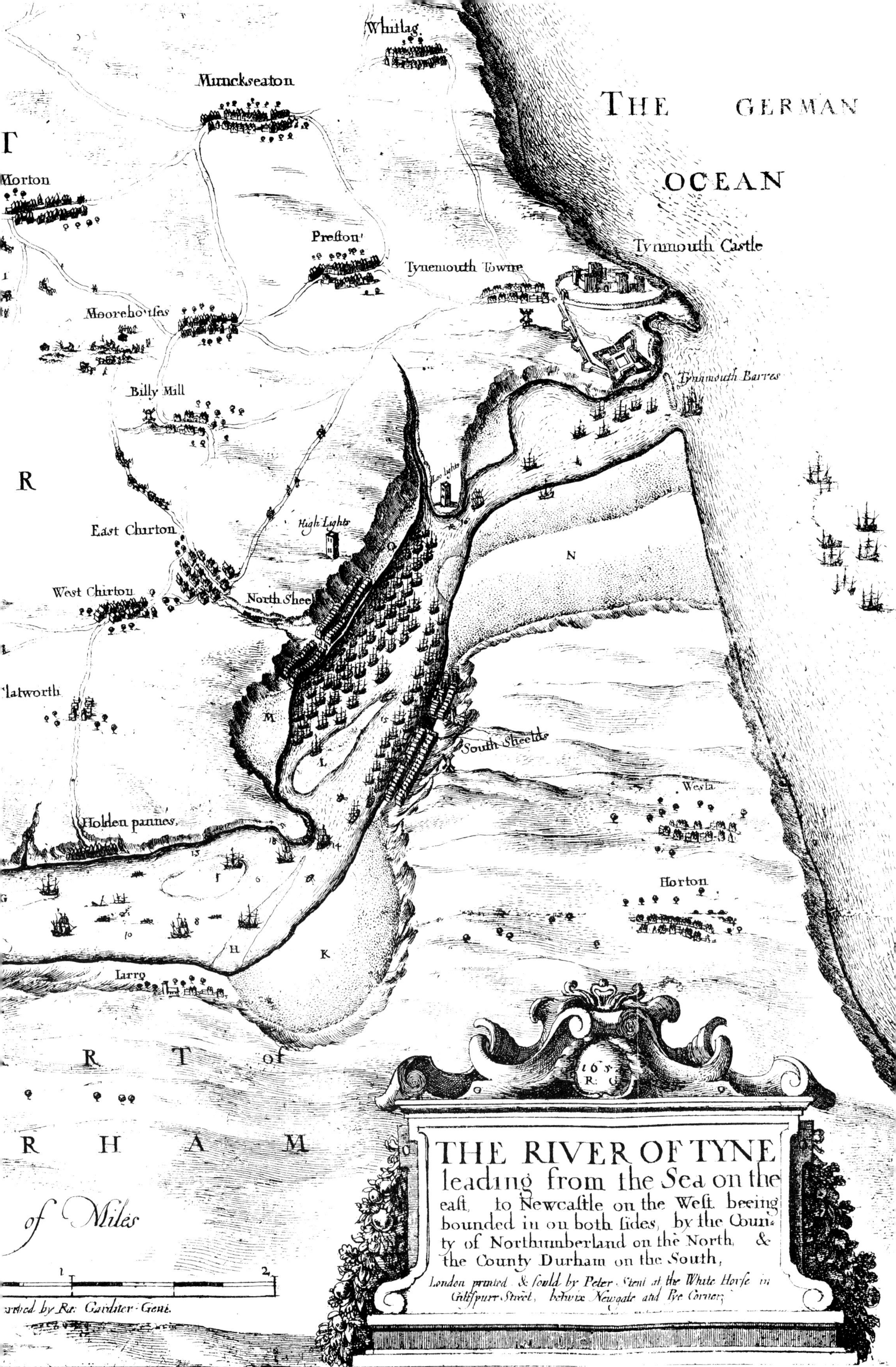

Whitlag
Munckseaton
THE GERMAN OCEAN
Morton
Preston
Tynmouth Castle
Tynemouth Towne
Moorehouses
Billy Mill
Tynmouth Barres
Low lights
High Lights
East Chirton
West Chirton
North Sheel
South Sheelds
Westa
Holden pannes
Horton
Larro
of Miles
THE RIVER OF TYNE
leading from the Sea on the east, to Newcastle on the West beeing bounded in on both sides, by the County of Northumberland on the North, & the County Durham on the South,
London printed & sould by Peter Stent at the White Horse in Giltspurr Street, betwixt Newgate and Pye Corner;

A year later, a royal proclamation forbade the burning of Newcastle coal in London because of the stench. This was largely ignored by the poor, who could not afford the more expensive, and cleaner, charcoal. A second, and more forceful, proclamation was made. It cannot have lasted long since shortly after there are records of coal being used in the royal palaces. Charcoal had become increasingly scarce as the demand for wood for shipping took precedence, and even the wealthy had to turn to coal. It would be another six hundred and fifty years before new laws were brought in to combat smog both in the capital and elsewhere.

By the second half of the fourteenth century, larger amounts of coal were being exported. Fifteen thousand tons every year were leaving on boats bound for ports in England and the Continent. Nevertheless the industry expanded slowly. The church exerted a strong grip over the quantities of coal allowed to be mined under expensive and short term leases. New ownership resulted in dramatic change. There was phenomenal growth in the industry. Gray wrote only a few years after the Dissolution that:

"Many thousand people are imployed in this trade of coales; many live by working of them in the pits; many by conveying them in waggons and waines to the river Tine; many men are imployed in conveying the coales in keels from stathes aboard the ships: One coal merchant imployeth five hundred in his works of coal".

With the keel boats passing through Newcastle, the town's merchants were able to exert an increasingly powerful control over the industry. The expansion of the Quayside area as the new commercial core ties in with the rapid increase in the importance of coal. All the administration and dealing was carried out in this area. By the sixteenth century the merchants formed a total monopoly, both on production and export. They often acted as middlemen between foreign merchants buying the coal and the Town Council, who charged levies on every chaldron exported (an old coal measure equivalent to 25.5 cwt).

The merchants were expected to entertain their counterparts on arrival in Newcastle. This hospitality, or 'hosting', gave rise

Collier boats at Shields.

to their guild name of the Company of Hostmen. The hostmen usually specialised on either the continental or domestic side of the coal trade. Examples of this are shown in surviving records. An Edward Baxter usually hosted French ships, whilst George Bird dealt exclusively with East Anglian boats.

During Elizabeth's reign the merchants became even more powerful. In 1600 she granted a new charter to the hostmen, formally incorporating them into 'The Fraternity of Hostmen of Newcastle'. In this new charter they were charged a shilling for every chaldron of coal exported. In return their rigid monopoly over the whole industry was reinforced. They were made responsible for *"the loading and better disposing of sea coals and pit coals....in and upon the river and port of Tyne"*. Up until the Civil War the coal trade boomed, with over three hundred ships involved in the coastal trade and many foreign ships docking in Newcastle or Shields.

The Civil War brought this lucrative period of expansion to a halt. Parliament embargoed Newcastle's coal, and by the end of the war the industry had settled into a period of stagnation. With this uncertainty the hostmen began losing their grip on the industry. New entrepreneurs, such as powerful local landowners, acquired coal interests. The hostmen were increasingly involved with the keel traffic and the marketing side of the industry, becoming known as 'fitters'.

Glass

There had been a small glass industry in Newcastle from as early as the mid-fifteenth century, *"In 1570 Bertram Anderson, Alderman of the City of Newcastle Upon Tyne, obtained 10 dozen drinking glasses from a local glasshouse"*.

In 1615 James I banned glass makers from using *"Timber or wood, or any Fewell made of Timber or wood, within this Our Kingdom of England and Dominion of Wales"*. James had made the decision for two reasons; to appease the aristocracy in the glass-making areas of Sussex, whose land was being ravaged by pollution, and to conserve timber supplies for the navy. A new source of fuel had to be found.

At the time a new method of smelting glass was being pioneered, using 'Pit-cole'. In 1623 James appointed one of his favourites, Sir Robert Mansell, to head an investigation into the new techniques. The early experiments were carried out in various parts of the country, but were hampered by technical difficulties. Mansell made *"traill at Newcastle upon Tyne where after the expense of many thousand pounds, that worke for window-glasse was effected with Newcastle Cole"*.

Mansell decided to locate the industry along the Tyne. It was the perfect choice, both well placed for export and with plentiful coal reserves. He transformed the glass trade from *"an unstable and scattered art into a genuine industry."* He was also greatly assisted by the skilled Huguenot glassmakers, Protestant refugees who had fled persecution in Catholic France.

They had arrived in Newcastle around 1619, when they built several glasshouses along the Skinnersburn, just off the Close. Their stay at this site was brief. They were soon to move to Stourbridge in the Midlands. Mansell eventually persuaded them to return to the North East. This time the Huguenot's stay was permanent and new glasshouses were established along the Ouseburn. These are now long gone, although one link with the industry remains - the Glasshouse Bridge, built over the Burn by the glassmakers in 1669.

There was a further group of glassmakers, the Venetian Dagnia family. They had arrived in Newcastle in 1684 and established themselves along the Close. From their three glasshouses they produced high quality flint glass.

The Newcastle producers were in the fortunate position of being able to use sand ballast from the many boats arriving in the port, sand being the industry's main raw material. The finished product was then exported by collier boat, in crates packed amongst the coal, to protect the delicate glassware on the voyage to the continent.

With these two great traditions firmly established, the stage was now set for Newcastle to become the foremost glass centre in the world. The period from 1730 to 1785 is commonly known as the 'Era of Elegance'. It was during this period that the Newcastle glassmakers developed one of the finest types of glass ever, the Newcastle Light Baluster. This was produced in response to the Glass Excise Act which taxed glass by proportion of weight and led to the collapse of sixty per cent of glasshouses in England. The industry in Newcastle suffered a setback but the new glass cushioned it from the full effects of the tax, so that in 1825 the historian Mackenzie could write that *"More glass is manufactured on the River Tyne than in all the kingdom of France."*

The highlight of the glassmaker's year was their procession through the town. Over seven thousand glassmakers in *"glorious disarray"* weaved their way through the Close to take a salute from the Mayor at the Mansion House. They dressed in regalia made of glass; top hats, badges and swords - one even had a glass gun which fired blanks. They also carried birds in glass cages. Many of these items can still be found in the Laing Art Gallery.

The Hostmens' Plot.

Newcastle's freemen directly elected the town's Members of Parliament. A man became 'free' once he was admitted to his trade after serving his apprenticeship. These made up about one third of all the men in the town - an unusually high electorate.

Despite this fairly democratic façade, it is clear that the town was tightly controlled by a body of wealthy coal merchants, numbering perhaps only twenty. Problems arose because the freemen did not directly elect the town's governors. The same names constantly appear as mayors and councillors or as signatories to important documents. At a time when more power rested locally these individuals, comprising a select group of hostman known as the 'inner circle', virtually monopolised the town's government. Whilst in theory any freeman could become a hostman, in practice admission was strictly

limited. It was those hostmen who were also members of the Merchant Adventurers who formed the inner circle. Though many of these men no longer resided in the town, it was still the source of their wealth and political influence.

Attempts to broaden the town's government in 1516 failed, though it took the King's Council, the Star Chamber, to come to a final decision. A further attempt in 1595 was mediated by the Privy Council.

The events that surround this affair are complex and inevitably revolve around the coal industry. The mines at Whickham and Gateshead, the wealthiest in Britain, had been assigned, in 1582, in what was known as the Grand Lease. Elizabeth I, who owned the mines, leased them for ninety-nine years to Thomas Sutton. He was not from Newcastle but was one of the Queen's favourites - reputedly the wealthiest commoner in England. He worked the mines for six years.

The town's merchants were envious of his position, his wealth and his royal patron. They wanted both to protect their cartel and gain control of his profitable mines. They excluded him from the Newcastle coal market by preventing him from becoming a freeman, even though many of the leading merchants were outsiders themselves.

Sutton's exclusion from this busy market place meant he was forced to sell the lease. Henry Anderson and William Selby bought it on the pretext of giving it to the town, but in reality they shared it out amongst the leading merchants. The lease had been secured with town funds, at a cost of around £5,000. Though purchased through the civic treasury the lesser guilds received nothing. This gave them the opportunity to try and secure a new charter and widen the political base.

The cause was taken up elsewhere. London's coal merchants were stirring for a change in Newcastle's charter because of the unfavourable cartel. As early as 1590 the Mayor of London complained to Burleigh, Elizabeth's Chief (and most trusted) Minister, about the price of coal, which had risen from six to nine shillings during the 1580's.

An attempt to form an alliance between the London Merchants and the lesser guilds was doomed to failure since the two groups had different ends. Unlike the London Merchants, the lesser guilds did not want to see an end to the prosperous cartel, they merely wanted the inner circle to be expanded to include themselves, the so called outer circle.

Elizabeth's Charter

The Council of the North supported the lesser guilds, but the Privy Council, short of money, invoked an old idea of charging a tax on coal exported from Newcastle. In return they allowed the hostmen to retain their lucrative cartel, confirmed in a charter of 1600. Only one mayor between this date and the Civil War was not a hostman, and every mayoral hostman was a Merchant Adventurer. The London merchants were appeased by a secret clause ensuring that the price of coal would not rise above ten shillings.

The tax raised amounted to £8,000 a year, a vast contribution to the government's revenue. Henceforth the crown and inner circle's interests became closely associated, an association which partly explains Newcastle's royalist stand in the Civil War.

The leading merchants had to act carefully: the town's privileges had been wrought from the crown over many years and were guarded jealously. If they were seen to be too closely linked there would undoubtedly have been widespread disruption. There is considerable intrigue surrounding the affair and even now we cannot be sure that we have a complete picture of the episode. As it was, the tax on coal was not included in the charter incorporating the hostmen but in another charter dated the 8th April 1600, two weeks after the first. The *"grant"* of one shilling was made *"in gratitude for their incorporation"* rather than as a tax.

Prosperity and Change.

The Expanding Town

The revenue generated by the coal trade and the spread of related industries helped Newcastle ride out the economic recession that was hampering growth in other parts of the country during this period. Sir William Brereton described Newcastle as *"beyond all compare the fairest and the richest towne in England, inferior for wealth and building to noe cittie save London: and Bristow and whether itt may nott deserve to be accounted as wealthy as Bristow I make some doubt."* He also thought Newcastle had the *"the fairest key"* and *"the fairest built inne"*.

Towards the end of Elizabeth's reign the threat of war with Scotland was steadily diminishing. Industrial expansion led to an increase in population which in turn put pressure on housing within the walls. Newcastle's suburbs date from this time with steady building along the main routes into the town. Fine houses, with large gardens, were built along Northumberland Street and Westgate Road. The villages around Newcastle were also steadily growing, although it would be several centuries before they began to merge to form the city we know today.

Newcastle's dominant features had changed little: the Castle, the walls and the churches; with new buildings being slotted into the old, haphazard, medieval street pattern. New building projects usually consisted of small scale clearances and the redevelopment of the vacant plots. The prime sites for new building were on the riverside, the heart of the commercial town. This was where nearly all the wealthy and merchant classes now lived: this was where they built their *"lofty and commodious"* houses.

The block of timber framed houses opposite the Guildhall, dating largely from the sixteenth and seventeenth centuries, is probably the oldest group of buildings in Newcastle. They give an idea of the type of homes that stood along the Quayside during the time. The best known is Surtees House, made famous by the elopement of the young John Scott and Bessie Surtees. The window through which she climbed in the mists of the night was marked by a blue pane. The building has been restored and is now the regional headquarters of English Heritage, who have opened part of the house to the general public.

Other houses of the era include the Cooperage and Red House. The Cooperage was, as the name suggests, a barrel making factory and was in use from 1730 to 1970. Its wooden beams are thought to come from a ship that sunk in the Tyne. Although it originated in the sixteenth century it has expanded since then, each storey predating the one above by approximately one century.

The houses contain many fine rooms, with oak panelling, ribbed pillars and decorations of cherubs' heads - typical of the 1600's. The Red House pub still contains the original arched brick work of what was once the old cellar. The low beamed and oak panelled rooms can still be seen inside the building.

A reflection of the wealth being generated at this time can be seen in the extensive refitting of the Merchant Adventurers' banqueting hall, the Maison Dieu, in 1636, and improvements to the Trinity House. Many streets were paved for the first time, with the luxury of gutters. Although a Norwich Lieutenant still *"found the people and the streets much alike, neither sweet nor clean"*.

Little of this money found its way to the poor. Beggars were still a common sight - Newcastle had twice as many licensed beggars as other towns. The poor lived in such streets as Low Friar and Gallowgate. There were also large numbers of artisans living in the south west corner of the town, around the Forth Banks and behind the Close, near to the new industrial sites.

The bustling Sandhill in the eighteenth century, with the Red House on the left of the print. Dr. Stukely described the locals: ***"They speak so broad; so that, as one walks the streets, one can scarce understand the common people, but are apt to fancy oneself in a foreign country."***

Trinity House

The chapel of Trinity House.

Trinity House was built for the Guild of Pilots and Mariners, originally known as the Guild and Fraternity of the Blessed Trinity - a religious group closely associated with All Saints. In 1492 Ralph Hebborn, a local merchant after whom Hebburn is named, donated part of his estate, Dalton Place in Broad Chare, as a meeting place or Trinity House. For this the guild were pledged to pay a red rose, if demanded, every summer.

In 1505 the building was remodelled to create a hall of assembly, a chapel, and an almshouse *"for aged and infirm brethren"*. In 1525 Ralph's son, Robert, donated further land, this time on payment of a bottle of red wine *"on the vigil of St. Peter and St. Paul."*

The mock Tudor façade of 1841 hides the secluded court. The south side was built in 1721. Behind it is a smaller courtyard and the school, which still has a library of some three thousand books. In the main courtyard are the late eighteenth century almshouses and north range, together with the chapel of 1800. The chapel is still used by the brethren once a year. Those present received a half crown as a memento, though this has now been updated to a five pence piece.

The two lighthouses at Shields built by Trinity House

Over the years Trinity House gained more and more control over the river and its navigation, appointing pilots, training people at its own school and collecting various charges and duties. In 1791 they were excused from the obligation to bear arms or serve on juries which demonstrates the importance of their work.

Henry VIII granted a charter of incorporation in 1536. The new guild was allowed to erect two lighthouses at North Shields, to be lit by candle and built with stones from the dissolved friaries. They charged foreign ships four pence and English ships two pence for entry into the port.

The Guildhall

The original Town Hall, or Exchange, was built on the Sandhill early in the 1500's. Bordering the Town Hall was the Town Court or Guildhall - appearing then almost as a lean-to. Indeed, in Elizabeth's time it was known as the Pentice, or Penthouse, meaning a lean-to. This was also the public weigh-house. As such it was probably supported by pillars and left open like a market.

Many of the town's incorporated companies held their thrice-yearly guild meetings here. It was also the venue for the Mayor's Court, Sheriff's Court, the Quarter Sessions and Borough Courts - as well as other civic occasions.

The old Town Hall was demolished in 1655, probably as a direct result of the fire in 1639 which destroyed the Town Clerk's office. The new Guildhall was built between 1655 and 1658 by Robert Trollope. It cost some £10,000, though the original quote was for only £2000. The ceiling was adorned with paintings, and the floor laid with chequered marble.

That building bears little resemblance to the Guildhall of today. Having suffered riot and fire damage in 1740 and 1791 respectively, the north face of the building was extensively remodelled and repaired in 1796. The south side underwent similar treatment in 1809, to a design by John Stokoe.

In 1783 *"a pair of crows built a nest and reared their young above the weather cock on the very top of the steeple, in a truly singular situation, as the nest shifted about with every change of the wind."*

The Maison Dieu, literally 'House of God', was on the east side of the Town Chamber, above which was the *"stately court of the Merchant Adventurers"* from 1480. It was founded as a hospital by Roger Thornton in 1412 for nine poor women who would pray for his soul. The hospital, hall and kitchens were later granted to the mayor and town for young couples to be married in.

In 1823, having survived years of town redevelopment, it was replaced by Dobson's covered fish market. A new merchant's court and offices for the town clerk, complete with fireproof records room and innovative double glazing, were also added. The new fish market enabled Sandhill to be cleared of fish stalls, and widened the entrance to the Quay. It was walled up in 1880 and turned into a newsroom.

The Tudor Guildhall. The inset shows the remodelled building which can be seen today.

Town Life.

Drinkers and Players

After the Dissolution, life in the town lost many of its more colourful scenes, such as the Corpus Christi performances. In the sixteenth century secular plays had begun to take the place of the medieval mystery plays, which had been the *"delight of the populace"*. The Council's records are scattered with payments to itinerant players, such as the twenty shillings for the Duchess of Suffolk's players who performed before the mayor in 1561. Performers would tour the country, under the loose patronage of a gentleman, and often received such gratuities for performing before the corporation.

The Puritan Commonwealth saw all plays banned, although they continued illegally in the Sandgate area. Punishments for actors caught were severe: one record is of actors who were *"all whipt in Newcastle for rogues and vagabonds"*. In the post Restoration period performances were taken up with a new zeal. The Moot Hall became the main theatre with performances fitted in between the assizes.

In 1554 the Merchants banned their apprentices from listening to or playing music, *"What use of gitterns by nyght"*, (a gittern was a kind of guitar). Elsewhere music was immensely popular. The carpenters' guild spent three fines they had collected *"in meten hous upon ij [the] mystreles, and in shorte cackes and aylle"*. There were many companies, particularly of pipers, perhaps because the local watchmen would pipe the hour and so learnt how to play the instruments.

Lord Keeper Guildford's visit to the town on the Northern Circuit during the assizes was recorded by one of his entourage: *"The magistrates were solicitious to give him all the diversion they could, and one was going down to Tinmouth Castle in the town's barge. The equipment of the vessel was very stately; for, a head there sat a four or five drone bagpipes, the north country organ and a trumpeter astern; and so we rowed merily along"*.

The Forth was always the most popular site for recreation. In the time of Queen Elizabeth there are records of payments to the *"tumbler that tumbled before Mr. Maior and his brethren"* and players were rewarded for *"playing with a hobie horse in the Firthe before the Maior."* It was also the site for archery and later a bowling green, which was overlooked by a tavern *"whence the spectators, calmly smoking their pipes and enjoying their glasses, beheld the sportsmen below."*

It was here that many of the guilds held their meetings. The Fraternity of Smiths' records show an order for thirty pence worth of *"Beare of the Foorth"*. The bowling green and tavern proved too strong a distraction for many of those present, not only were those who failed to attend fined but also *"such as misbehaved themselves whilst there."*

The *Frith* or Forth Tavern.

An event in 1542 illustrates the importance of beer to the town. Orders had been issued to the gentlemen and sheriffs of the North of England to be at Newcastle with their tenants to march into Scotland on the 2nd October. The men of the North were ready to descend on the town, but the ships coming from London with beer had not arrived - the campaign had to be delayed twice, until the 7th and then the 11th. When it did arrive there was not as much as expected - the commander, the Duke of Norfolk, wrote to Henry VIII that he only had enough for a six day campaign.

With the whole of the English army in the town he had no choice but to head north. He marched to Berwick and crossed the border on the 22nd. Either his quartermasters miscalculated or his soldiers drank more than their ration, but the beer ran out after only four days. Rather than face a mutiny, Norfolk retreated. The Scots misread this as a sign of weakness and invaded unprepared. In the battle of Solway Moss they were decisively defeated.

Fairs

There were three fairs, St. Lukes, Lammas and Martinmas, held on the 29th March, the 12th August and the 22nd November respectively. The first two lasted for a week, the third for just a day. Thousands of cattle and horses would be herded into the town from all over the North to be traded at Cow Hill. The local merchants would also set up stalls for the influx of people. The Cordwainers noted in 1690 the *"publick merkett for shooes att the two faires of Lamas and St. Luckmas, [where] no forraine shoe makers have any liberty to sell any shoes or other waires in any other liberty of the towne"*.

The Cordwainers had earlier been the subject of a Papal Bull. In the fifteenth century an Act of Parliament had forbidden the wearing of pointed shoes, and the Pope scolded the Newcastle cordwainers for continuing to make them.

During the fairs an amnesty was given to the *"King's outlaw, or ane traitor or sic ane malefactor"*. The great bell in St. Nicholas became known as the *"thief and reever bell"* as it was used to pronounce the start of the fair and the entry of criminals into the town. During the fairs flags would be raised on the Castle, attracting people from far and wide. In 1590 John Hardcastle was employed in *"peynting the banners which wer sett upp at the Newgate in the fair tyme"*

A fair on the Town Moor in Georgian times. The painting by J. Wilson can be seen in the Joicey Museum.

'Justice'

The Branks.

The Newcastle Coat.

Punishments were public and thousands would gather to witness executions or the humiliation of a person in the pillory.

The condemned were taken through Gallowgate to the gallows on the Town Moor, though sometimes executions would take place in the town itself. In 1577 *"a newe paire of gallowes was set up in the market place, and a souldior hanged for quarellyng and fightyng"*. The town's executioner was kept busy by the steady flow of moss-troopers (reivers) found guilty of border raiding. Between four and six were hanged on each gallows, and as many as twenty-one were executed in a single session.

There are also records of religious dissenters executed in the town. The North long remained sympathetic to the Catholic cause with priests celebrating Mass clandestinely. In 1592 James Watson was hunted from Newcastle with sleuth hounds but escaped, probably the same James Watson who was captured a year later and executed.

In 1593 there are records of an Edward Waterson being executed in Newcastle. He attempted to escape from the prison at Newgate by burning down his cell door. His arms were tied and he was taken by horse-drawn sled to the gallows where he was hanged by another prisoner. The aptly named William Sever, a member of the Barber-Surgeons' guild, was employed to draw and quarter him. Waterson's bowels were cut out, he was then decapitated and his body divided into three pieces. The head was placed on the magazine gate and other portions were placed around the town.

John Ingram was executed at Gateshead, and his quartered body taken to Newcastle to be displayed. Ingram had been transferred to the Tower of London to be tortured in the hope he would reveal information on other Catholics. He gave nothing away and was executed for his pains. Following Catholic executions the gallows were burnt so that pieces could not be cut off and used as holy relics of martyrs

There are records of the *"ducker in the water"* receiving regular payment. Quite often women were drowned during a ducking. The Branks, an 'iron engine', was kept, and regularly used, for gossips. It consisted of a crown which fitted over the head leaving the face clear. An iron tongue then fitted into the mouth which prevented the culprit from speaking. The 'Newcastle coat' was kept for drunks. This was a hollow barrel which rested on the felon's shoulders. Once these instruments were in place the victims were paraded around the town to be humiliated before the public.

Seven witches at the gallows, the executioner has just pushed one off the ladder. The bellman is calling for witches to be brought out. On the right, the witch-finder receives his pay.

Witch hunts

More barbaric still were the frenzied witch hunts. In 1647 fewer trials were taking place following the execution of the self-styled witch-finder general Matthew Hopkins, who had himself confessed to witchcraft. The Newcastle historian, Oliver, still records an event in 1650 when fourteen witches, a wizard and nine moss troopers were executed in the town.

In 1649 a person had been sent for from Scotland who *"pretended to be possessed of the knowledge of distinguishing those wretches who, for the sake of being able to hurt their neighbours, had sold themselves to the devil. Thirty women were brought into the town hall and stripped, and then had openly had pins thrust into their bodies, and most were found guilty; near twenty-seven of them by him were set aside. The magistrates sent their bellmen through the town, ringing his bell and crying, all people that would bring any complaint against any women for a witch, they should be sent for and tried by the person appointed."* They had been picked by Ann Armstrong, herself a witch. *"So soon as the witch finder had done in Newcastle and received his wages, he went into Northumberland, to try women there...upon the gallows he confessed he had been the death of two hundred and twenty women in England and Scotland for the gain of 20s. a piece."*

Civil War.

Bishops' War

Although a Stuart king sat on the English throne, the Scots were by no means subdued. Attempts to anglicise the Scottish Presbyterian church in 1640 led to the Bishops' War. A new invasion of England by Scottish troops was mounted under the leadership of the gifted commander, General Leslie. Newcastle, facing overwhelming odds, was evacuated of English troops who left the town defenceless by removing the ordinance. Leslie entered the town peacefully. There does not appear to have been a great deal of opposition to the Scots on their arrival. Indeed, there may have been some sympathy with their cause. The Mayor even entertained Scottish officers on their first day in the town. Leslie helped matters by forbidding his troops from pillaging or looting.

Any sympathy that the town had was soon eroded by Scottish actions. Leslie seized church and crown property and demanded £200 a day from the corporation for the cost of billeting his troops, a vast sum the town could ill afford, since nearly all trade stopped during the entire length of the occupation. The town was *"altogether unable to supplie the inhabitants, being so wasted and spoyled by the forces which have lyen and lived upon it."* Despite Leslie's desire to keep his troops well-behaved the townsfolk considered them an unruly mob. An alderman wrote to a friend living outside the town telling him that the *"Common Soldiers are intolerable, insolent and voyolent in their actions and discourse."* When the Scots finally left the town, in August 1641, Leslie demanded a loan of £40,000. The town was later compensated £60,000 for their stay.

The Bishops' War left Charles I short of money and forced him to call the notorious Long Parliament. The hostility between the king and his Parliament put England on the road to Civil War. Charles recognised that Newcastle would play a pivotal role in the conflict. He garrisoned the town a full two months before raising his standard at Nottingham.

Royalist Newcastle

Charles was able to make one of his staunchest supporters, the Earl of Newcastle, governor, while Sir John Marley, as Mayor, was another ardent Royalist. Given the evident allegiance of the town's governor and troops, it would have been difficult for the town not to have supported the King. There were many other reasons. The town's people had little sympathy with puritanism, so powerful a force in Parliament. Puritans had only once managed to elect a mayor, in 1639. There was also the traditional and long held distrust of the old enemy, the Scots, particularly after the recent occupation. At this stage, although they were officially independent they were seen to be more closely aligned with Parliament.

Then of course there was the question of coal - the interests of the town forever bound by the coal merchants. In 1637 Charles had imposed a further tax of one shilling a chaldron in addition to Elizabeth's tax. It was a crude attempt to make his finances independent of Parliament. The London merchants and East Anglian collier owners combined to boycott Newcastle coal and end the cartel. Sir John Marley was typical of the local merchants: *"I will not speak of what loss I sustained by the contract, but the Ipswich Puritans have so wrought the ship-men that for six weeks I did not load one chaldrons of coal, so that my staithes were so full they are likely to fire."*

Charles had to cancel the cartel. The London merchants then formed their own, 'the Society of London Coal Merchants', and themselves set about raising the price of coal. In 1641 the Long Parliament ended the crown's right to collect duties on coal. The antipathy between the two groups was strengthened when the London merchants actively encouraged the Scottish occupation.

Unable to form an army large enough to besiege Newcastle, Parliament placed an effective embargo on the town's coal, *"Until that Towne of Newcastle be freed from the forces there are now raised, or maintained against Parliament."* It is difficult to assess who was worse hit by the embargo. The fuel situation in London became critical during the harsh winter that followed and Parliament began losing its grip on the capital. Newcastle's trade was at a standstill as hardly a boat set sail from the Tyne. Once Parliament had taken Sunderland and began to encourage mining there, it looked as if Newcastle would lose its monopoly. Sympathies soon began to sway and Marley was forced to run the town under strict military lines to keep order. But in the end it was another event that swung the outcome of the war - Scottish declaration for Parliament.

In the freezing Winter of 1644, Leslie, now the Earl of Leven, crossed the Tweed a second time on his way to Newcastle. By the time Leven reached the town, the Earl of Newcastle had left with his Royalist army to try and stop the northward advance of Parliamentary troops in Yorkshire. Leven captured South Shields and from here was able to control the mouth of the Tyne, but he had more pressing matters than besieging Newcastle. He, too, left to travel south, to join with Parliament's forces which met with the Royalists at Marston Moor in July, the turning point of the War.

In many respects Newcastle's defence after this was *"merely a display of stubbornness"*. The town faced thirty thousand troops with only fifteen hundred men guarding two miles of walls. Leven returned to Newcastle in August. His time away had allowed Marley to strengthen the town's defences. The King's Dyke around the town was deepened and lined with clay so that it could not be easily climbed and any gaps in the battlements were lined with *"lime and stone"* to leave slits from which to fire. Two forts outside the walls at Sandgate and Shieldfield were also constructed. Others may have been planned on other heights but time was short. Carr's battery was built on the Quayside and a bastion added to the castle.

Leven made his headquarters in the village of Elswick. He was joined by General Callender with ten thousand more troops who set up his headquarters in Gateshead. From here he constructed a bridge of keels across the river.

During the siege John Marley supposedly saved St. Nicholas from ruin by putting prisoners in the tower. Brand retells the story:

"In the Time of the Civil War, when the Scots had besieg'd the Town for several weeks, and were still as far as at first from taking it, the General sent a Messenger to the Mayor of the Town, and demanded the Keys, and the Delivering up of the Town, or he would immediately demolish the steeple of St. Nicholas. The Mayor and Alderman upon hearing this, immediately ordered a certain Number of the chiefest of the Scottish Prisoners to be carried up to the Top of the old Tower, and place below the Lanthorne, and there confined; after this they returned the General an Answer to this Purpose, That they would upon no Terms deliver up the Town, but would to the last Moment defend it: That the Steeple of St. Nicholas was indeed a beautiful and magnificent Piece of Architecture, and one of great Ornaments of their Town; but yet should be blown up into Attoms before ransom'd at such a Rate: that however, if it was to fall, it should not fall alone; that the same Moment he destroyed the beautiful Structure, he should Bath his Hands in the Blood of his Countrymen; who were placed there on Purpose either to preserve it from Ruin, or to die along with it. This Message had the desired Effect. The Men were kept Prisoners during the whole Time of the Siege, and not so much as one Gun fired against it."

The town withheld for three months without the walls being breached. On the 19th October the mines under the walls, and the bombardment from Gateshead and the Castle Leazes, were successful in creating a large breach. Leven led a final successful assault. Marley drew back to the keep but his cause was lost and he surrendered on the 22nd. He was taken to be imprisoned at the Tower of London but escaped on route and headed to France. He returned after the Restoration in 1660.

Charles I

It was from this defence that Charles is believed to have awarded the town its motto, 'Fortiter Defendit Triumphans'. Charles was to enter the town once more, in 1646, now a prisoner. Many historians believe he received a royal welcome but eyewitness accounts suggest otherwise: *"There were none out of the Toune...to meet his majestie, neither the Scotish Lords that were in the toune, nor the Deputy-Mayor therof; nor any other, either inhabitant or other. His Majestie was not recieved in triumph...nor did they in Solemne manner take notice of his Majestie. The King rid in a sad coloured plaine suite, and alighted at the General's quarters....There were no guns discharged...by way of triumph. There was no acclamation by shooting of muskets, sounding of trumpets, or beating of drums."* One of his own entourage noted that his entry into the town was *"In a very silent way, without bels ringing, or bagpipes playing, or Maior and Alderman, not as at Doncaster."* He most probably stayed in the town's premier building, Anderson Place. He must have been well known to the townsfolk, as he played golf at Shieldfield (one of the first records of golf playing in England) and attended Parliamentary Commissioners waiting for an answer to their demands, whilst making two escape attempts. The Scots finally gave him up to Parliament for a ransom of £400,000 - a king's ransom.

Charles I entering Newcastle, in 1646, as a prisoner.

Newcastell 2. June 1646.

Nicholas / since I saw you, I receaued but one letter from you wch was of the 5th of May; & this is but the 3d that I haue written unto you, hauing sent a Duplicat of my last, about 9 Dayes agoe: For directions, I shall in substance repeate what I last sent you; wch is, that, because [illegible] I giue you leaue treate for good conditions; let those of Exeter be your guyde [illegible] hauing a particular care that my Sone & two Nepueus haue permission to come to me wherseeuer I shalbe, as lykewais that the freedome of the Vniuersity be preserued, & that all my Servants, who ar willing, may come to me with the few goods that I haue there. Touch Newes at this tyme, because it will doe litle good to you, & troble me: So, comanding you to assure all my Frends, that no change of place shall mealter my Affection to them; I rest

Your most assured frend
Charles R.

[illegible] by the grace of god [illegible]

When my goods ar sent, forget not all the Bookes wch I left in my Bedchamber

This letter was sent by Charles to Edward Nicholas, Secretary of State, shortly before he was removed to London. It is surprisingly legible and details his instructions concerning the move. The postscript tells Nicholas *"When my goods are sent, forget not all the Bookes wch I left in my Bedchamber."* The letter is now owned by Lloyds Bank and kept in the Grey Street branch.

Regicide

Despite Newcastle's evident Royalist sympathies two men closely associated with the town were to be signatories of the King's death warrant.

John Blakiston became one of Newcastle's Members of Parliament in 1641, following a long disputed election in 1640, after the other candidate died. His career began unspectacularly. It was not until later that his name increasingly can be seen in records of debates and as a member of committees - a sure sign of a blossoming career. After 1644 he began taking more interest in Newcastle politics - the importance of the town to the Parliamentarians having been shown in the first Civil War by the effectiveness of the coal blockade. He became one of the key members at the King's trial, and was one of the signatories on the death warrant.

Another of the signatories was Robert Lilburn. The Lilburn family played an important role in the Civil War. The most famous was the leveller theorist, John. His form of ultra-republicanism was crushed by Cromwell in 1649. Robert did not share his brother's views. George Lilburn was the mayor of Sunderland; Henry Lilburn turned Royalist and took part in the abortive revolt centred around Tynemouth.

Robert was born in County Durham in 1613. In 1647 he was Governor of Newcastle, later second-in-command of the Northern Army, and then Governor of Scotland. After the Restoration in 1660 he was put on trial with the other regicides. A tract described him as *"a most implaccable Enemy against Kingly Government and a most insolent Infringer of the Peoples Liberties, one that had more wit than Honesty, but despised Good Old Law called Magna Carta."* He was condemned to death but the sentence was commuted. He died in 1665.

Newcastle sided with Parliament in the second Civil War. Parliament had learnt its lesson and had left Sir Arthur Hazelrigg as the Town's Governor. He was perhaps more famous as one of the *"birds that had flown"*, one of the five Members of Parliament that Charles had tried to arrest in 1642. The inhabitants of the town were woken every day at six in the morning to prepare the defences and were fined eight pence a day for non-attendance, but most of the fighting was in the West and Newcastle avoided another conflict.

Considering the town was on the losing side, and had seen the coal trade come to a standstill, Newcastle fared extremely well after the Civil War. The coal trade soon picked up but it remained in the hands of a privileged few, albeit a different group than before the war. New faces joined a group of Civil War neutrals who had remained in the town during the siege but had no particular adherence to the crown.

The Glorious Revolution

In 1688 the town supported William of Orange's claim to the throne. A mob dragged down a brass statue of James II and threw it into the Tyne. The statue was later salvaged: one leg was given to St. Andrews, the rest to All Saints for a new set of bells.

The brass statue of James II which was thrown in the Tyne.

The Age of Reason.

Chapter 6

This chapter covers a period when Newcastle was at its most confident. It was an age that saw two of Newcastle's finest sons, Eldon and Grey, an age when Tyneside's industry came to dominate the world. Above all, it was an age of coal.

The eighteenth century saw Newcastle increasingly run by an oligarchy of families, a small powerful group like the Blacketts, the Claytons, the Ridleys and the Andersons, names still familiar in the area. We can take the Claytons as an example of this type of political dynasty. Nathaniel Clayton was the son of a Yorkshire rector who was appointed sheriff in 1715, and became mayor in 1725 and 1738. His son, William, was mayor three times. A close relation, Robert Clayton, was the mayor in 1804, 1812 and 1817. Robert's brother, Nathaniel, bought the office of Town Clerk for £2,100 which he held from 1785 until he passed it onto his son in 1822, who kept the post until 1867. Gradually, often through intermarriage, new faces would be introduced. Many of the old families slowly moved out of Newcastle to take a step up the social ladder and join the rural squirearchy.

Not surprisingly men began to expect a voice in their own affairs. The American War of Independence and the Napoleonic Wars ended disquiet at home for a spell. During the Napoleonic Wars there had been a great fear of invasion, Jacobinism was suppressed; press gangs were used on an ever increasing basis and even, in 1797, a 'home guard' was formed in Newcastle.

In 1815 the panic of revolution returned to Europe which, under Lord Liverpool's Government, led to widespread repression and restrictions on liberties. Popular condemnation of the Peterloo Massacre in Manchester led to a mass protest on the Town Moor in 1819, where a crowd of up to

Sir Walter Blackett was mayor five times between 1734 and 1771. He also represented Newcastle in seven different parliaments.

one hundred thousand gathered. Fortunately this new age of upheaval was not accompanied by widespread violence in Newcastle, although the Riot Act was read to a crowd in 1822.

Grey's 1832 Reform Act failed to stem the demand for change and the Chartist Movement emerged as a new popular voice for universal suffrage. In 1839 parliament rejected a Chartist petition with one and a quarter million signatures demanding radical reforms such as yearly elections. During that summer the country seethed with unrest. On August 20th and 30th there were riots on the Side. On the second occasion the Riot Act was read four times and the mayor was stoned. The disorder was finally broken up by cavalry. As the century progressed it was not a political solution but an economic upturn that finally dampened the people's demands.

In Newcastle during the 1830's the corporation was unable to keep pace with political developments. It was inadequately funded and failed to adapt to the needs of the swelling town. With the passing of the Municipal Corporations Act of 1835, the corporation was finally brought under the popular control of the ratepayers.

The reformed Town Council was to consist of forty members elected every three years by the ratepayers. Fourteen aldermen were chosen from amongst the councillors. They held office for six years, and a mayor was elected by the councillors on an annual basis. Though conceived partially to allow greater funding, the council was sometimes even more frugal. For the first time they were responsible to their electorate, the ratepayers, at a time when tax paying was even more unpopular than it is now.

Earl Grey

Earl Grey, the Father of Reform, must be considered one of Newcastle's greatest sons - the town's only Prime Minister. The Reform Bill which he steered through parliament was one of the most important pieces of legislation of the day. He was first elected to parliament in 1787 and became First Lord of the Admiralty in 1806. In the same year he became Leader of the House and Secretary of Foreign Affairs, he also piloted a Bill for the Abolition of the Slave Trade through parliament. Following his father's death in 1807 he left the Commons and entered the House of Lords, although by now he was semi-retired, only sitting when important measures were being considered.

Following the resignation of Wellington in 1830, William IV persuaded Grey to come out of retirement and form a new Whig government. The country was in near tumult. Grey soon presented a Reform Bill that was defeated. He turned to the country for support and after the election was able get the Bill through the Commons. He faced much stiffer opposition in the Lords, and the Bill was defeated. A third Bill in 1832 was again defeated. Grey resigned. By now the country was at fever pitch, events being closely followed throughout the land. On October 17th fifty thousand people demonstrated on Cow Hill to protest against the Lords' decision and vitriolic attacks were made on those peers, such as the Duke of Northumberland and the Bishop of Durham, who had voted against the measure.

Eight days after his resignation Grey returned, but on one condition, *"The Bill, the Whole Bill, and nothing but the Bill."* The King persuaded opposing peers to be absent from the House and the measure was passed. In 1834 Grey was able to lead a government made up of members elected by the wider franchise. This done he resigned from government for good. He died in 1845.

Central Newcastle.

As the eighteenth century progressed, the pressure within the walls that had been experienced towards the end of the last century became even greater as more and more land was needed for building projects. It was clear that the walls would have to be demolished to make way for new developments. Improvements did come, but they were slow to begin with. The first stage was the demolition of stretches of the walls near the Quayside and Sandhill in 1763. The plans were set back when the medieval bridge over the Tyne was destroyed by the 1771 flood. Its replacement was not completed until 1781, at a cost of £30,000. This done, much needed improvements within the town could resume.

The most pressing need was for a new road to link the Sandhill and the Quayside with the upper part of the town. Traffic coming off the bridge had to weave its way through the cramped chares or go up the steep and narrow Side. The best new route was that carved out by the Lort Burn. It had become *"a vast, nauseous hollow"* as the twenty-seven butchers on Butcher Bank used the burn to dispose of their putrid offal. Over the centuries the lower part had been gradually paved over. This allowed the construction of Dean Street. It took five years to complete under the supervision of David Stephenson. The finished road provided much easier access to the upper part of the town. The valley of the Lort Burn can still be seen today as the large dip in the middle of Mosley Street.

A busy scene from the Bigg or Barley market around the 1820's. The row of houses in the centre of the print, along Middle Street were torn down in 1838.

It was not until the 1830's that the burn was completely filled in, with two hundred and fifty thousand cart loads of rubble from the grounds of the recently demolished Newe House.

The new Mosley Street linked the top of Dean Street to Pilgrim Street and, with Collingwood Street at its western end, provided a new thoroughfare to the Westgate. These roads soon became the premier shopping district with oil lighting, which was introduced in 1763, and new style glass-fronted display windows.

Building work spread beyond the town walls which were systematically being demolished. New residential squares with central gardens, such as Hanover and Charlotte Squares, were built. Large houses with gardens were also constructed off Northumberland Street at Saville Row, Saville Place, Ellison Place and Eldon Square. They were the *"genteelest and best built part of the town....the pleasure abodes of the affluent."*

The Old Assembly Rooms

Planned by local architect William Newton, this Grade One listed building was built between 1774 and 1776 in what were then the grounds of St. Johns Church. This area was rapidly becoming the most fashionable part of town. A special act of parliament was needed before work could start, as the vicar of St. John's held the lease. The building cost £6,700, the money being raised largely by a share issue.

Its main use was for concerts and balls in the huge ballroom, with its seven magnificent chandeliers - one of which is reputed to have cost 600 guineas. There was also a coffee room, saloon, card room, library and news room.

The building comprises a brick body with polished stone façade, and is now used for private functions - gaming, dining, and dancing. The front portico was added early this century.

Liberal Club

The Liberal Club on Pilgrim Street was once Alderman Fenwick's House and is said to stand on the same site as the medieval Pilgrim's Inn. Its name changed to the Queen's Head in 1781, when it was used as a coaching inn - the yard stretched back to Grey Street. Passengers would gather in the yards waiting for the heavy waggons and stagecoaches which left daily from here and the other inns around Pilgrim Street, Bigg Market and Sandhill on journeys to London, Edinburgh, Leeds, and Carlisle.

The building ended its life as a hotel in 1884 and was taken over by the Liberal Club. It closed during the 1960's and its future hung in the balance until 1981 when it was bought by the Tyne and Wear Preservation Trust. Since then the building has been slowly restored to its former glory.

Quayside

The new developments accelerated the movement of the professional classes away from the now decaying buildings around the Sandhill and Quay, a movement which the historian Henry Bourne had commented upon as early as 1736. They went to the elegant new houses in the upper parts of the town, leaving behind their businesses. For the first time the merchants no longer lived above their workplaces.

The seeds were sown for the area to decay into a classic Dickensian slum as the riverside was unable to compete with the new Georgian developments. By the time Mackenzie wrote his history of the town in 1827, the Quayside had become *"a dirty and inconvenient street."* The chares had declined in quality, some of the properties being over three hundred years old. Fenwick's Entry was *"dirty and disagreeable"*, whilst Plummer Chare had, at the turn of the century, been a red light district, a centre for *"Cyprian nymphs"*. Despite this, many diverse businesses stayed or moved into the Quayside and it remained the economic heart of the town.

Mark Akenside's house on Butcher Bank, later named Akenside Hill. He was Newcastle's most important contribution to literature, ranked amongst the best of English poets.

The demise of the smaller workshops - weavers, potters and smiths - indicates the end of the medieval craft industries in the area. Most of the small industries that survived were those related to the river: mast and block makers; sail makers; rope and twine makers and anchor smiths. By 1827 manufacturing had fallen to only twenty per cent of business on the Quayside.

As the area declined the shops no longer served the town as whole. Many moved into Grainger's new covered markets. Those that were left were often small and cramped and could not offer the range of goods found in the upper part of the town. There were grocers and tea dealers; chemist shops; hairdressers; pawn brokers and cloth dealers, together with thirty-three butchers.

Industrialisation had commenced in earnest along the Tyne by 1815. With very little new building, conversions were necessary to accommodate the port's expanding trades. Mackenzie describes the conversion of buildings in six of the chares to warehouses. In Fenwick's Entry a Newcastle merchant, Sorbie, had converted a building into a tobacco warehouse. The large buildings were ideal and streets such as Quayside, Sandhill, Broad Chare and Dog Bank experienced the most change in property usage. Mackenzie found *"shops, warerooms, offices and public houses"* where *"the property is very valuable"* which indicated continued importance.

The port of Newcastle, the centre of which was along the Quay, experienced increasing trade during the eighteenth century. It became *"one of the largest and most commodious wharfs in the kingdom"*, its organisation based in hundreds of offices around the Quayside. This growing trade was international - wine and port from Portugal; raisins from Spain; timber from Norway; hemp and flax from Russia; corn from Danzig and brandy from France.

A new customs house was built in the centre of the Quayside in 1766. The original Customs House had been at the western end of the Quayside which proved inconvenient. The building was later remodelled by Sidney Smirke and is the oldest surviving building along this section of the Quay. By 1828 eight hundred and sixty-two ships were registered at the Customs House, and by 1835 Newcastle was ranked the second most important port in England.

The busy Quayside around the 1820's. It was described as ***"one of the largest and most commodious wharves in the kingdom".***

Forge And Furnace.

Industry spread both east and west along the banks of the river. In eighteenth century Newcastle, small factories and workshops, typical of the period, crowded around the various burns entering the river such as Ouseburn and Skinnersburn. Here, glasshouses and chemical plants flourished. The new industrial districts included Walker and Elswick, where there was metal working and some shipbuilding, whilst a variety of factories and workshops could be found at Felling and Hebburn.

Daniel Defoe, on his journey around Britain in 1727, wrote of Newcastle: *"They build ships here to perfection, as to strength and firmness and to bear the sea, as the coal trade requires."* The rise of shipbuilding on Tyneside had begun with the area specialising in brig colliers. By 1800 it was the third largest producer of ships in Britain. A century later it would be building almost forty per cent of the world's shipping.

All these industries benefited from the abundant supply of cheap local coal to provide power. It was the coal industry which fuelled Tyneside's bid to become the major industrial centre of the eighteenth century, a coal industry that was itself to be revolutionised by the steam engine.

The Coal Industry

The latter part of the seventeenth century had seen a steady drift of the mines towards Newcastle itself, as the reserves in the earliest pits in the west were exhausted. Deeper eastern pits were made possible after the introduction of Newcomen's Steam Engine, in the eighteenth century, which partly solved the age old problem of drainage. Other improvements included innovations in shaft and tunnel construction and the wide use of waggonways, so pits further away from the Tyne could be exploited.

These improvements allowed the reopening of many old pits which had workable coal in them but had shut because

The bottom of the pit shaft at Walbottle Colliery in 1844.

The Church Pit at Wallsend which exploited the highly productive Main Seam.

they had been unprofitable. New mines opened in Jesmond, Heaton and Byker in the 1720's. These were all linked by waggon-ways to coal staiths on the river for export out of the area. At Longbenton the difficult Ninety Fathom Fault seam was opened up, which was later to become the largest producer of coal in the country. The pits around Newcastle fed a virtually insatiable appetite for coal as British industry switched from charcoal.

The latter half of the eighteenth century saw even greater expansion in production. Pits to the east of the town, along the Main Seam, were opened for the first time, around Walker in 1758, Wallsend in 1780-1 and Percy Main four years later. The Wallsend Basin was to radically change the fabric of the coal industry. Being nearer to the coast, collier boats could now come virtually to the back door of the pits. The Wallsend pit once received a visit from Tsar Nicholas I of Russia, who looked down the main shaft and commented, *"Ah my God, it is the mouth of hell; none but a madman would venture into it!"*

Although the industry was hugely profitable for the owners (the Wallsend pit made over £1000 a week profit at its peak), the men and boys who worked underground had to endure dreadful conditions for pathetically low wages. Jars, a French commentator on the industry, noted on a visit to Walker in 1765 that the use of child labour was common; boys as young as seven and eight worked over ten hours a day riding pit ponies. Older boys could be expected to work up to an eighteen hour day. The men, seemingly better off, only worked between eight and ten hours a day. The conditions were wet and dark, with pickaxes being used to hew coal from seams as narrow as eighteen inches.

Lighting was another problem in the industry. In the early part of the seventeenth century some mines had even resorted to using phosphorescent fish to provide illumination!

Perhaps the greatest problem faced by the miners was the lack of ventilation. In the late eighteenth century an effective system had been discovered by the use of two pit shafts. Men and equipment used the 'downcast' shaft, whilst a small furnace drew any unpleasant air out of the mine through the 'upcast' shaft. The result was a steady flow of air through the mine. Unfortunately for the men underground, many owners refused to have the extra shaft installed because of the high cost. The invention of the Davy and Stephenson Lamps should have improved safety but merely led to deeper and more dangerous mines. Another risk of working underground was the possibility of contracting the lung disease pneumoconiosis, which was rife and disabled or killed hundreds of miners.

One of the most hazardous and unpopular jobs faced by a miner was that of 'robbing'. As the mine was depleted, large pillars of coal were left to support the roof. With the deeper mines more coal was being left behind in the solid pillars. Robbing consisted of hacking the coal pillars away to such an extent, that the roof of the mine tunnel collapsed. Owners found that using this dangerous technique increased the capacity of a mine by as much as a third. Profits went up but then so did the number of men being killed.

During robbing the presence of gas increased, which led to more underground explosions. One of the worst incidents occurred in Wallsend in 1835 when one hundred and two men died in a huge underground explosion.

The pits along the Tyne Corridor were reaching their zenith at the turn of the nineteenth century. There were new sinkings in Wideopen and Gosforth in the 1820's. The Gosforth mine exploited the Ninety Fathom Fault further along from Longbenton. This had proved such a difficult task for the owners that a celebration ball was held, not in a hall but in a chamber over a thousand feet underground. It was attended by over two hundred people involved with the pit.

As the century progressed and the Main Seam was at the point of exhaustion, it was to be other parts of Northumberland and south-east Durham which overtook Tyneside in terms of output. Newcastle remained the 'capital' of the Great North Coalfield. It had the merchants, the know-how and the men to supply the demands of the industry, both home and abroad.

As the eighteenth century had witnessed innovation so did the next. Production rose to even greater peaks when steam was adapted to power cages that could take men even deeper. In 1813 came the frightening innovation of gunpowder. Unfortunately the owners' drive to produce more coal saw inevitable increases of deaths underground.

Events like this saw institutions set up to improve safety in the mines. The Institute of Mining and Mechanical Engineers was one such body which had its headquarters on Westgate Road in Newcastle. The building still stands near the Central Station.

The first unions emerged in this period, formed by men hardened by years of exploitation and dreadful working conditions. The first attempt to form a North East Union came in 1831 when a Durham miner, Thomas Hepburn, led a group of men demanding better pay and conditions. The strike, which lasted almost ten weeks, was organised following a meeting on the Town Moor. They did manage to secure some improvements but the leaders were sacked and Hepburn was blacklisted by his employers.

The first attempt to form a national union came in 1841 with the foundation of the Miners' Association of Great Britain. It became involved in a bitter dispute in the North East coal field which resulted in an all out strike. The owners won the day with constant intimidation and violence against the union's members. The union was disbanded only two years later.

Keelmen.

"A Species Of Watermen"

The keelmen carried goods (chiefly coal) from shore to ship before wharves came into common use. They are first mentioned in 1516, in a decree of the Star Chamber, as a craft, later to become an independent society in 1556. They were never to be an incorporated company mainly because of the opposition of the hostmen, who thought they would have to pay higher rates if a cartel was allowed to be formed, something at which the hostmen themselves were past masters. By the early eighteenth century sixteen hundred keelmen worked the river on four hundred boats.

The keel boats were double ended craft, crewed with a skipper, two keel-bullies, (from an obsolete term meaning 'of friendly familiarity') and a boy known as a pee-dee. After the coal was loaded the keels sailed down river, often with the help of the tide, three of the crew using a large oar called a swape, the other steering. On reaching the bigger collier boats, the keelmen emptied their twenty-ton load. The men needed to be strong as the collier boats they loaded were considerably higher than their small keels. The largest chunks of coal were emptied first, by hand, followed by the smaller pieces by shovel through a large porthole into the vessel's cargo hold. Before the nineteenth century river improvements, the shallow bottomed keel boats were essential to the industry as the colliers were unable to navigate the river.

The keelmen are associated with Sandgate where most lived, close to their place of work. *The Keel Row* immortalised them in song:

As I came through Sandgate
the Sandgate, the Sandgate
As I came through Sandgate
I heard a lassie sing
Weel may the keel row, the keel row the keel row
Weel may the keel row, the keel row the keel row
The Boat that my loves in.
Oh who is like my Johnny

The Wallsend Staiths heralded the end of the keel industry on the Tyne. The inset shows a group of keelmen, with time on their hands, playing cards on the Sandhill.

So leish, so blithe, so bonny
He's foremost among the mony
Keel lads o' Coaly Tyne.

In 1763 the area was described by Bourne as a *"vast number of narrow lanes....crowded with houses"* and *"chiefly inhabited by people that work upon the Water, particularly the Keelmen"*. John Wesley, visiting the district, commented, *"So much drunkenness, cursing, and swearing even from the mouths of little children, do I never remember to have seen or heard before in so short a compass of time"*.

The keelmen were bound for one year to the colliery fitters. Binding day was at Christmas, and on being bound the keelman was given one guinea and his supper. They were often paid in beer.

Strikes

The industry suffered from many strikes. A 1671 entry in the Gateshead Parish Church register records, *"paide for powder and match when the keelmen mutineyed, 2s."* Press gangs were used in an attempt to break a strike in 1719. One of the press gangs captured an American sailor, who was of course exempt from service and released by the town's magistrates. A pressed keelman, on arrival at the magistrates box, spoke in his finest broad Geordie: *"Aa's a Yankee tee, hinny"*.

The 1822 strike was one of the most famous in early labour history. It was over the use of staiths to load and unload coal. There were frequent attempts by keelmen to destroy the 'spouts' and they had previously struck in 1708 and 1794 over their use. The keelmen argued the staiths were destroying the navigation of the river by the accumulation of mud and sand and, more importantly, they were destroying their livelihood. There were also grievances over reduced wages and non-payment of binding money. Another problem faced by the men was the end to the practice of rebinding three months before the end of the year. This meant that the keelmen would not know until shortly before the start of the season if they had a job that following year.

It was a violent strike. Pitched battles were fought at North Shields, at Scotswood and in the Castle Garth. The authorities took the threat seriously, calling up the military and placing seven men of war in Shields harbour. The keelmen were supported by the river seamen, who had themselves unsuccessfully struck in 1815. The keelmen were able to prevent ships coaling at staiths and the marines were unable to manage the keels. The *Tom and Jerry*, one of Hedley's locomotives, was placed on a keel and used as a tug. It was the only boat able to break the blockade. It towed other keels but failed to make a decisive impression. The strike lasted ten weeks but eventually failed.

The keelmen decided to take legal action to close the staiths. They claimed the Wallsend Colliery Company was ruining the navigation of the river. Three judges at the York Assizes took eighteen months to decide in favour of the defendant. Undeterred, the keelmen took the case for retrial at Carlisle in 1828. Here the matter ended with the judges in favour of the coal owners. They did agree with the keelmen on their grievance but declared that the staiths had greatly boosted trade on the river.

In 1876 the building of the Swing Bridge, coupled with the Tyne improvements, meant larger boats could sail up the Tyne and in 1872 binding was finally abolished. The keelmen gradually faded away and by the start of this century only a handful were left working the river.

Keelman's Hospital

In 1700 one penny, the keelman's groat, was deducted from their pay to help keelmen in need. In 1701, an increased levy was used to found the Keelman's Hospital, which was built by the men themselves at a cost of some £20,000. The Trustees of the fund were the members of the Company of Hostmen and they provided the first governor, Matthew White. The keelmen were not allowed to run the hospital themselves, despite having built and funded it. In 1707 they mutinied over the rights to the hospital and three years later one hundred men signed a petition *"complaining that the money collected for the hospital was partly detained and partly wasted and misapplied"*. In 1723 the hostmen made an order that the charity should be run solely under their management.

Transport.

Although the steam engine had been invented in 1710, the early machines were liable to frequent breakdown. At first they were used for pumping water out of mines, but as the century progressed entrepreneurs gradually recognised their potential and they were slowly adapted to other uses. In the coal industry they were used to power the cages taking miners underground but it was in transport, at the turn of the nineteenth century, that the most dramatic advances were made.

In 1814 Tyneside's first steamboat was built. The *Tyne Steam Packet*, later called *Perseverance*, was used as a small ferry along the river. By 1827 the larger twin engined *Hylton Joliffe* was running a regular summer service from Newcastle to London.

The new screw propelled collier steamboats could ship coal to London in only fifty-six hours, instead of the two weeks it had previously taken. All these early boats were built from wood. It was not until 1842 that an iron boat, *Prince Albert*, was built locally - at Coutts Yard in Walker.

Railways

The railways spread the Industrial Revolution throughout Britain. By the 1830's virtually all the local collieries were linked to ports along the North East coast. From here coal could be shipped all over the world. Newcastle was soon connected to other towns, as a national railway network slowly moulded together. By 1838 Carlisle could be reached by train and North Shields the following year.

The most important links were south to London and north to Edinburgh. Gateshead was connected to London as early as 1844 but bridges had to be built over the Tyne and the Tweed before the two capitals were final-

ly connected by rail in 1850. At Berwick the impressive Royal Border Bridge was finished by Robert Stephenson that year, whilst in Newcastle the ingenious High Level Bridge had already been completed.

The twin deck High Level bridge was built between October 1846 and June 1849 by Stephenson and Harrison. The six cast iron arches span some one hundred and twenty-five feet each, and marked the first use of curved iron in Newcastle. Some five thousand tons of local cast and wrought iron were used. The pillars are hollow to a point just above the water line and then rise an impressive eighty-five feet above the river. Apart from being strengthened in 1922 to take trams, the structure has changed little since it was built. On the very first crossing of the bridge the engine driver turned to his fireman and is reputed to have said: *"Weel Geordie mun, 'ere's for 'eavan or Gaitshed"*.

Central Station

Another impressive piece of railway architecture was added to the town in 1850, the Central Station. Despite being the largest nineteenth century building in Newcastle, the original design for the Central Station, which won an award in Paris in 1858, was for a far more magnificent building. It would have had two parallel porte-corcheres supported by thirty-four pairs of Classical doric columns. This is compared to the present single porte-corchere which, although similar in conception, is supported by only seven arches. Unfortunately the railways were suffering from a lack of public confidence and the money for the project could not be found. The architect, Dobson, had to compromise on his original design, leaving out his colonnade front and grand entrance. The present entrance was added by Thomas Prosser in 1863.

The iron-worked roofing was unique at the time. Dobson devised a process which pressed the iron out between rollers, instead of cutting it from flattened plates. The work was provided by Hawk, Crawley and Co. of Gateshead, and Dobson's invention, now universally copied, won him a prize at the Paris Exposition.

This drawing by John Dobson represents his original exalted design for the Central Station which won an award in Paris in 1858.

The costs were shared by the Newcastle and Carlisle Railway, and the York, Newcastle and Berwick Railway - each of which had their own platforms and staff.

The Central Station was opened by Queen Victoria and Prince Albert on August 29th 1850. The day was declared a public holiday and local manufacturers were asked to put their fires out between 11 am and 2 pm so as not to cloud the momentous occasion. Local legend has it that this was Victoria's last visit to Newcastle. After the celebration banquet the manager of the hotel had the cheek to present the Queen with the bill! In future, whenever she passed through the town the blinds were always pulled down in her carriage.

Industrial Pioneers.

The Stephensons

The Stephensons' contribution to the Industrial Revolution was outstanding. They are recognised the world over as designers and builders of many of the great railway projects in the first half of the Nineteenth century. Who has not heard of the Stockton and Darlington Railway or the *Rocket*?

George Stephenson was born in Wylam in 1781, the son of a colliery fireman. His cottage still stands, owned by the National Trust and is open to the public. He spent his childhood on the move between different pit villages in the North East. George consequently had a poor education and during most of his career he was largely illiterate. In 1802 he married Frances Henderson and later settled down in Killingworth with their son Robert. It was here that he established a world reputation as an engineer, inventing a miners' safety lamp - the *Geordie Lamp*.

George Stephenson.

He also worked on better designs for iron rails for the numerous waggonways in the area and explored the possibility of developing powered haulage. Trevethick had already built such an engine in South Wales in 1804. Ten years later George followed with his own locomotive, *Blücher*, used on a local colliery line. In 1819 George became involved in his first major railway project, the Hetton Colliery line, near Sunderland.

The rapid development of the early railways attracted the attention of a group of local businessmen headed by the Darlington Quaker, Edward Pease. Having obtained permission from parliament, the men invited George to leave his job at Killingworth to construct the Stockton and Darlington Railway, the world's first-steam powered public railway. It was now, in 1824, that Robert became formally involved in his father's business when they founded a small workshop on Forth Street in Newcastle to build the engines for the nearby railway.

Robert Stephenson.

The locomotives proved to be unreliable and at one point it was considered whether they should scrap them and revert to traditional horse power and stationary haulage engines. In 1829 trials were held, at Rainhill on the Liverpool and Manchester Railway, to finally end the dispute between horse and steam. It was here that the Stephensons stunned the crowd with their revolutionary engine, *Rocket*. The engine not only achieved a world record speed of thirty-six miles per hour but shattered a popular misconception at the time - that people were unable to breath at such speeds.

George completed the Liverpool to Manchester line and left Tyneside to live in Derbyshire. He still worked on new routes as well as branching out into coal mining. He died in 1848 in Chesterfield. Newcastle honoured him with a monument in 1862. It is situated at the bottom of Westgate Road on the site of the old West Spital, and is now sadly sandwiched between two modern office blocks. It cost £5,000, and was designed by J. G. Lough, a local artist, who is also responsible for Collingwood's statue at Tynemouth. Around the base of the plinth are four figures; a smith, a pitman, an engineer and a platelayer, symbolising a century of industrial progress on Tyneside.

Robert stayed in Newcastle and continued to build engines. They were exported all over the world from the Forth Street workshops. He was also recognised as one of the nation's great civil engineers, building the High Level Bridge and the Royal Border Bridge. A lifetime of overwork finally took its toll and Robert died in 1859 at the age of fifty-six. He was laid to rest in Westminster Abbey.

The Stephensons' company carried on in Forth Street, building all kinds of engines, boilers and turbines for the international market. In 1901 the Forth Street workshops were sold to their great local rival Hawthorn Leslie's when the company moved to new premises in Darlington.

The Hawthorn Brothers

The Hawthorn brothers, like the Stephensons, were involved in the early pioneering days of the railways. Their father had at one point employed George Stephenson at Willington Quay. The two brothers were the only survivors of eleven children. The eldest son, Robert, opened a small engineering workshop on Forth Street in 1818, six years before the Stephensons, and was joined two years later by his younger brother, William. They were involved in the Stockton and Darlington Railway and in later years supplied the Newcastle to Carlisle Railway with engines.

The brothers saw the early potential of marine engineering. There was already a steady expansion of shipyards along the Tyne making revolutionary steamships, and they supplied engines for Leslie's steamships being built at Hebburn.

Robert Hawthorn died in 1867 leaving William in control of the Company. The Forth Street workshops were not large enough for all the Company's interests and the marine division was moved in 1872 to St. Peter's workshops in Walker, after buying the site from the Smith's Dock Company. William died three years later.

The Company formally amalgamated with Leslie's in 1885 to become R. and W. Hawthorn Leslie and Co., and went on to be one of the most famous shipbuilding and engineering firms in the world. It reached its peak in the run up to the First World War, expanding its Forth Street workshops by buying the Stephensons' old premises.

A chronic lack of orders during the Depression led the two great companies of Stephensons and Hawthorn Leslie to merge in 1937. The threat of war loomed again and the Company was able to work at full capacity once more. After 1945 the firm's four sites were split into separate companies.

Unfortunately the story of the early Tyneside Pioneers ends in the post-war period. English Electric took over the railway side of the Company, closing the Forth Street workshop in 1959, and ending locomotive production at Darlington in 1966. Thus one hundred and forty-three proud years of engine design and building in the North East came to a close. The other two sites suffered a similar fate: both the Hebburn and Walker sites were closed, victims of the post 1973 recession.

Healthcare.

During the seventeenth century a Town Physician was employed for the benefit of the corporation's members and staff. By the eighteenth century there were a number of private practitioners, largely concentrated around Pilgrim Street.

In January 1751 a letter appeared in *The Courant*, simply signed 'B.K.', urging the opening of a new hospital. Soon after Richard Lambert, a young surgeon and possibly the writer of the letter, opened a public subscription for the building of a General Infirmary. The hospital opened in temporary accommodation at the Gallowgate in May 1751 and was soon using rooms in neighbouring buildings. In October 1752, the hospital moved to a permanent site on the Forth with two resident surgeons.

After the formation of the General Infirmary developments in hospital care came swiftly. In 1760, the Lying-in Hospital for Poor Married Women in Rosemary Lane was opened, followed in 1767 by a lunatic asylum in Warden's Close beyond West Wall. The lunatic asylum was, by all accounts, Draconian. It was crowded, little attention was paid to cleanliness and the patients were kept in dungeon-like cells - sometimes chained to the walls.

In 1822 Doctor Fife opened a Hospital for Diseases of the Eye in Brunswick Place. The need for the hospital was demonstrated by the seven thousand patients who were treated in the first nine years. This was the same Doctor Fife who, in 1829, lectured on anatomy over several days using the body of *"a most disgusting and abandoned female"*. The woman in question had been sentenced to death at the Assizes and taken by cart to the gallows on the Town Moor sitting on her own coffin. Twenty thousand people came to watch the spectacle of her execution, after which her body was exhibited for six hours in the Surgeons' Hall.

The eighteenth century at last saw physicians beginning to take the study of anatomy seriously. The profession became increasingly unpopular as the lack of bodies

The General Infirmary.

meant that surgeons had to resort to the services of the body snatchers. In 1771 a human skeleton fetched a handsome £6.6s., whilst that of a gorilla, being understandably much rarer, fetched £35. One of the prime sources of bodies was from public executions, a supply which steadily increased as the eighteenth century progressed.

In 1752 a nineteen year old trooper, Ewan Macdonald, killed a man in a brawl in the Bigg Market and was sentenced to death at the Assizes. After he was hanged his body was taken to the Physicians' Hall and the surgeons were on the point of dissection when they were called away. They returned to find the young Ewan sitting up begging for mercy. A surgeon, not to be done out of his body, promptly took a large mallet and killed him.

The lack of well trained doctors was rectified in 1832 when the Newcastle School of Medicine and Surgery was formed, later to become the School of Medicine at Durham University.

Even though there were more trained doctors they could do little about the way people lived. With the growing influx of people into the riverside area, health standards plummeted. The area consisted of thirty-three streets without drains or sewers. The ancient housing suffered from chronic overcrowding. Mackenzie described the chares as *"narrow, dark and stinking alleys"*. Rubbish and excrement were simply thrown out of windows where it lay uncollected for months on end. The corporation did employ twenty refuse collectors but their efforts were largely concentrated on the main streets or the well-to-do suburbs. The atmosphere of the slums was further polluted by the stench of the slaughter houses, chemical plants and various factories in the surrounding areas.

In such an unhealthy environment disease was a recurrent problem. During the 1820's and 30's the oldest parts of the town gained the unfavourable reputation as the 'fever districts'. A combination of overcrowding, unpurified water, poor education and low wage levels saw the rapid spread of disease. Smallpox and typhus were virtually endemic. Mackenzie had written about the typhus outbreak in 1825/6 but he himself died six years later from cholera.

Cholera

Nobody knows what triggered the 1831 epidemic. It originated from India and advanced across Asia and into Europe. The British Government was complacent over the whole matter, blaming poor foreign hygiene and diet. When spring came to Europe in 1831 cholera came with it. The Government was unprepared. The first case was found in Sunderland. The arrival of a single infected person in a district was sufficient to cause a countrywide epidemic.

Cholera thrives on stagnant and slow flowing water, poor sanitation and a dire lack of even rudimentary cleanliness - a combination the Quayside had in plenty. It was a hot summer, the river was running low and full of stagnant pools. The epidemic was further perpetuated by a water shortage caused by the previous mild winter. The reservoir above the town was virtually dry. Emergency water was pumped from the Tyne and was distributed to the population by carts.

A contemporary writer, Sykes, described this first outbreak: *"It was most distressing, to hear the greatest fatality of the disorder the constant tolling of the bells of the churches from morn to night."* Corpses were collected by cartmen *"holding the bridle at its utmost stretch"* - reviving images of the Plague centuries earlier. The corporation was unable to tackle the crisis, other than by laying down basic guidelines. The owners of the chares were ordered to wash their property down with hot lime and the dead were buried in lime outside the town walls. Although the town had a fever hospital, poor people were unable to pay for any treatment and by staying at home infectious diseases spread all the more quickly.

What the epidemic did more than anything was to concentrate minds on the festering problems of poverty and the strains of industrialisation, putting into question the abilities of the corporation. The fear of revolution returned, magnifying social tensions.

Law and Order.

Punishment

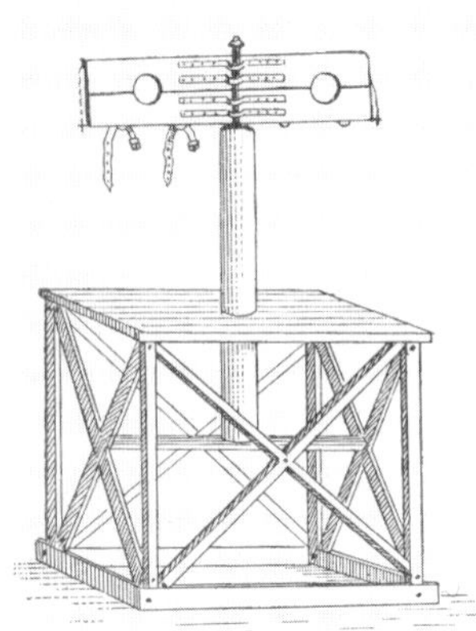

There were few hangings on the Town Moor in the early part of the eighteenth century. Between 1703 and 1733 there were none at all, and over the next thirty years only ten, together with a further two at Westgate. As the century advanced this trend reversed and the death penalty came to be used on an ever-increasing basis.

The crime rate rose remorselessly throughout the eighteenth century and the only response the authorities had, prior to the formation of the police force, was to increase penalties. This led to the infamous anomalies in the penal code, so that in 1789 a Newcastle man was only fined 6s. 8d. for manslaughter in a tavern brawl, whilst a woman who stole a handkerchief in 1790 faced seven years transportation. She may be considered lucky since this was a capital offence. Paradoxically, these severe penalties frequently had the opposite effect by making the juries less willing to convict defendants.

The pillory was still used as a form of punishment and was kept for the *"vile and seditious"*. Death was not unknown, particularly for short men or women since if their feet did not touch the ground they could well be throttled. Sometimes the occupant's ears would be nailed to the wood so they were unable to put their heads down. The use of the pillory ended in Newcastle in 1790. It was still used in Sunderland until 1811, when the last offender drew a crowd of twenty thousand - more than Roker Park gets on a Saturday afternoon!

Winter's Gibbet, near Elsdon. In 1791 the body of William Winter was hung here in sight of the place he murdered Margaret Crozier.

Riots

Another regular problem which faced the town authorities was that of large scale rioting. The riots, in 1709, 1710, 1740 and 1750, were nearly always preceded by a bad harvest and a subsequent harsh and hungry winter, so they earned the title 'rebellions of the belly' - despite the town's paternal efforts of soup kitchens and relief funds.

The keelmen were often involved in these riots. The winter of 1739-1740 was severe - even the Tyne froze over. It was so cold that Alderman Ridley allowed the poor to take coal from his own stocks. The bitter winter led to a shortage of food that following summer. On the 25th June *"the keelmen entered Newcastle in terrible numbers and with all sorts of weapons"*. An angry meeting with town officials led to the death of one of the crowd. The rioters then attacked the Guildhall, destroying many of the Council's records. The town's treasury was robbed. There is some speculation that £1,200 was distributed to the poor. In the evening three companies of soldiers dispersed the crowd, making forty arrests. At the following Assizes six men were sentenced to be transported to the Colonies.

In 1761 the balloting of militia brought further riots. The trouble began in Gateshead and quickly spread into outlying Northumberland. Mobs seized the militia lists and destroyed them. By the time the seething mob reached Hexham it was five thousand strong, but it was now faced by two battalions of Yorkshire Militia. The militia stood their ground for three hours under constant provocation from the rioters. Then one rioter grabbed a trooper's flintlock and shot him. The militia responded by opening fire, killing eighteen people.

The Police Force

Events such as these eventually provoked the first attempts to form an organised police force, although no proper force existed in Newcastle until well into the nineteenth century.

In 1763 a night watch had been formed. By 1827 twenty-six watchmen, under the supervision of a constable and his two assistants, patrolled the town between ten at night and six in the morning. They were equipped with a lantern, a stick with a hook and a rattle. For one guinea a week, and a further guinea at the end of the season, they walked the streets in their uniform, a great coat, calling the half hours. The problem with this arrangement was that the night watchmen were paid one shilling for every arrest made. This made walking the streets at night a worrying time, as much from the fear of over-zealous watchmen, eager for their supplement, than from any criminal element.

In November 1832 the first attempts were made to form a regular police force. Robert Peel's revolutionary new force, the Bow Street Runners, though unpopular, had reduced the level of crime in London. Unfortunately many of the felons had simply moved into the provinces and created a fresh crime wave that drove many towns to consider the formation of similar bodies. The new force formed in Newcastle was despised. It was viewed as an affront to civil liberties and had to be abandoned in September 1833 after a popular outcry. However the high level of crime meant the town could not live without regular policemen, so in May 1836 the force was re-established. This was followed later in 1845 by creation of the separate River Police, the first in Britain.

The Moot Hall

The Old Moot Hall.

Criminals were kept in the town's prisons until they were tried at the Assizes held in the Moot Hall. The original Moot, together with the Great Hall in the Castle Garth, was pulled down in 1809 as the building was not considered suitable for the County Assizes. Parliament and the Crown sanctioned the demolition, and Earl Percy laid the foundation stone on July 22nd 1810. The replacement Moot Hall was designed in an early Greek revivalist style by John and William Stokoe, and completed in 1812. The first Assizes were held there that August. The building was extensively remodelled in 1875 by William Crozier, the architect to Durham Council.

In 1986 the building was acquired by the Property Services Agency who have carried out a full renovation at a cost of some £1.6m. The old designs of Crozier have been reproduced as closely as possible. The carpets for the principal rooms are based on a section of Brussels carpet, decorative plasterwork has been reproduced and new lamps have been designed from fragments of the original glass. Cheap glass was imported from Russia, as glass of the necessary (and authentic) poor quality could not be found in Britain. The building is still used as the Crown and High Courts.

The recently refurbished replacement next to the Castle keep.

The Assizes

During Norman times the Assizes were held at irregular intervals and often the accused would have to wait years before coming to trial. In 1216 Henry III made the system more efficient by making the visits more fixed. A record exists of the Sheriff of Northumberland who was ordered *"to be attendant upon"* the king's justices itinerant in 1218. The Sheriff would meet the assize judges with his entourage of knights, gentlemen, freeholders, coroners and bailiffs in a display of medieval pageantry befitting the king's justices. The group would ride out to Sheriff's Hill, outside Gateshead, and the Sheriff would escort the judges into Newcastle. In 1835 the Assize procession consisted of:

"Bailiffs two and two Bailiff errant in the Sheriffs livery.
Two trumpeters in the sheriffs livery with banners bearing the sheriffs arms attached to their trumpets.
The gaoler with a black rod.
The undersheriff with a white rod and sword.

The Assize day procession winds its way down the Side.

J.W. Carmichael's painting of the
1827 Ascension Day.

Classical Newcastle.

Chapter 7

The Georgian improvements in Newcastle were aimed at the town's professional classes. New houses, shops and offices were built along elegant streets in the upper part of the town. Some of these buildings can still be seen today, at Leazes Terrace and Crescent and the eastern part of Eldon Square. Sadly many have disappeared in the building (or demolition) zeal of the 1960's. Examples of this include most of the buildings on Blackett Street, to make way for the Eldon Square shopping centre, and the Royal Arcade at the bottom Pilgrim Street.

The men involved were a new breed of architect and builder; John Dobson, Thomas Oliver and Richard Grainger. These forward looking men, however, left two parts of the town untouched by development, the archaic riverside and a twelve acre site comprising Newe House and the adjoining Nuns Field in the centre of the town. This prime land was owned by the builder George Anderson who had renamed it Anderson Place.

John Dobson had tried to put through a major development plan in 1825, but it was not to be until the death of George Anderson and the subsequent sale of the land to Richard Grainger that the Classical Newcastle we know today could be born.

The developments of the 1820's and early 30's had given Grainger the capital needed to buy Newe House and its surrounding land. This was to be the heart of the elegant commercial and residential plans.

The Triumvirate.

Grainger

Born into a poor background on Low Friar Street in 1797, Richard Grainger was the second son of a Quayside porter. He began his education at a charity school on Percy Street, whilst his mother struggled to make ends meet following the death of her husband. Grainger set up in the building trade in 1816 with his brother George, who tragically died the following year.

Through the Methodist Church he met influential members of Newcastle society such as William Batson. This prominent merchant gave the young builder his first major contract to build houses, at Higham Place. The success of this project established Grainger's reputation and he was soon working on more houses on New Bridge Street and Carliol Street. The £5,000 dowry his wife, Rachel Arundale, brought with her enabled Grainger to begin developing his own ambitious plans for houses on Blackett Street and Eldon Square. Eldon Square was designed by Thomas Oliver and planned by the rising young architect John Dobson. Only the east row of these once fashionable terraces remains. The size and spaciousness of the old square was unheard of at the time. High quality ashlar masonry was used, which was expensive as stone was rarely used in domestic architecture.

The Royal Arcade

The building of Leazes Terrace and Crescent followed. Before they were finished Grainger had embarked on his next project, the Royal Arcade. The Royal Arcade was built to a design by Dobson on the site of the present day Swan House, between 1831 and 1832. It took less than a year to build and cost £45,000. It could be compared with modern day shopping centres such as Eldon Square or even the Metro Centre in that it housed not only shops but also offices and other amenities; banks, auction rooms, a post office and a steam and vapour bath.

The interior of the arcade was floored with chequered stone and black marble, and lit by eight conical skylights set in domes high up in the roof. There were eight shops on either side of the mall.

Unfortunately the building was poorly sited, and never became the commercial success it should have been. Only the western entrances opened towards the town centre, which was some distance away. The east end exited at Manor Chare, which was an unsavoury area at the time. Because of this the arcade was never used as a thoroughfare - unlike most successful arcades which join two main streets. This state of affairs was not helped by the opening of Grey and Grainger Streets. The place may well have been ideal for the lady of fashion, but she did not want to walk down to this area of the town.

The interior of the Royal Arcade, 1823.

Gradually the offices emptied. By the end of the nineteenth century they were occupied by furniture brokers and second hand dealers. It became a mecca for socialists of all shades of opinion in the 1950's and 60's and was also associated with intellectuals and artists. The People's Theatre was conceived here, as was the Tyneside Film Society. Having been left to decay the building was demolished in 1963. During demolition every piece of stonework was numbered - with chalk - the intention being to rebuild the arcade elsewhere. The pieces were stored on various outdoor sites and, Tyneside weather being what it is, it was not long before the numbers had washed off. Not even the Americans could be persuaded to buy ten thousand assorted stone pieces, so the rebuilding plan had to be scrapped.

What remains is a replica of the inside of the old Arcade, which actually cost more to build than the original. It sits uneasily beneath the Orwellian gloom of Swan House.

Clayton

In contrast to his close friend Grainger, John Clayton was born into a wealthy and powerful family. John was the son of the Town's Clerk, Nathaniel Clayton, and was educated in Northumberland. He became involved in the town's politics, becoming Under Sheriff at the early age of twenty-two. At this time he was also working as a lawyer at his father's practice. He inherited his father's prestigious post of Town Clerk in 1822 and immediately took great interest in the improvements of this period. Clayton was a very quiet man who lived with his brother, Matthew, in Fenkle Street.

Dobson

John Dobson was born in North Shields in 1787. From an early age he displayed a talent for drawing and he became an apprentice at the office of the celebrated architect David Stephenson. In 1809, he headed for London where he met influential architects and artists such as Varley and Turner. Dobson returned to Tyneside the following year and set up his own business, near North Shields. His first project was the design of the Royal Jubilee School on New Road (now called City Road) in Newcastle. It no longer stands.

Leaving North Shields in 1812, he opened an office on Pilgrim Street. By this time, he became increasingly sought after as a designer of country houses in the North East. Dobson was involved with Doxford Hall, built in the Greek style, and improvements to Cheeseburn Grange. He matured as an architect of country houses during the 1820's and in the process built up a reputation amongst the aristocracy. It was during this decade that he arguably produced some of his best designs; at Mitford Hall, Lilburn Tower and his own house on New Bridge Street in Newcastle.

Leazes Terrace, once thought to be by Dobson, but in fact designed by his colleague Thomas Oliver.

Dobson was also involved in several schemes in and around Newcastle. The cholera epidemics had given rise to the need for more cemeteries. He responded with designs for graveyards in Gateshead and Jesmond. Newcastle's rapid expansion saw more churches built. Dobson's early work in this sphere of architecture included a Presbyterian chapel on Blackett Street and the Church of St. Thomas the Martyr on the Haymarket. This church established Dobson's reputation as an ecclesiastical architect. It was consecrated on October 19th 1830, built partly with funds from the corporation. It is an early example of the neo-gothic design of that time. The design was chosen from two others submitted as models to the Committee of Newcastle Common Council in July 1827.

A year before this submission Dobson had built the Lying-in Hospital, designed in the Gothic style. It was occupied by the combined charities of the Lying-in Hospital and the Outdoor Charity for Poor Married Women. It eventually became the home for BBC North East, who recently moved out to their new studios in Fenham - the 'pink-palace'. There have been plans to convert the building into an *'up market'* neon pub, not quite what Dobson intended.

Eldon Square.

The Plans.

In 1834 Grainger submitted his plans for extensive town centre improvements. They received council approval, with the persuasive help of Clayton. Grainger knew the influence Clayton had over the corporation. He tactfully moved his lucrative account to Clayton's own law firm just prior to the presentation, a move which not only secured Clayton's support but also started a friendship that was to last until Grainger's death in 1867. This may be classed as somewhat dubious today, but business ethics were less stringent in those days and moves such as Grainger's were often common practice.

Grainger presented his ideas whilst he was still in negotiation with George Anderson's son, Thomas, over the purchase of Anderson Place. In June 1834, the outline of the plan had been printed in the local press and had received widespread public acclamation. The council's main objection to the elaborate plans was that the old Theatre Royal and the relatively new Meat Markets would have to be demolished in the construction of what is now Grey Street. After Grainger had assured the councillors that he would build a new theatre and a covered market (now called Grainger Market) the plan was quickly adopted. He secured the purchase of Anderson Place for £50,000. This was to be the heart of the elegant commercial and residential developments.

The scheme was financed using a number of different means. The biggest sum came from mortgages; each new building erected was mortgaged to provide capital for the next building. This was a risky and very speculative means of raising finance, but it worked well as confidence in the project was riding high. The scheme also received cash injections from leading citizens, often thanks to Clayton. Other funding came from the Northumberland and Durham District Banking Company.

The first part of the scheme involved the construction of Upper Dean Street (now Grey Street), to provide a thoroughfare between Dean Street and Blackett Street. There was also the building of the New Market and the laying of the four streets that surrounded it; Grainger Street, Clayton Street, Nun Street and Nelson Street.

Grainger Street, showing the Central Exchange on the right, and the Grainger Market on the left. By J Christie.

New Buildings.

Grainger Market

The original 'new' Flesh Market was only thirty years old when the new plans were unveiled. As it lay on the site of the Grey Street developments, it had to go. Grainger paid £15,000 for the Market, which was just to the south of High Bridge, so that he could redevelop the land. Designed by Dobson, the new building housed the largest covered market in the country. They were divided into the butcher and the vegetable markets, together covering two acres and protected by a massive glass roof. Many of the traders had moved from the Quayside, keen to take advantage of the new developments - at the same time accelerating the decline of the riverside. The Grainger Market was described as the *"most magnificent in the world"*, the opening being celebrated by a huge dinner complete with an orchestra.

Central Exchange

The Central Exchange was built between 1836 and 1838, with the Central Exchange Hotel being added in 1862. The triangular exchange with its domed roof contained apartments, a coffee room, and a news room.

It had many connections with the art world and housed the Victorian School of Art and Northumberland Institute for Fine Arts. There was also an art gallery situated here in the 1870's. In the early 90's it was home to the Vaudeville Theatre which held concerts and pantomimes. Unfortunately the original domed structure was gutted by fire in the early 1900's, and was rebuilt as the picturesque Central Arcade in 1905. Window's music shop in the Arcade is said to be haunted by ghosts from the fire.

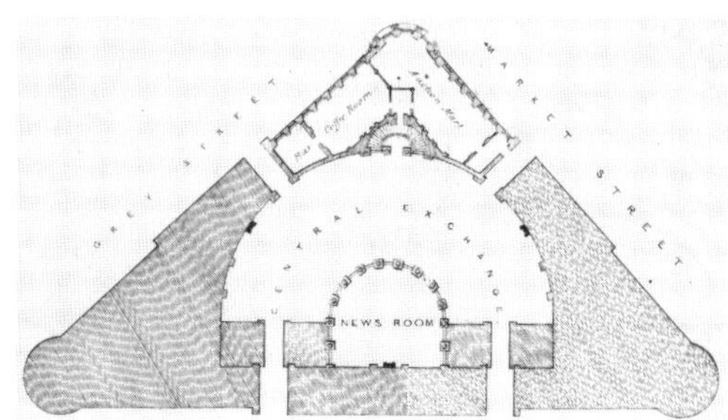

The plan of the Central Exchange.

When plans were put forward for the building of a new Town Hall in the 1850's, there was public dismay as the proposed site for the building would destroy the fine view of St. Nicholas from down the Bigg Market. Grainger offered the Exchange as an alternative site for the council's home but it was deemed unsuitable and the proposal went ahead.

The Monument

The one hundred and thirty-five feet tall Grey's Monument, with its one hundred and sixty-four steps to the top, was built to mark the passing of the Great Reform Bill in 1832. It was designed by John and Benjamin Green, who were also responsible for the Theatre Royal. The foundations were laid in September 1837. A sealed chamber cut into the stone holds; a glass bottle containing a sketch of the building; a list of those who paid for it; a collection of silver and copper coins; and several local medals and tradesmen's tokens. The Monument was completed when the statue, by E. Bailey, was lowered into place on the 24th August 1838.

During the summer the Monument is open to the public on Saturdays and offers one of the finest views of Newcastle.

Theatre Royal

The 1788 Theatre Royal.

The original theatre was situated midway along Mosley Street and opened on January 21st 1788. This again lay in the path of the proposed Grey Street development. It cost Grainger £45,000 to buy the theatre and the surrounding properties.

The new theatre was started in 1837, to a design by John and Benjamin Green. It was opened on February 20th 1838 with a performance of *"The Merchant of Venice"*. It has been said that the graceful portico,with its six Corinthian pillars, helps to break up the smooth curve of Grey Street.

In 1899, four years after extensive renovations, the theatre was severely damaged by fire, following a performance of 'the Scottish play'. It was renovated by Frank Matcham, and reopened in 1901.

The theatre was bought by Newcastle Council in the early 1970's and then leased to an independent trust who were responsible for its administration and upkeep. In June 1986 it was again closed for major renovations. Much of the original work in the auditorium was in poor condition, and the cramped backstage facilities were out of date. When the work began it was discovered that the building was riddled with dry and wet rot. Also, the foundations were inadequate and major cross walls lacked stability, with some parts being dangerous. The new restoration work involved fully renovating the auditorium, with its plaster and fittings, to their former glory. There was also a newly laid out and enlarged foyer, a new staircase in similar style and materials to the old, and vastly enlarged and improved back stage facilities. Neighbouring properties

were merged into the complex, bringing in a coffee shop, bar and restaurant; turning the whole building into the concept of 'all day theatre'.

Restoration was carried out only after extensive historical research to ensure that everything returned to its original state. The final cost of the entire restoration programme was £6,333,000.

The grand reopening took place on the 11th January 1988 with Hollywood legend Charlton Heston and Roy Kinnear in Bolt's *"A Man For All Seasons"*.

The Results

The whole scheme was completed in 1839, at a cost of £640,000, using an assortment of architects and builders. John and Benjamin Green designed most of the buildings at the top of Grey Street, whilst the area between Shakespeare Street and Mosley Street was built to the plans of Dobson. Grainger and his two leading architects, Wardle and Walker, concentrated on most of the other street elevations. Today the different styles of these Victorian architects can be seen along these *"broad and stately thoroughfares"*. The simpler designs usually belong to Dobson, whilst the more elaborate tend to belong either to Grainger's own architects or to the Green brothers.

The end result was a vastly improved Newcastle centre. Nine new streets had been built, along their lengths were thirty-two new inns and pubs and three hundred and twenty-five shops, offices and houses. Grey Street, the centre piece of the new developments, with its impressive curve, was described as *"the finest street in Europe"* and even today few people would argue with this.

In 1948 John Betjeman visited the street: *"As for the curve of Grey Street, I shall never forget seeing it to perfection, trafficless, on a misty Sunday morning. Not even Regent Street, even old Regent Street, London, can compare with that subtle curve."*

Later Years.

Even before the scheme was completed, Grainger was seeking another area of Newcastle to develop. The town centre improvements would not show a return for some time and he wanted to reduce the debts incurred over the previous five years. After consultation with Clayton he bought the Elswick Estate in 1839, for £114,000 from John Hodgson Hinde. Clayton still acted as his solicitor and was a great help in raising the finance necessary from the forty-one creditors who invested in the scheme. After the huge success of the town centre improvements, Grainger was given a free hand to develop the estate. Building started soon after Clayton had finalised the legal work; the capital invested could then be recouped as soon as possible. The idea was to create a semi-industrial suburb close to the town centre.

By 1841 it was clear that there was little interest in the area. Grainger's speculative building was heading towards financial disaster, with much of the property lying empty and money from rents and sales barely covering interest payments.

To avoid the public humiliation of being arrested for bankruptcy in his home town, Grainger left for Liverpool. He spent several months on the move, finally ending up in Scotland. Clayton went to great lengths to preserve Grainger's good name, and informed him by letter every few days on the situation in Newcastle.

Grainger eventually arrived back in Newcastle in November 1841, with his creditors threatening legal action. John Clayton managed to appease most of them by his skilful mediating and by 1847, with the sale of two plots of land to William Armstrong, Grainger's desperate situation began to improve.

He drifted out of the public eye in his later years and lived in modest middle-class comfort at his house, 5, Clayton Street West. He died in 1861, leaving a huge debt of £128,582 with only £16,000 in his will. It was not until forty years after his death that all his debts were cleared, by which time Elswick had become the industrial suburb that Grainger had envisaged.

John Clayton continued as Town Clerk, living a quiet life as a bachelor. He managed the huge amounts of legal work left by Grainger; even by the 1890's his firm was working on the complex issues of mortgages and debt clearances. He died in 1890 a wealthy man, leaving an estate of almost £750,000.

Dobson drifted away from Grainger and Clayton during the troubled Elswick years and continued designing a multitude of buildings for various clients. He still pursued his passion for designing country houses, but it was the age of railway mania and Dobson became increasingly involved in industrial and railway architecture. He also worked on several projects on Newcastle's Quayside, the design of Central and Manors Stations and various warehouse and dock schemes around the North East.

He became associated with the 'railway king', George Hudson, who was chairman of three separate railway companies. The two men embarked on what was to become Dobson's largest single project. Hudson ordered the building of four hundred high quality houses in Whitby, North Yorkshire, using Dobson as chief architect. Unfortunately for Hudson the scheme proved to be a failure and all but ruined him.

In 1859 Dobson was elected to the esteemed post of President of the Northumberland Architectural Association, but his glittering career was brought to an abrupt halt in 1862 when he suffered a severe stroke. He retired to Ryton, along the Tyne valley, and died two years later at his other home in Newcastle on New Bridge Street. Dobson's work is still found all over the North, a testament to Newcastle's finest architect.

Victorian Newcastle.

The Great Fire

The Great Fire of Newcastle and Gateshead began on October 6th 1854. A local policeman on his beat, John Ewart, first spotted a fire in the Worsted Manufacturing Mill of Wilson and Son at 12.30 am. This factory stood on the site of a warehouse which had been burnt down only three years previously. The fire quickly spread along Gateshead's water-front and within an hour of the alarm being raised the nearby Bertrams warehouse was fully ablaze. This was a threatening development, as a large quantity of sulphur and highly inflammable nitrate salts were stored inside.

Word was spreading faster than the fire. A large crowd was beginning to assemble at various vantage points, to view the awesome spectacle. By three in the morning the sky above Newcastle was filled with yellow and purple flames from the burning timber and sulphur inside Bertrams. A major disaster, unknown to the onlookers, was imminent.

The crowds heard two dull explosions in rapid succession. At first people were not too alarmed. Then a gigantic third explosion followed. The sheer force of the blast is difficult to imagine. It left a crater thirty feet deep and some fifty feet wide, hurling large stones in all directions. Some ended up going through buildings as far away as Pilgrim Street, whilst the shock wave blew out hundreds of windows along the riverside area. Some people at Shields thought the blast was an earthquake, whilst folk in Sunderland thought it was a factory on the Wear exploding.

There was pandemonium as the blast instantly killed many who had gathered on the bridge and in the immediate vicinity. It also put most of the fire engines out of action. Burning timbers fell onto the north bank, starting fires which worked their way along Newcastle's Quay. Panic messages were sent to most North East towns to send any available fire engines. As most were horse drawn it would take several hours before engines could arrive.

By midday more fires had broken out on both sides of the river - the fire service was helpless. The crowds swelled and by Saturday the streets of Newcastle were overflowing with sightseers and sympathisers - even special trains were laid on.

In the aftermath the death toll was finally calculated. It is estimated that over fifty people had died, many immediately after the third explosion. The exact toll was never known as many victims were incinerated in the intense heat. One casualty was John Dobson's son, Alexander, who was accounted dead on the discovery of his snuff box. Another was the owner of Bertrams who was identified by his keys. The fire left many properties destroyed and it completely razed six chares along the Quay.

A dramatic painting of the Great Fire.

Chapter 8

The Newcastle Fire Service

The Great Fire highlighted the inadequate provision of an organised fire service on Tyneside. In 1751 the corporation and Trinity House had bought two fire engines from Nuttals in London. The early firemen were all volunteers and were paid 2s. 6d. every time they manned the pumps. The only response prior to this was the provision of fire hydrants along the major thoroughfares of the town. By 1845 there were between ten and twelve fire engines owned by fire assurance companies or by large businesses. If the building did not have a policy the assurance companies would simply let it burn to the ground.

Despite the fire, it was not until 1885 that a fully organised fire service was deployed by the corporation. It was housed in the same building as the Police Station on Thorton Street. Other fire stations opened soon after. In 1891 the West End station was opened at Arthur's Hill, whilst the east side of the city was served by the Headlam Street station.

There were also several private fire services operating at the turn of the century. The Elswick Works Brigade was formed in 1896 at the sprawling Armstrong works which stretched several miles along the river bank. Their pride and joy was the fireboat. The Brigade lasted until 1982 when the whole complex closed to be replaced by the Vickers tank factory on Scotswood Road. Another private service was organised between Armstrongs and the Durham and Northumberland Coal Owners but this arrangement lasted only two years. The mine owners carried on without Armstrongs until the National Coal Board was formed in 1946. The NCB finally ended cover during the 1950's.

The present day City Fire Station was built in 1933 after the old site at Thorton Street became too cluttered. The service was extensively modernised in 1952 under the Local Authority. The present Tyne and Wear Fire Service came into being in 1974 after the Government reorganisation of Local Authorities.

Expansion.

Each successive era in Newcastle's history saw growth in employment and population, but in the Victorian era growth was unprecedented, an expansion that finally warranted Newcastle gaining City status. The population explosion saw the pressing need for a reformed Diocese and in 1882 St. Nicholas Church rose in stature to become a cathedral. In the sixty years this chapter embraces Newcastle's population grew from almost ninety thousand to around its current size of two hundred and eighty thousand. This was the era of the great industrialists such as Armstrong and Palmer, of huge immigration of Irish, Scots and dispossessed rural Northumbrians, and of the start of the sprawling suburbs that are so characteristic of modern British cities.

One of the first areas to be developed by the Victorian builders was the old Quayside. This was the first time in hundreds of years that large scale development had occurred in the old commercial core of Newcastle, and conditions in the area were appalling. The Quay had become very unstable, caused by the deepening of the river, and was rebuilt by the corporation between 1866 and 1884 from the Swing Bridge to the Ouseburn. This led to the demolition of many of the old chares, allowing many of the families that had been packed into the converted tenement blocks to move into the ever expanding suburbs.

The 1854 fire had destroyed six of the most westerly chares, ensuring that much needed improvement could begin. Three new streets were built; Queen Street, King Street and Lombard Street, which surround the palatial Exchange Buildings, completed in 1866. Young local architects rose to prominence, like William Parnell, who was responsible for many of the Italianate buildings along the river front. Developers, such as Ralph Water, worked their way along the Quay. The old fever districts were gradually demolished and with them several historic sites and buildings. Lord Eldon's birthplace in Love Lane was torn down, as was Akenside's old house in Butcher Bank (present day Akenside Hill) making way for The Granary Warehouse and new offices. The building of Milburn House on Dean Street saw the similar destruction of Bewick's workshop on Amen Corner and Collingwood's birthplace down the Side.

Victorian Newcastle was a time of tremendous commercial growth, closely linked to industrial progress. There was the arrival of new banks, with the Midland and Barclays establishing in the City. The TSB buildings on Grainger Street were completed in 1862, and the Provincial Bank of England on Mosley Street in 1872. Elegant new office blocks, such as the Collingwood and Cathedral Buildings have their origins in this period, whilst shops and businesses, which are still household names today, such as the famous Stewarts the Tea Dealers, and the great department stores, like Bainbridges and Fenwicks, also have their roots in Victorian Newcastle. Bainbridges itself was the world's first department store.

Commuting

With the building of the suburbs it became clear that the City needed an organised transport network, as private carriages proved unable to bring in large numbers of people from the outlying areas. The corporation responded with the Newcastle and Gosforth Tramways and Carriage Company, established in 1879.

Rails were laid from Scotswood, through the city centre and up to Jesmond and Gosforth, along which ran horse-drawn trams. Further routes were leased to private operators, on twenty-one year contracts. By the 1890's there were forty-four trams operating on various routes throughout Newcastle, using two hundred and seventy horses. There was a brief attempt to use steam trams, but unreliability soon led to their withdrawal. Electric trams using overhead cables were introduced at the turn of the century to make the system more efficient.

By 1904 the new, and much faster, trams were operating on virtually all of the old routes with a major junction at the Central Station. The electric trams, and the introduction of electricity to the rail loop out to the coast in 1903, meant people were able to live further away from their workplace - the commuter was born. By the outbreak of the First World War the coast line was carrying over nine and a half million passengers a year.

A tram outside the Central Station in 1903.

This industrial expansion saw the need for new links across the river and the Tyne's skyline changed with the addition of four new bridges. The old Redheugh Bridge was designed by Thomas Bouch, who also designed the Tay Bridge, and was built in 1871. The iron girder cantilevered structure, supported by brick piers, was reconstructed in 1901. There was also the Swing Bridge (opened in 1876) the King Edward VII rail bridge (opened in 1906), and further down river, a new bridge at Scotswood.

The Old Redheugh Bridge.

Industrial Supremacy.

Tyneside's industrial growth in the first half of the nineteenth century had been made possible by such pioneers as the Stephensons and the Hawthorn brothers. The second half of the century belonged to new men - Armstrong, Parsons and Palmer. Tyneside produced a steady flow of great innovators unlike any other area in Britain. It was the reign of the great industrialists, far sighted men who employed many thousands in the shipyards and engineering factories along the Tyne. In 1860 the area was described in a guide to Newcastle: *"The whole distance betwixt Blaydon and the sea, on both sides of the river, forms one huge manufacturing town, so thickly are the factories and the works strewed overall the district."*

Tyneside rose to unparalleled peaks of prosperity, even as other areas in the region overtook it in terms of coal output and iron manufacturing. As the nineteenth century progressed the factories, shipyards and engineering workshops grew larger and more efficient.

Shipbuilding

This growth can be illustrated by the meteoric rise of the Palmer's Shipyard in Jarrow. As a young coal owner Charles Palmer became involved in a fledgling steamship business. He saw this as a means to export his coal from Tyneside in response to the opening up of the Midlands coalfields which were being linked by rail to Tyneside's major customer, London. He leased a small plot of land in the village of Jarrow as a site for his yard. The first ship down the slipway was the *John Bowes*, which could carry as much coal in a five day round trip as a traditional sailing collier could in two months. The yard expanded and was soon building ships for the Royal Navy. *HMS Terror*, built for the Crimean War in 1854, was the yard's first order from the Admiralty and was completed in only three months. The Navy was impressed with the speed and quality of the yard's work, and it soon gained the reputation as one of Britain's premier shipbuilders.

By the 1880's there had been a massive expansion of both the town and the

One of the many battleships launched at Elswick during the warship fever years of the 1890's. The *Blanco Encalada* was commissioned by the Chilean Government and completed in 1894.

A striking photograph of *HMS Superb* passing through the Swing Bridge after being fitted out at Elswick. Armstrong had built the bridge between 1868 and 1876. Its two hundred and fifty feet wide swinging span was the largest in the world at the time.

yard which was inundated with international orders for both merchant and naval shipping. The yard covered one hundred acres and had three quarters of a mile of river frontage. It was totally integrated, having an ore smelter for the steel required, boiler shops, construction docks and slipways that could build a ship from start to finish. These large integrated sites became the norm for the companies along the river.

At the turn of the century the industry was dominated by five major companies. The last of these, Swan, Hunter and Wigham Richardson, Ltd. had been formed in 1903 from the three companies that had controlled the north side of the river between Walker and Wallsend - C.S. Swan and Hunter Ltd., Wigham Richardson and Co. Ltd., and the Tyne Pontoon and Dry Dock Company. The combined yards covered seventy-eight acres with a river-frontage of almost a mile. Shortly after, the Wallsend Slipway and Engineering Co. was brought under the umbrella of the firm adding a further fifty-three acres. Up to the War the firm averaged ninety-three thousand tons a year from its seventeen building slipways.

The other big four, apart from Palmers, had been formed from the same process of amalgamation. At the mouth of the river the Smith's Dock Co., which had moved to North Shields in 1871 after the sale of their yard to Hawthorns, merged with the Edward's yard of South Shields in 1899. The other two firms, Sir W.G. Armstrong, Mitchell and Co. and R. and W. Hawthorn, Leslie and Co. Ltd., were formed in 1882 and 1885 respectively.

In the run up to the 1914 conflict these five yards were building the best ships in the world, in one year alone they launched one hundred and sixteen vessels. Competition between them was stiff and each firm clamoured for orders as 'warship fever' swept the world. Governments placed large orders for huge battleships with demand especially strong from South American countries.

In 1904 the naval Battle of Tsushima, between Japan and Russia, had seen Tyneside yards supply nineteen of the warships used in the conflict. Armstrong's ships had been used by the victorious Japanese fleet, a triumph over their rivals Swan-Hunters and Hawthorn Leslies, the suppliers to the losing navy. It was, all in all, a disastrous campaign for the Russians. Travelling from the naval port of St. Petersburg the Russian fleet came across a small group of British trawlers in the North Sea. Their commander mistook this to be an advance flotilla of the Japanese Navy and bombarded the unfortunate fishermen. It was only with profuse apologies and financial compensation that the Russians avoided another war.

These firms transformed villages such as Jarrow, Hebburn and Elswick into sizeable industrial towns. They attracted large numbers of immigrants who lived in the familiar terraced housing around the yards. At Hebburn, a rural village before the arrival of Leslies in 1852, huge numbers of Scottish workers earned the town the name of 'Little Aberdeen'. These were tough areas and brawling was common, especially on pay day after the pubs closed.

The men started work in the shipyards at just after six in the morning. Before this they went through the traditional ritual of going to the pub. The pubs outside the yards opened five minutes before the gates were locked to sell tea, coffee, rum and whisky. The landlords guaranteed the fastest service in town. The workers had just enough time to gulp down their drinks before they *"burst out into the darkness and ran towards the yard - to the bright lights and thunder of machinery"*. (David Dougan)

Men coming off the nightshift at Armstrong's Elswick works.

Reshaping The River

The industry could not have risen to such prominence without the major work on the river carried out by the Tyne Improvement Commissioners. Much of the work was necessary to make the Tyne a deep, navigable river. Up to the 1850's the river was full of treacherous sandbanks and was often cluttered with grounded ships. At one time it was even possible to wade across at low tide. On board the Tyne ferry to Shields, passengers were given long staffs to help 'pole off' the boat if she ran aground.

The Commissioners rejected several schemes before opting for an imaginative proposal put forward by J.F. Ure, who had already carried out improvements to the Clyde. Ure designed the two largest dredging buckets in the world. These were capable of the daunting task of deepening the river to a depth of thirty feet at low water up to Jarrow, and to twenty-five feet up to Derwent Haugh. The dredging began in 1861. Sixteen thousand tons of silt were removed from the soft river bed every day. By 1914 over one hundred and thirty million tons had been removed.

The improvements not only included dredging the river but also straightening it at key points. The biggest task was the cutting of the loop between Scotswood and Newburn. The river was widened or narrowed where necessary to speed up the flow of water. This prevented silt from settling and avoided the need for continual dredging.

To maintain its domination of trade and in response to other North East river improvement schemes, two large docks were built near the river's mouth in the 1850's. The Tyne and Northumberland Docks were quickly linked by rail to Newcastle and to the local coalfields. The Tyne Dock soon became the world's largest coal exporter. The final task was the completion of two stone piers at the mouth of the river, which took forty years to build.

The whole project enabled the Tyne to become Britain's second busiest river and allowed the industrial expansion along the river to forge ahead uninterrupted.

Coal

By the middle of the nineteenth century Tyneside had declined as a coal producing area. There were still plentiful supplies of coking, gas and steam coal near to and under the sea. The industry that had begun in the west, far up the Tyne Valley, had finally reached the coast. Any further mining would now have to stretch below the sea bed.

Towards the end of the nineteenth century two powerful unions emerged. The Northumberland Miners' Association was founded in 1864 and led by Thomas Burt. To the south, the Durham Miners' Association, headed by William Crawford, was soon the largest mining union in Britain. When the first national union was founded in 1888, The National Miners' Federation of Great Britain, the two North East unions refused to join. They had already secured a seven hour day, whilst the national union had set its sights on an eight hour day. The two unions did eventually join but it was not until 1907 that most miners in Britain were members of the National Federation.

In the run up to the First World War the North East's coal industry boomed, reaching a peak in 1911 when fifty million tonnes were mined.

The Great Industrialists.

Armstrong

William George Armstrong was born in Shieldfield, Newcastle, in 1810, the son of a corn merchant. He trained to become a solicitor at the offices of the eminent lawyer Donkin, becoming his partner in 1835. Armstrong's real interest, however, lay in science and engineering. He frequently gave lectures at the Literary and Philosophical Society and was well respected by his peers in Newcastle.

Armstrong's earliest commercial venture was the setting up of a company to build the hydraulic cranes he had invented. The first cranes built were sold for use on Newcastle's Quay. This small company was a success and led him, in 1847, to set up W.G. Armstrong and Co. at Elswick, employing just twenty people.

The factory grew quickly. In just ten years, over one thousand cranes and engines had been built. He then turned his attention to the development of armaments. His eighteen pound breach loading gun was considered the most superior weapon in the world and was soon adopted by the Government as standard military ordinance - he was rewarded with a peerage in 1859 for this work. Armstrong was appointed as Engineer of the Rifled Ordinance at Woolwich. The Government spent £50,000 on a new ordinance factory at Elswick. Armstrong was unable to have any involvement with the project as it was considered unethical to give contracts to himself, so Andrew Noble was appointed as manager. After only three years the Government switched production to London, which prompted Armstrong to resign from the War Department and return to his native North East. He merged the ordinance factory and the engineering plant into one company in 1864. Blast furnaces were built to supply all the steel required for the now unified site.

Armstrong struck a deal with shipbuilders Mitchells, in 1868, to build his warships. His chief salesman, Sir Hugh Tennyson d'Encourt - a cousin of the famous poet - secured large contracts from foreign governments for the world's most fearsome battleships, built at Mitchell's Walker yard and armed with Armstrong's guns. The ship's huge guns often took a whole year to complete, work on them going on uninterrupted night and day. The opening of the new Swing Bridge, coupled with the deepened river, meant warships sailing up the Tyne to be fitted out at Elswick became a common sight.

Armstrong bought the Mitchell yard in 1882, splitting production between merchant shipping at Walker and warships at the newly built yard at Elswick. In 1897 he bought out another industrial giant, Whitworths, in Manchester, together with the

Inside the Boring and Turning Shop at the Elswick Works.

Scotswood Shipbuilding Co., to form the largest industrial empire in Europe, employing twenty-five thousand people.

His last twenty years were spent in semi-retirement at Cragside, the mansion he built near Rothbury. The day to day running of the company was left to Andrew Noble. Cragside benefited from his continuing fascination with new technology. It was the first house in the world to be lit by hydro-electricity - Armstrong was a partner in Swan's Electric Light Company. The house, set in beautiful grounds, is now owned by the National Trust and is open to the public.

Armstrong was a man of contrasts. He had a reputation as a harsh employer who never yielded to his employees' demands for a shorter working day. At the same time he donated a large part of his Newcastle estate to the people for their recreation, including Jesmond Dene and Armstrong Park, and made regular donations to charities and the Literary and Philosophical Society. Armstrong died in 1900, at the age of ninety, leaving behind one of the greatest industrial legacies in British history.

Parsons

Charles Parsons is another Tyneside legend, known as *"the man who invented the twentieth century"* - world famous as the inventor of the steam turbine. The youngest son of the Earl of Rosse, he was born in 1854 and spent his childhood at the family's home, Birr Castle in Southern Ireland. From Trinity College, Dublin, and then Cambridge, he paid £500 for a 'premium apprenticeship' at Armstrong's in Elswick.

This apprenticeship secured Parsons a job at Kitsons in Leeds, though he returned to Tyneside in 1884 to take a job as a junior partner at Clarke-Chapman. It was here that he developed the turbine, the first being only seven and a half kilowatts in power. Some of these were used to provide lighting on ships.

Parsons formed his own company in Heaton, which made a major breakthrough by producing a one hundred kilowatts turbine, the first ever to be noticeably more economical than a traditional steam engine. Shortly afterwards Parsons began looking into the possibility of harnessing the turbines to propel ships. He formed the Marine Steam Turbine Co., at Wallsend, and set about building *Turbinia*, a one hundred feet experimental vessel powered by turbines. The first tests were a disappointment due to cavitation, a phenomenon caused by the propellers turning so fast that a vacuum cavity was formed and slowed the boat down. Undefeated, Parsons isolated the problem and a modified *Turbinia* was given marine trials off Spithead in 1897. The result stunned the naval world as the small ship achieved a world record thirty-four knots.

Turbinia at speed during her marine trials in 1897.

The Admiralty ordered two ships, *Cobra* and *Viper*, to be powered by Parson's turbines. The turbines were quickly adopted for use in merchant and passenger vessels. Perhaps the most famous was the Tyneside liner, *Mauretania*, built by Swan, Hunter & Wigham Richardson, Ltd. Over eighty thousand people turned out in 1907 to watch the launch. The Times reported: *"The occasion was of unusual interest, even in a river where many great giants have been built, and the crowd of spectators was enormous."* The ship quickly captured the much prized *Blue Ribbon* by sailing across the Atlantic in under five days. During the War the liner had to sail without escorts as no convoy could keep up with her.

The company branched out and started building turbines for the rapidly expanding electricity industry, supplying the first power stations on Tyneside, at Neptune Bank and Carville in Wallsend.

Parsons was knighted in 1911 and continued to run the company until his death in 1931. He was laid to rest at Kirkwhelpington in Northumberland. The company is now part of the engineering giant NEI, and still builds turbines, some generating over a million kilowatts, for a variety of international customers.

Swan

Born in Sunderland in 1828, Joesph Wilson Swan was to become an apprentice chemist, eventually working for the Newcastle chemist Mawson. The two men became great friends and were soon involved in the scientific circle that surrounded the Literary and Philosophical Society, exchanging ideas and views with others and attending lectures.

Mawson gave Swan a free hand to pursue his ideas at the company and he worked on the concept of a carbon filament light bulb for many years. He also became a consultant in chemistry and photography.

In 1862 he married Fanny White and after living in Gateshead they moved to 21, Leazes Terrace, in Newcastle. Swan's life was marred by tragedy in the late 1860's. Mawson was killed handling nitro-glycerine. Later he was to lose his wife and then his twin sons. He left Newcastle and returned to Gateshead. In 1871 he married his sister-in-law, Hannah, in Switzerland, as English law forbade such a union.

After years of research Swan finally managed to produce a durable and realistic light bulb. The first public demonstration was given at the Literary and Philosophical Society on 20th October 1880 in front of an eminent audience. It was a resounding success and he was quick to set up the world's first electric light bulb factory at Benwell. The new form of lighting was soon installed at the British Museum and the Savoy Theatre in London. In 1882 Swan formed a new and larger company in London and he left Tyneside the following year.

Swan's invention is shrouded in controversy because around the same time as his demonstration in Newcastle, Edison, in America, was involved in the discovery of a similar bulb. Several legal battles began over who actually should have rights to the lucrative patent. The two men eventually came to an agreement, to avoid the expensive legal costs, and formed a united company with the inclusion of Edison's name to Swan's company. The partners were never to meet.

During his life Swan acquired over seventy different patents for a variety of inventions including batteries, artificial silk and new photographic processes. He was awarded the Freedom of the City of Newcastle in 1914, the year of his death.

Victorian Life.

Vices?

"Whilst the middle-classes withdrew to their parlours, the working-classes advanced to the gin houses." It was a time of the rise in Victorian moral values. The middle-classes reacted to what they saw as the moral collapse around them, a reaction expressed in a lecture given to the Temperance Society in 1854. The speaker declared that Newcastle had a high arrest rate; one in twenty-seven people compared with one in forty-five in Liverpool and one in ninety in London. He believed the high crime rate came from alcohol abuse.

There were over five hundred pubs or brewery shops in Newcastle; that is, one for every thirty-nine families - every twenty-second house was licensed to sell drink! There were also seventy-one brothels with an average of four prostitutes to each house. Casinos and Music Halls were criticised: *"The evils of such entertainments are, that they blend the fascinations of music, with the meretricious decorations of artistic skill and the pernicious influences of intoxicating liquor"*. Tobacco was similarly condemned: *"The mere boys in our*

The 3 Bulls Heads - Sandgate.

streets, apeing manhood, may be seen equipped with their penny cigars and cutty pipes". Pawnbroking was, *"for the indulgence of the vicious and the intemperate....Too frequently the working man has his home robbed of its comforts, his house stripped of its furniture and movable utensils, his clothes disposed of, his children starved, naked and neglected, in order to satisfy his insatiable thirst for drink".*

The speaker draws a vivid picture of one area of the town through the experience of the local vicar: *"in the eastern part of Ouseburn...out of four hundred and forty-four protestant adults [there are] three hundred and ninety-five who do not attend my place of worship, fifty-nine adults who cannot read and ninety-three children who receive no instruction. The number of public houses in the district is ten - being one for every twenty-two families. Several of these are of the lowest description, where dancing is allowed every night, and where there is every reason to suppose drinking goes on the whole of Sunday....The sanitary condition of the district is very bad; some of the dwelling houses are almost inaccessible from filth."*

These attitudes may say more for the narrow minded Victorian middle-classes than they do for the people they were describing. The working-classes had no choice but to live in very poor conditions, caught up in a vicious downward spiral of poor education and wage levels.

Black Bull's Head - Westgate Road.

The New Tyne Theatre

The Victorians constructed various impressive buildings for their leisure pursuits. The largest and best equipped theatre for a time in the North, the New Tyne Theatre, was built in 1867 to a design by Parnell. It played an important role in the social and intellectual life of Newcastle. Not only did the owners put on plays, but they also held a series of Sunday lectures, including one by Oscar Wilde.

In 1919 it was leased by Sir Oswald Stoll when it became the Stoll Picture House - the first in Newcastle to show 'talkies'. It became a theatre again in 1971 after major renovation. Sadly it was badly gutted by a fire on Christmas Day 1986, although a trust fund raised over £1 million to renovate the theatre to its magnificent former glory.

Music Hall

Another popular Victorian pastime was the Music Hall. In the 1850's 'harmonic meetings' were held at places such as the Royal Hotel and The Music Room on Grainger Street. It was at the Wheatsheaf in the Cloth market, run by John Balmbra, that the 'Blaydon Races' were first sung by Geordie Ridley in 1862.

The Geordie Music Hall flourished until the end of the century. But competition from the Variety Theatre became too strong and Balmbra's closed and became a billiard hall. It was reopened in 1961 and was Britain's only surviving music hall for a spell.

An 1854 poster advertising the Geordie Music hall at The Wheatsheaf Inn.

For all those who do not yet know the words to the Geordie Anthem - A full rendition of the Blaydon Races.

Aa Went to Blaydon Races, Twas on the ninth of June
Eighteen hundred and sixty-two on a summer's efternoon
As tyuk the bus fra Balmbra's and she was heavy laden,
Away we went alang Collingwood Street that's on the road to Blaydon.

Chorus:
Oh! lads ye shud a' seen us gannin,
Passin' the folks upon the road just as they were stannin,
Thor wis lots o lads and lasses there all wi smilin faces
Gannin alang the Scotswood Road to see the Blaydon Races

We flew past Armstrong's factory an' up to the "Robin Adair",
Just gannin' doon to the railway bridge the bus wheel flew off there;
The lasses lost thor crinolines an' the vails that hide thor faces;
Aa got two black eyes an' a broken nose in ga'n to Blaydon Races.

Oh! lads, etc

When we gat the wheel put on, away we went agyen,
But them that had thor noses broke they cam' back-ower hyem;
Sum went to the Dispensary, an' sum to Dr. Gibb's,
An sum to the Informary to mend thor broken ribs.

Oh! lads, etc

Noo when we gat to Paradise thor wes bonny gam begun,
Thor wes fower an' twenty on the bus, man hoo they danced an' sung,
They caaled on me to sing a song, aa sang them "Paddy Fagan";
As danced a jig an' swung me twig that day aa went to Blaydon.

Oh! lads, etc

We flew across to the Chine bridge reet intiv Blaydon Toon,
The bellman he wa callin' there - they called him Jacky Broon,
As saa him taakin' te sum cheps an' them he was persuadin'
te gan an' see Geordy Ridley's show in the Mechanics' Haall at Blaydon.

Oh! lads, etc

The rain it poored a' the day an' myed the groonds quite muddy,
"Coffy Johnny" had a white hat on - they yelled, "whe stole the cuddy?"
Thor wes spice stalls an munkey shows, an' aad wives sellin' ciders,
An'a chap wi' a ha'penny roondaboot shootin' "Noo me lads for riders".

Parks

Public parks were being opened in Britain for the first time, the earliest in Manchester in 1847. The medical profession had long argued that clean air was important for health; there was also a greater demand for recreation facilities from the general public. The town already had plenty of open space. The Nuns Moor had been given to the corporation from a charter of Richard I: the Town Moor and Castle Leazes had been granted to the town by Edward III in 1357, although the townspeople had thought of it as common land long before then.

In 1873 sixty-eight acres of the Leazes became Leazes Park, soon after Bull Park and Brandling Park were created. Elswick and Heaton were given recreation grounds and parks. Armstrong donated the park named after him and Jesmond Dene was later added to it.

These parks were not simply for 'promenading' - there was bowling, lawn tennis and quoits, as well as Sunday concerts.

Jesmond Dene.

Health and Living.

By 1851 over half Newcastle's population had been born outside the town, with people coming in from the local countryside to provide the workforce for industry in constant need of labour. More came from the remoter rural areas of Northumberland, from Scotland and from Ireland. It was this great expansion that was to lead to the poverty so noted in the Victorian Period.

The Irish had been forced off the land and into British cities by the devastating potato famine. They formed one tenth of Newcastle's population, living on the Quayside and Sandgate, often five to a room with no sanitation or clean water. The Sandgate was a popular Irish area because there was vacant, cheap property left by the people who were moving out to the suburbs. The men often worked as unskilled labourers or in shops, whilst the women worked as cleaners or maids. Many in the town considered them to be the lowest stratum of society. A town official noted uncharitably: *"Place them in any habitation, they will turn it into a noisome hovel. If they have drains they will allow them to become obstructed - if free of ventilation they will close it up, if the clearest sun shine, they will shut it out by negligence and filth."*

The Victorian era is renowned for very high mortality rates. Most of the Quayside's housing was geared towards renting which devoured the working-classes' low wages. This led to chronic overcrowding, with large families living in one or two rooms and taking in lodgers to help pay for the rent. The water system was a natural breeding ground for diseases such as cholera and typhus.

The issues were highlighted by public and philanthropic efforts but they could do little more than advertise the problem. One such body was The Health of Towns Commission of 1845, which reported on the levels of overcrowding, the accumulation of refuse, smoke pollution and open sewers. Another was The Cholera Commission which was highly critical of the corporation. Between 1851 and 1903 there were twenty-eight major Public Health Acts but enforcing them was left to local authorities. Newcastle's corporation, despite its power to

Paddy's Market at the Sandgate. This was a popular area with Newcastle's Irish population.

help, had done very little to clean up the town. Its main efforts were channelled towards the expansion of the new suburbs and not the decaying riverside area. Most of the time, this area was conveniently forgotten by the corporation. The advancement of medicine and the major clearance of the slums belonged to the last twenty years of the nineteenth century.

In 1865 the corporation managed to gain the 'Newcastle upon Tyne Improvement Act' which enabled it to clear some of the unsanitary conditions. Within two years, five hundred buildings had been emptied, and some fifty demolished. Still, in 1867 an eighth of all houses in Newcastle were without water or drainage. Although the Act was a start the corporation was still left with pockets of total deprivation and despair, at Sandhill, the bottom of Pilgrim Street and Pandon. Pandon had the worst slum in the town in the 1870's. A large block of tenements on the lower reaches of Pandon Burn had one of the highest death-rates in the country at forty-eight per thousand.

From 1875 onwards there was a marked drop in the number of cases of certain infectious diseases; mainly cholera, typhus and smallpox, although there were later sporadic outbreaks. They were replaced by new killers, industrial diseases that evolved in the crowded and smog ridden cities; diphtheria, tuberculosis and scarlet fever - TB was to become the nineteenth century's biggest killer, accounting for one death in every six.

Children playing outside a sweet shop on Akenside hill towards the end of the nineteenth century. Most could only afford to look at the treats through the window.

The Public Health Acts of the 1870's made it compulsory for councils to appoint a Medical Officer for Health. Newcastle's first officer was Dr. Henry Armstrong who made some dramatic changes to the town's health service. One of his first reforms was to allow the poor free admission to the fever hospital. Up to 1873 the hospital averaged two hundred and thirty admissions a year but by the outbreak of World War One this had dropped to none as conditions improved with cleaner water, better health education and improved hospital cover.

The Royal Victoria Infirmary.

The new Royal Victoria Infirmary was a major step by the corporation to help raise the City's health standards. The corporation and the Freemen provided a ten acre site at Castle Leazes. Work was started in 1900, and the new infirmary was officially opened by Edward VII on July 11th 1906.

Overcrowding remained a major problem until well into the twentieth century. In 1914 the average number of persons per house, at just over eight, was the same as in 1851. The population of the city was still growing faster than new houses were being built. There were still large numbers of families living in two roomed tenements down near the river and in suburban areas like Walker. The situation did not improve until the 1920's when the Council began building extensive estates on the periphery of the City.

The Suburbs.

Some of the villages, which for so long had been separate from Newcastle, were incorporated into the town's administrative boundaries in 1835. This doubled the town's population at a stroke, although to all intents and purposes they were already part of the town, having been linked by the urban sprawl that characterised the nineteenth century. The villages had grown at a tremendous pace, Elswick from a population of under four thousand in 1851 to over fifty thousand in 1891. In only thirty years from 1871, thirty-five thousand people had moved into new housing in Byker.

Shops and churches were built to serve the growing population. St. Michaels Church in Elswick, St. Augustines on Brighton Grove and Holy Trinity in Jesmond are all examples. There were still outlying villages, like Gosforth, which were not linked to the town until the twentieth century.

The suburbs were built to a better standard, thanks to new laws between 1850 and 1871 - collectively called the 'Town Improvement Acts'. These laid down strict guidelines on new house building with minimum levels of standards, which had to be strictly observed by the builders. The new houses were a vast improvement on the old tenements scattered in and around Newcastle.

The most common style of housing adopted was the familiar Tyneside Flat. These all had sewerage and drainage facilities and much improved interiors. There are several variations on the flats. Examples of those built to a high standard can be found in Rye Hill and in Jesmond, which often have small gardens. In other areas, for example Byker and Scotswood, many of these old flats have been demolished. They were built to the barest minimum legal requirements, squeezed together with shared facilities.

Elswick

Aefsige's wic - Aefsige's dwelling.

The original Elswick village was situated where Elswick Park is today. It was owned by a series of Norman Barons. One of them, Gilbert, gave the estate to the Prior of Tynemouth around 1120. King David of Scotland's son, Henry, as Earl of Northumberland, was granted the profitable fishing rights to the Elswick estate in 1147.

The estate remained under Church control until the Dissolution when ownership passed to Henry VIII. Elswick was one of the first areas around Newcastle to be extensively mined. It was later sold by Charles I, providing a handsome profit. Ownership remained in private hands for the next two hundred years. In 1839 Richard Grainger bought the entire estate, for £114,000, and he briefly lived in the sumptuous Elswick Hall.

He divided the land up into development plots. William Armstrong bought the two most westerly fields as a site for his engineering factory, which was to be central to Elswick's growth. The factory was slowly surrounded by rows of terraced housing, built by Grainger and later by Armstrong himself. The expansion of Elswick continued at a rapid pace during the nineteenth century. By 1903 it had linked up with Benwell and both were incorporated into Newcastle's boundaries the following year.

Benwell

Binnan wealle - Within the wall.

The recorded history of Benwell stretches back to the Romans, when Hadrian's Wall was built over Benwell Hill. A fort, *Condercum*, was positioned at the top of the hill, manned by a cavalry regiment - the *Ala I Astures*. The horsemen were originally a tribe from the wild northern reaches of Spain. It is more likely that by the time of the building of *Condercum* the regiment was composed of more local soldiers.

Benwell Tower. It was designed by Dobson and completed in 1831. Fifty years later the house was handed over to the newly appointed Bishop of Newcastle.

During the medieval period the area was owned by the powerful Delaval family. The centre of the village, which lies underneath the modern town, was dominated by Benwell Hall. The Hall was a popular summer residence for the Priors of Tynemouth, who owned the estate before it passed to the Crown. It remained a royal manor until 1628 when it was sold to private owners. One owner was Mr. Stoney Bowes, a Member of Parliament for Newcastle. He was to end up in prison for sadistically beating his wife, the Countess of Strathmore. Benwell Hall fell into disrepair while he was in prison and was demolished in 1831. It was replaced by Benwell Tower.

Coal mining was an important part of the local economy until 1936 when the Charlotte Pit closed. One infamous mining incident occurred in 1826, when a small fire got out of control in a Benwell pit. The fire, which lasted for thirty years, gradually spread along the seam and caused miniature 'volcanic' explosions near Cowgate.

***"A bird's view of Elswick"* drawn in 1887. Some of the surrounding terraced streets were named after Richard Grainger's children.**

Scotswood

Scott's wode.

Scotswood also expanded rapidly during the second half of the nineteenth century. The village obtained its name in 1368, when the king allowed Richard Scott of Newcastle to enclose a wood in the area known as 'le westwode'. During the early nineteenth century the rural village was transformed into a large industrial town. Around the 1860's Scotswood Road had more pubs to the mile than any other road in the world! There were forty-four, virtually one on every corner. Now only two remain, names which reflect the area's industrial heritage - The Forge Hammer and Armstrong's Hydraulic Crane.

Fenham

Fenn ham - At the marshes.

In the twelfth century, Fenham was owned by the Knights Templar, who fought in the Crusades. They were a monastic fighting order who protected the pilgrims' routes through the Holy Land. Fenham later passed to the Knights Hospitallers of St. John of Jerusalem, who kept possession until 1540. These knights spent huge sums of money on hospitality and banquets, often as a bribe to corrupt judges and officials to keep their privileges. The manor was let to the Chief Justice of England, Geoffry le Scrope, under very dubious circumstances, rent free for life.

Eventually the land passed to the Ord Family who built the impressive Fenham Hall in 1745. The old Hall eventually became the home of the Sacred Heart Convent School and a teachers' training college. The Ords ran the rural estate until 1835. Four years prior to this the Boundary Commission investigating Fenham stated: *"the township of Fenham is agricultural and being situated to west of the moor it is improbable....Newcastle will ever extend into the township"*. How wrong they were.

Much of the property development in Fenham was directed at the middle-classes. It was pleasantly rural and being on the west side of the city the prevailing winds ensured most of industrial pollution from the riverside areas did not blow this way. Its expansion mainly started at the turn of the century with the sale of Blackett-Ord land to private builders. New spacious houses were built along such streets as Wingrove Road and Gardens just before the outbreak of war in 1914.

Byker

By kiarr - neighbouring upon a marsh.

The iron Ouseburn Viaduct. It replaced a wooden viaduct in 1868 and it was built to the same design.

On the east side of the City there was similar expansion. Byker, was owned by the de Byker family, Crown Bailiffs for South Northumberland. They also owned land nearer to Newcastle, including parts of the industrial village of Pandon. Ownership passed to the powerful Percy family and then to the king in 1428. Byker was the main centre of the Newcastle glass industry, which spread along the Ouseburn. The last trace of this once flourishing industry is the Glasshouse Bridge of 1669, built by the glass makers themselves.

Dent's Hole, a deep water berth on the river, close to Byker, was at one time used as a winter anchorage for the Greenland Whaling Fleet. The town's rapid growth occurred in the 1870's when hundreds of Tyneside flats were built for the workers of the nearby Ouseburn industrial area and the men and women who gained a living from the river.

Heaton

Hea tun - High Farm.

The village is first mentioned in the early twelfth century when Henry I granted the area, part of the Barony of Ellingham, to Nicholas de Grenville. The estate later passed to Adam of Jesmond, who built a fortified manor house here in the 1260's, the remains of which can still be seen in Heaton Park. Adam was loyal to Henry III and fought in the Barons War holding the 'new castle' against the insurgent barons.

Heaton Hall - built by the powerful Ridley family.

Heaton had strong connections with the Kings of England. An ancient chapel stood near the centre of the village. In 1299, a child Bishop performed the Vespers of St. Nicholas in front of Edward I. Another royal visit came from James I in 1617. He knighted the estate's owner, Henry Babbington, here. A large part of the estate was then purchased by the merchant Nicholas Ridley and it was his son who built Heaton Hall.

Heaton, like most areas of Newcastle, had working pits in the eighteenth and nineteenth centuries. The Heaton Pit has a particularly tragic tale. In 1815 the mine flooded. Thirty men managed to escape with the sounding of the alarm but seventy-five men and boys were trapped underground. At first the men must have thought themselves fortunate as they were trapped in a blocked-off tunnel and rescue was not far away. It took nine months to drain the mine and by the time they were discovered they had starved to death. The miners had eaten their pit ponies, candles and had even resorted to chewing the bark off the pit props to stave off starvation.

The marriage between the children of two of Newcastle's most influential merchants brought about the important and powerful Victorian family, the White-Ridleys. They sold half the estate to the Potter family and the other half to the solicitor Donkin. He left the land to his one-time partner Armstrong. He, in turn, gave this to the people of Newcastle in the form of two parks. In Heaton Park there was a bear pit and a monkey house. In the 1880's private builders turned the area into a pleasant Victorian suburb. It remains little changed to this day.

Jesmond

Gesmemue - Mouth of the Yese or Ouseburn.

Like Heaton, Jesmond was part of the Barony of Ellingham and passed to the baron, Adam. It is possible he came from this area as he took his name from it. Adam died childless and his relatives sold Jesmond, or Gesemue, to Richard Emeldon, a mayor of Newcastle eighteen times.

Emeldon built a housestead at Barras Bridge, where the Grand Hotel building now stands. In 1736 Henry Bourne described it as, *"the great waste barn called Emeldon Barn"*. Emeldon led three hundred Newcastle men at the Battle of Halidon Hill near Berwick in 1333. Not one returned.

The remains of another important medieval building can still be seen near Jesmond Dene Road. St. Mary's Chapel and the nearby well were important shrines of Christendom in the Middle Ages. Miracles, including the appearance of Jesus, were said to have happened at the well and were accepted by Popes. The small chapel was built during the thirteenth century, and Kings of England made presentations of gifts to it until 1449. The chapel was eventually sold to the Squire of Jesmond, John Brandling, and it was converted into a barn and slowly fell into disrepair.

It is recorded that the village was surrounded by three large fields around 1600. Jesmond kept its rural appearance well into the nineteenth century, until it was incorporated into Newcastle's boundaries in 1832. Six years later Jesmond Road was planned by Dobson and built by the corporation. The other main road into Jesmond, Osborne Road, was built during the great suburban expansion of the late Victorian era. The emphasis was on building high quality housing for Newcastle's professionals. Villas were built first during the 1850's. As the century progressed terraced housing became the norm, built in a variety of sizes and styles.

Walker

Wall Car - Marshy place beside the wall.

Walker stands on the route of the Roman Wall, and it is from this that the district gained its name. It was originally part of the Barony of Morpeth. The Fenwick family acquired all the land in Walker by marriage in the fourteenth century. They controlled the area until it was sold by Sir John in 1692. He met a grisly end five years later, executed at Tyburn for plotting to assassinate William III. Walker was the birthplace of the once important Tyneside chemical industry with plants taking advantage of a salt spring. William Losh located a sulphuric acid plant here in the eighteenth century.

Coal mining was also important. It was here that the Safety Lamp was first used as part of a miner's standard equipment. A local song records one miner's impressions of the town:

"When aw cam to Walker Wark,
Aw had ne coat nor ne pit sark;
But noo aw've getten twe or three -
Walker pit's deun weel for me.
Byker Hill and Walker shore,
Colliery lads for evermore."

The land around Walker ended up in the hands of the corporation in the eighteenth century and it used the land to dump ballast from local shipping. Several small burns were filled in and factories built on top of the ballast heaps. In the 1840's and 1850's shipyards were established such as Coutts, later to become the Neptune Works of Wigham Richardson, and Mitchells. The metal industry also flourished, the largest site being The Walker Iron Works.

By the turn of the twentieth century Walker suffered from overcrowding. Over a thousand families in the town lived in two roomed tenement buildings. It was not until after the 1914 war with new house building, that overcrowding was partially solved.

The Japanese battleship, *Yashima*, sliding down the slipway and into the Tyne.

Tyneside's industrial peak came in the run up to the First World War. It was *"just about the richest part of the richest country in the world"*. Unfortunately, because of the massive rise in these heavy industries, other areas of traditional employment were neglected and this was to be Newcastle's downfall over the following two decades. There was a marked decline in glassmaking, pottery and chemicals, but this was ignored as any redundant workers could easily get jobs in the shipyards or engineering plants. The result of this concentration in the heavy industries after the war was catastrophic as the demand for munitions and shipping plummeted. The seeds of decline had been sown.

The Twentieth Century.

Tyneside at War

The threat of war loomed over Europe in the long, hot summer of 1914. Fears of shortages quickly brought queues at stores and shops for food and other essentials. Newcastle, like many other cities, saw panic buying amongst the population. A local paper reported: *"At Newcastle Co-op stores there was a distinct desire on the part of customers to abandon the underlying ideas of co-operation and to look after number one."*

Newcastle also faced a tram strike and there were rumblings of discontent in the coalfields which feared a drastic fall in exports. Two men were charged with espionage. Frederick Sukowski was detained for having maps and plans of the naval yards in his possession, whilst another was arrested for drawing the High Level Bridge.

Kitchener's *"call to the colours"* received a tremendous local response in the city. Two recruitment offices were quickly opened on Westgate Road and at the Corn Exchange. Those coming in were described as *"men of a hardy type, full of the right spirit"*. The first parade of the war in Newcastle was by the Sixth Battalion of the Northumberland Fusiliers, inspected in St. Nicholas Square.

The Army Council had sanctioned the formation of three battalions in Newcastle: the Tyneside Irish; the Tyneside Scottish and the Tyneside Commercial Battalions. They were to have eleven hundred men each and were virtually at full strength within a month. The Royal Navy also reported brisk recruiting.

In September, as more men from Newcastle left for the front amidst cheering crowds, the other side of war was cruelly brought home. The first casualties from the Western Front arrived on Tyneside by train for treatment at the Royal Victoria Infirmary.

The Lord Mayor led the way in raising cash and rallying men for the war effort. He launched 'The War Relief Fund' and gave many speeches around the city, including one at St. James Park during a cup tie between Newcastle United and West Ham United. The Government sold War Bonds and War Saving Certificates, often during appeal weeks. In Newcastle £680,000 was raised in just a week from the 'tank bank'-

The Queen Mary, leaving the Tyne in 1913.

bonds sold from a tank named *Julian* parked in the city centre. Other efforts included 'Lest We Forget Day', 'Feed the Guns Week' and the appeal for people to invest in the 'War Loan' which raised over £18 million locally.

The Licensing Justices' contribution to the war effort was to close all the city's pubs at nine pm prompt.

Men and women working along side each other at the Wallsend Slipway and Engineering Co. Ltd. This photograph, taken in 1916, shows work being carried out on turbine blades inside the iron foundry.

1915-1917

During 1915 women were employed as conductors on the city's trams for the first time. This precedent was followed in other industries - previously all male domains. By the end of the war over one million women around the country were working in essential industries, with seventeen thousand at Armstrongs. Their vital contribution during the war played a major part in promoting women's suffrage.

That same year there was a Zeppelin attack along the North East coast with six bombs dropped on Wallsend. Casualties and damage were minimal but it was still enough to shock the council into suspending tram and train services.

By 1917, the war was being brought ever closer to home with the growing shortages in essential goods. The campaigns of the German *U-Boats* in the North Atlantic sank hundreds of Allied ships. This had a twofold effect on the Tyneside economy. Not only were the shipyards working flat out to replace lost tonnage but there were also shortages of food. The council urged people to try and buy food in local stores rather than the city centre shops which were swamped with customers.

The war naturally generated strong feelings in the city which sometimes spilled over into the streets. One of the most serious incidents was in 1917 at a meeting of *"The Workers' and Soldiers' Council"* - a pacifist group. The City had banned the organisation from giving a meeting in the Town Hall so the rally was switched to the Central Hall. Angry scenes soon erupted. Soldiers just back from the Front stormed the stage and fighting broke out both inside and outside the hall.

There were also attacks on German descendents living in Newcastle and there were even reports of Alsatian dogs being killed.

One of the most infamous incidents was early on in the war when a riot started on Newgate Street as an angry mob stoned a German butchers. Matters got worse at nine pm when the pubs closed and further attacks began on Westgate Road. Mounted police were needed to quell the unrest and eventually water-cannon were called in to disperse the last of the crowd.

Armistice

By the summer of 1918 it was clear that the war was coming to an end. Allied troops finally broke the stalemate of trench warfare and made swift advances into German held territory. News of the *"All Quiet on the Western Front"* on November 11th 1918 reached Tyneside quickly. Most of the shipyards and factories were closed and the Scotswood Road workers walked into the city centre burning an effigy of the Kaiser. Hundreds of others congregated outside St. Nicholas Cathedral to celebrate the news.

Despite the tragedy of war the people of Tyneside fared better than most. The unprecedented demand for armaments and ships had brought about big increases in wages for those working in key industries. A shipyard riveter saw his pay double to over 74s. a week. The Daily Mail reported shortly after the armistice that, *"There are now no poor in Newcastle upon Tyne"*. It was not to last.

A father bids farewell to his daughter, a detail from the city's war memorial at Barras Bridge

Between the Wars.

The Depression

The end of the war heralded the promise of a 'land fit for heroes' and for a brief spell prosperity did reign. Britain's shipyards produced over two million tons in 1920, replacing wartime losses. The Treaty of Versailles, followed by the Washington Conference of 1921, imposed strict arms limitations on the countries of Europe. Tyneside's long concentration on heavy industry, which had made Newcastle one of the mightiest industrial cities in the world, now proved to be the area's downfall - a problem which remains to the present day.

By the end of 1921, virtually all shipping orders had dried up. Coupled with falling coal prices the first bout of unemployment took its grip. In Willington three-quarters of the insured men were out of work by 1923, as were almost half those in North Shields and Wallsend.

In 1927 there was a short lived recovery with an order for tankers, but the overall trend was a continuing spiral downwards. Companies were forced to rationalise and several mergers took place between the foremost yards. It became imperative for the area to pull together. The first major merger was between Armstrongs and Vickers in 1927. This managed to secure some jobs but the following year the naval yard at Walker was forced to close, putting hundreds more out of work.

The fate of Palmers in Jarrow was typical. In 1930 they launched their thousandth vessel, the oil tanker *Peter Hurll*. Tankers had been the mainstay of the yard during the troubled twenties. 1931 proved to be the worst year in Tyneside shipbuilding history and the Jarrow yard only launched one vessel. By the end of that summer eighty per cent of the insured population in the town

A march that received far less publicity than the one from Jarrow was the Unemployed Marchers to London. This North East contingent left Newcastle from the Bigg Market in May 1930.

were unemployed. Time for the yard was running out and the following year creditors' meetings began. In June 1933 the Jarrow firm finally had to concede defeat along with two other yards, The Tyne Iron Shipyard and Eltringhams.

By some form of perverse irony Palmer's first ever ship the *John Bowes*, which had been renamed the *Carolina*, sank off the coast of Spain in a violent storm that same year.

In the year preceding World War One over two hundred and thirty-eight thousand tons of shipping had been launched on the Tyne. In 1933 a mere seven thousand tons were launched. The world's shipping market had collapsed.

Tyneside's other large employer, the coal industry, also suffered. Demand slumped as the largest consumer of coal, the steel industry, crashed. Meanwhile in Europe the Polish and German coalfields were expanding rapidly. These two factors helped to halve exports from the Tyne. Coal tonnage available for shipment, a useful indicator to the state of the industry, dropped from over twenty-one million tons in 1922 to only thirteen million tons. This had a knock on effect for Tyne Dock, from where most of the shipments sailed.

Unable to make any profits, the last remaining pits around Newcastle began to close. Pit owners imposed wage cuts which eventually culminated in the General Strike of 1926. The last mine in Walker, the Ann Pit, had closed just before the war and others followed. The Charlotte Pit at Benwell survived until 1936. The most tragic closure was the Montague Pit in Scotswood - it never reopened after a flood which had caused the deaths of thirty-eight men.

As the recession bit deeper the Government had to step in to avert a national disaster. With backing from the Bank of England they formed the National Shipbuilders' Security Company. This set about converting shipyards to other uses in an attempt to reduce excess capacity. Nine firms in the North East were bought, including Palmers at Jarrow. Meanwhile, Armstrongs began to produce cars and electrical engines at their Elswick and Scotswood sites. The Company also ventured into paper making in Canada - a huge mistake that cost them millions of pounds.

The psychological impact of the Depression was particularly difficult to bear for a people so accustomed to hard work. David Dougan, in his book on Tyneside Shipbuilding, reflected the mood of many:

> *"No wonder the men felt they were living through terrible times. Even middle aged men would have remembered that once they were kings of the world. Then there had been the cruellest war, followed by the cruellest peace - a peace mixed with prosperity and pitiless despair".*

General Strike

In 1925 miners refused to accept new wage cuts and job losses. The mine owners would accept nothing less. It seemed nothing could stop a national strike, then the Government stepped in and offered to set up a commission to look into the coal industry. The miners considered this a victory. They thought they had an overwhelming case for nationalisation which the Government was bound to accept. Unfortunately the Commission thought otherwise, and while they deliberated, the Government was able to arrange contingency plans for a national stoppage.

A soup kitchen organised for the miners during the 1926 strike.

When the strike was called it was generally well supported by workers from other industries, many of whom had joined in sympathy, but the strikers, unlike the Government, were ill prepared. Traditionally, when the miners came out on strike they did not need organising - they simply downed tools and left the pit. With a national strike things were different. For maximum effect events had to be co-ordinated between industries and areas. The first attempts to organise anything were left until two days before the stoppage.

Both the local press and local councils were hostile to the strikers - it would be another ten years before the Labour Party began to take control of the North East's local authorities. On the Government's side the Northern region could count on twenty thousand volunteers and twelve thousand special constables, fifteen hundred of whom were based in Newcastle. These were made available to man essential services.

In Newcastle, on the 8th May, the police had to lead two baton charges against a crowd of up to ten thousand people, driving them down Grainger Street and across the High Level Bridge. On the whole, though, the dispute was very peaceful, better known for the friendliness shown between strikers and the police - and for the football matches arranged between the two sides. A stark contrast to the scenes of violence on the picket lines during the miners' strike of 1984.

Transport was seen as the key to the dispute. Trams and buses were brought to a halt in Newcastle on the first day and remained out solidly. The managers even refused student offers of blackleg help. In the coalfield areas pickets were successful in bringing transport to a near standstill.

During the first few days after the strike ended many of the workers thought they had won, they had been ready to stay out longer. They had, after all, only been out nine days, and the second wave of workers had been brought out only a few hours before the announcement of the strike's end. Despite assurances to the contrary there were many cases of victimisation of strikers, many workers lost jobs and had their pay cut.

The miners were to stay out for another seven months eventually being driven back by sheer poverty. William Straker of the Northumberland Miners commented: *"I may be told that I speak extravagantly in saying this. I do not; I speak but plainly; I speak the facts bluntly and I speak what I know. Under the terms of settlement to which the miners in Northumberland have had to submit there will be thousands in a state of semi-starvation."*

Social Conditions

Such large numbers of unemployed led to serious problems of overcrowding and poor health. Nearly a quarter of Newcastle's inhabitants were officially classed as over-crowded in 1930, compared to less than a tenth nationally. The 1930's Housing Act meant that the council was able to demolish many of the city's slums. In total the inter-war years saw the council build over twelve thousand flats and houses, and the private sector provide a further sixteen thousand. Between 1934 and 1937 as many as twenty thousand people were rehoused.

"Atrocious housing conditions under which many lived in the mid-nineteenth century could no longer be tolerated"(Dr. M Barke).The emphasis was on low-density housing. Pendower, with its gardens, trees and grass verges, was typical of the pleasant estates that were built, a huge improvement on the old back to back flats of the previous century. Surprisingly, owner occupation increased during the period as the middle-classes moved into new semi-detached houses in the suburbs.

The Depression was a time of contrasts. Whilst thousands of new houses were being built, the impoverished men of Jarrow were setting off on their famous march. The job situation in Jarrow was so bad that in the twenties and thirties the population fell by over a third. Newcastle, being a regional centre, had fared better than the outlying industrialised suburbs and towns, though nothing could hide thirty thousand men on the dole or the resultant poverty. Infant mortality remained high at ninety-one per thousand - nationally it was only fifty-three. Over a third of working class children were undernourished and physically unfit. The rate of tuberculosis was forty per cent above the national average. A third of the working classes could not afford real milk and had to buy cheaper condensed milk.

With little help from central government until 1934, the council had to try and provide jobs for the thousands of men on the dole. With money from the rates, which had held up well, the City Council was able to improve social services and start solving the inherent problem of housing. At the same time there was a new spate of building in the city. It was this period of construction that led to the North East's most famous landmark - The Tyne Bridge.

This photograph epitomises the dreadful conditions endured by thousands of families on Tyneside during the 1930's. It shows a one roomed home at Clive Street, North Shields.

The Tyne Bridge

Towards the end of the nineteenth century it had become clear that there was a need for a new bridge to span the Tyne. As early as 1893 a committee had been formed between Gateshead and Newcastle Councils to probe the possibility of a new link between the two centres. The High Level Bridge was the major crossing point for road traffic and was always a scene of confused congestion.

In the 1920's, with increasing numbers of lorries, cars and even tram lines across the High Level, plans for a new bridge, the Tyne Bridge, were laid. By the middle of that decade the work was put out to tender. The final design was by Mott, Hay and Anderson, with construction by Dorman, Long and Co. of Middlesborough. By its completion seven thousand tons of Cleveland steel had been used. The roadway stands an impressive ninety-three feet above the river.

Whilst the 1,254 ft. long bridge was being built hundreds of people turned up on the Quay each day to watch the steady progress - the unemployed of 1926 had a lot of time on their hands. King George V declared the bridge open on October the 10th 1928. The ceremony was a magnificent affair. Thousands of people turned up to line the Royal route, with many more watching from the Quayside. The cheering was accompanied by the sounding of factory sirens and a twenty-one gun salute.

Today the bridge carries more traffic than the Humber, Severn and Forth road bridges combined, and has become the symbol of Tyneside, recognised the world over.

Recovery

The Bridge again altered the centre of the commercial and retailing core of the city centre. The flow of traffic coming off the bridge meant that Grey Street, Mosley Street and Collingwood Street were bypassed, and the commercial centre shifted towards Pilgrim Street, Blackett Street and Northumberland Street. New buildings followed such as Carliol House, home to the NEEB, the Central Police Station and Fire Station on Market Street, and new shops along Northumberland Street. Other buildings of the period include the Co-operative Building on Newgate Street and the Medical School on the University campus.

In 1934 more positive action was taken when parliament passed the Special Areas Act. The Act provided capital for the establishment of industrial estates and factories, leading to investment in the new 'light' industries that had saved the South East from the ravages of the Depression. It helped set up the infrastructure necessary to attract newer industry and much needed new jobs. As a result the Team Valley Industrial Estate was built in 1936, the first of its kind in Britain. It brought two and a half thousand jobs over the next three years.

By 1935 the world's economy had begun a slow recovery. Several small shipping orders were secured and the naval yard at Walker was reopened after seven idle years. By 1936 the world was beginning to rearm, and a large contract for seventeen warships brought hundreds of jobs to the Tyne. The world was once again preparing for war. By 1939, order books were full.

FULL MOON
HOTEL
JOHN
BOYD

PUCK

World War II.

By the outbreak of the war in September 1939 Tyneside had already started to supply arms, shipping and engineering products. During the 'phoney war' thousands of children were evacuated, though most of these had returned to their families by the end of October when the predicted bombing did not materialise.

Bombing did start in the summer of 1940. The Luftwaffe concentrated on the ordinance factory at Elswick, the docks, railways and the bridges spanning the Tyne. The first large raid was on the 2nd July, when thirteen people were killed. More raids followed that summer as the Germans were determined to disrupt the vital war industries on Tyneside. By the end of the bombing over a thousand people had been made homeless. After the Battle of Britain, bombing raids became less frequent and as the war progressed the North East became a safe area for evacuee children with thousands coming from London to seek refuge with Tyneside families.

Work in the shipyards and arms factories continued at a frantic pace as men and women worked side by side to feed the nation's insatiable appetite for war products. The shipyards produced record figures and built some of the most famous vessels of the war. Hawthorn Leslies built *HMS Kelly* which was captained by the late Lord Mountbatten. The ship was attacked in the North Sea in 1940 and, although badly damaged, endured and survived a constant onslaught during the ninety-one hour return journey. The vessel was refitted and returned to sea at breakneck speed but was lost later in the war together with one hundred and thirty men.

The Neptune Yard at Walker built over sixty ships including their largest naval vessel, at thirty-five thousand tons, *HMS Anson*. An-

The Naval Yard, Newcastle upon Tyne 1940, **by Montague Dawson. H.M.S. Eglinton, Exmoor, Nigeria, King George V and Victorius.**

other Tyneside-built ship, *HMS Edinburgh*, sank in 1942 with millions of pounds worth of Russian gold on board. In the 1980's the ship again hit the headlines when the gold was salvaged.

Swan-Hunters averaged an incredible one hundred and fifty thousand tons a year from their extensive eighty acre site and had built seventy-four vessels by the end of the war. Vickers-Armstrong also had an impressive record, building warships and thousands of tanks and guns. Parsons produced much of the machinery for the shipyards and massive generators to ensure the nation's electricity supply during those dark years.

Tyneside had four active Regiments between 1939 and 1945. The Royal Northumberland Fusiliers were one of the first Regiments involved in active service as part of the ill-fated British Expeditionary Force. The battalions of the regiment served in North Africa, Singapore, and later on in France. The Tyneside Scottish and 15/19 The King's Royal Hussars also served in France, being involved in both the Dunkirk and the D-Day landings. The other Tyneside Regiment, the Northumberland Hussars, spent much of their time in the Middle East as an artillery unit.

As in towns all over Europe, VE Day on the 8th May 1945 heralded much jubilation. There were hundreds of street parties, festooned with bunting and flags. As night time fell bonfires were lit and the parties carried on well into the early hours. The celebrations were rekindled three months later when the Japanese surrendered. Festivities on Tyneside were marred by the death of a woman at North Shields, killed by a shell fired from a Royal Navy ship by some youths.

Post War Tyneside.

After the Second World War there was a new found prosperity on Tyneside, order books were full and unemployment was at an all time low. Under the 1945 Distribution of Industry Act, the area became designated as the North East Development Area. There was a concerted effort to attract new businesses. Lighter industries such as textiles, electrical goods, clothing and light engineering came to the North East.

By 1952 twenty industrial estates had been built, providing twenty-six thousand jobs in one hundred and eighty-four factories. Throughout the 1950's the North East experienced low levels of unemployment (two to four per cent), partly due to a high demand for industrial staples, coal and steel.

Public health improved too, there were far fewer deaths from tuberculosis, and the introduction of smoke emission controls in 1958 helped reduce the previously high rate of chest disease. Indeed, the amount of sunshine reaching the city increased by a half.

During this period, however, there were undercurrents that went unnoticed. Tyneside had escaped virtually unscathed from the Luftwaffe's bombing and the bulk of post-war investment went to the Midlands and London, where vast areas had been decimated.

By the 1950's the shipyards, which had been working at full capacity throughout the war, had become outdated. There had been insufficient investment to bring them up to modern standards. Meanwhile, countries like Japan and Germany had been able to rebuild their own industries, virtually from scratch, using the latest technology. In the face of competition from these modern yards, and with the collapse in the tanker market following the Suez crisis in 1956, the yards began to founder.

Coal

The coal industry was nationalised on January 1st 1947. The new National Coal Board initially closed nineteen local pits, although production remained buoyant for a time. The turning point came when cheap Middle Eastern oil flooded the country in the late 1950's. There followed devasting closures in the Coal Board's North East Region - the number of pits fell from one hundred and fifty-six to twenty-eight in just two decades. The trend continued into the 1980's which saw another bout of closures after the 1984 miners' strike.

The coal industry on Tyneside is now a mere shell of its former self. Only one colliery remains, the 'long life' Westoe Pit in South Shields. British Coal has recently focused its attention on this type of 'super pit' which will ensure coal production into the next century. The discovery of over two hundred million tonnes of coal off the coast of Tyne and Wear led to millions of pounds being invested. Eventually Westoe will produce three thousand tonnes a day, securing two thousand jobs in the process.

The Dunston Coal Staiths, built by the North East Railway Co. to export County Durham coal.

One of the few remaining landmarks of the industry on the Tyne are the Dunston Coal Staiths. The staiths were completed in 1893, one of the largest wooden structures in the world. They were closed by British Rail in 1983. After renovation the staiths are expected to become a major attraction at the 1990 Gateshead Garden Festival. The Coal Board now operates only three sites for shipping coal on the river, Harton and the Tyne Coal Terminal near South Shields and the Jarrow Staiths. These export all over Europe and as far afield as Morocco. In 1987 these final outlets exported almost four million tonnes of coal.

Further Slump

With rising unemployment throughout the country, the Government had to act. The 1960 Local Employment Act pinpointed areas with the unacceptably high unemployment level of four and a half per cent, a figure which today's government would be proud (and unlikely) to achieve. By 1963 this covered the whole North East region. The main thrust of the Act was to provide and develop further trading estates, and the provision of a grants system aimed at attracting branch plants into the area.

Little, however, could stop the demise of heavy industry. Between 1961 and 1972 sixty thousand jobs were lost in mining alone, with the shipyards losing a further sixteen thousand. The task of bringing the area back to its feet was charged to Lord Hailsham who was designated as minister for the North East. He co-ordinated a programme designed to diversify and modernise the region. This involved investment in roads, factories and industrial estates; the redevelopment of town centres; improved housing; and land reclamation.

The region faced other problems, particularly about its image, perceived by some people as being grey, too far away from London and having poor labour relations. To combat this the The Hailsham plan also recommended the building of New Towns such as Washington, designed in 1964. These were to offer potential employers attractive Greenfield sites. The new industry that came to these areas offered employment to the residents of the old slums that were being cleared in and around Newcastle.

Despite these measures the last twenty-five years have seen continued high unemployment on Tyneside. The hardest hit areas have been in engineering and shipbuilding. Faced with competition from overseas and falling profits, several yards merged in 1968 under Swan-Hunter. This was not enough - by the early 1970's Tyneside had seen its share of the world's shipbuilding market fall from thirty per cent to just two per cent. The final blow came in 1973 with the OPEC oil price increases, virtually destroying the industry along the Tyne. The Labour government was forced to nationalise the yards in 1977 or be faced with the total collapse of the industry.

Overall, however, compared to the early 1980's the actual number of jobs lost was fairly low (just over three per cent). Throughout the demise of industry the city itself was changing. The growth of public sector services such as health, education and public administration soaked up losses from heavy industry.

The switch from heavy industry to these public services has been a major influence on the city's development. Together with the extensive city centre renewal this has served to strengthen Newcastle itself as a regional capital.

Regeneration.

The Good The Bad and The Ugly

During the 1960's and early 70's Newcastle city centre entered a phase of change and development that continues to this day. City planners in the 1950's recognised that Newcastle city centre was in severe danger of grinding to a halt. Changes in commercial activity, the insatiable public obsession with the motor car and the increase in leisure time, all had to be catered for. Something had to be done to give the people of Newcastle a city to be proud of.

As a result, a city wide development programme was born, on a scale unheard of since Grainger and Dobson's day; a programme designed to take Newcastle into the future. Pedestrians were to be separated from the traffic in a split level city, new amenities would be provided and a new educational quarter founded. At the same time the council, led by T. Dan Smith, recognized the importance of preserving the city's historical heart. Top planners and architects were consulted, as were the general public, to ensure that the new developments would be functional and yet would blend in with the history and traditions of the city. In Dan Smith's own words: *"[I] wanted to see the creation of a twentieth century equivalent of Dobson's masterpiece, and its integration into the historic framework of the city. If this could be achieved, I felt, then our regional capital would become the outstanding provincial city in our country"*.

The cheerless history of the Royal Arcade. Grainger's grand building in 1832, shortly after completion; its demolition in 1963; and its replacement.

The career of T. Dan Smith, the driving force behind the 60's 'renewal', is every bit as controversial as some of the projects he inspired. The son of an intensely political Durham miner, Smith entered the council in 1950. He did himself no favours by criticising them during his maiden speech. Smith eventually became council leader, and then moved on to become chairman of the Northern Economic Planning Council where he conceived and steered through many of the plans for the Newcastle redevelopments.

Whilst with the council, allegations of corruption and fraud arose over building contracts in which Smith had not declared an interest. In 1962 he met Yorkshire architect John Poulson, and became entwined in the infamous web of corruption. Eventually twenty-one people were sent to prison on corruption charges, including Smith who was jailed for six years.

The plans were very much a product of their age and have been justifiably criticised since. Despite the sentiment for preservation, space still had to be found for the new office blocks, shopping centres and motorways. The destruction of many old buildings was considered inevitable. Even though some of the areas cleared were run down, many feel that regeneration would have been more appropriate. Today many of the 60's and 70's buildings sit uneasily alongside the townscape of Grainger and Dobson or the remnants of the medieval and Elizabethan town.

Buildings that appeared bold and exciting as architect's models twenty years ago now present a rain-stained concrete, blot on the skyline. It is remarkable that office blocks such as the large and offensive Westgate House - sprawling over Westgate Road and in sight of the medieval church of St. John, Dobson's Central Station and the historic Literary and Philosophical Society - were ever given planning permission.

Perhaps fortunately, the city as it is now is very much a compromise on what might have been. The vision of a split level city - an ingenious way of separating people and traffic - never came to fruition. Though it is still possible to walk from the Central Library to Manors multistorey car park without having to descend to road level. Similar walkways, such as those linking Eldon Square with proposed offices on the other side of Percy Street, were never built.

The changing face of Eldon Square.

Eldon Square itself is much smaller than originally envisaged. Early models and plans of the Centre incorporated shops, offices and homes. The focal point was to be a thirty-two storey aluminium clad hotel situated in the south-west corner of Eldon Green. That project eventually proved too expensive. On the other side of the Green the last remaining terrace of old Eldon Square had originally been earmarked for demolition. A whole block of shops, with parking above, would have stretched along Percy Street almost to where the Haymarket Metro Station now stands.

There were also plans for a modern church, next to what is now the Percy Street multistorey car park, and a cinema, which eventually became the Recreation Centre. Building work on the ten-acre site was started in June 1973 and completed by September 1976, at a cost of some £60 million. Other building projects in the plan included the Newgate Shopping Centre and Hotel, the Central Library, Civic Centre and the new educational quarter.

The council recognised the importance of good educational facilities, and the benefits to be gained from building them within close proximity to one another. Having the University and Polytechnic within walking distance of each other would allow the sharing of facilities and the pooling of knowledge. It would also integrate the student population. During the holidays the facilities could be used for the conference trade, again attracting people into the city centre.

Drawing people to the city centre was a key part of the plans. The place would buzz with shoppers and office workers by day, whilst providing central living accommodation for locals and students alike would bring the city to life at night. The same theory was applied to the proposed regeneration of the Quayside areas. New offices were to be built there, along with student accommodation, shops, pubs and theatres. With the exception of a few office blocks, such as the All Saints Office Complex, few of these ideas came about - many of them, however, are reflected in the latest plans for Quayside regeneration.

A vital part of the plans was the removal of through traffic from the city centre. A new and complex motorway system was designed to divert traffic around the city centre. Two north-south routes and two east-west routes, one of which would pass under Northumberland Street and the Haymarket, were considered essential, even in the 1960's. There was a further proposal for another north-south route, a bypass to the central motorway east, which would have meant building another high level crossing of the Tyne.

Of these only the Central Motorway East and Claremont Road section have been built, completed in 1972. In order to relieve the Tyne Bridge, which is now overloaded, the concept of the Central Motorway West, from the new Redheugh Bridge to the Haymarket, has now been resurrected, albeit as a continental boulevard.

The 1980's

There have been further developments in the 1980's. Many of these are directly related to the original fifties ideas - though the presence of Europe's largest out of town shopping complex across the river has undoubtedly influenced the planners. Eldon Square appears in an almost continuous state of expansion. The first addition was the Eldon Square Food Court, which involved the demolition of a number of properties along Newgate Street; including an antiques centre, The Adelaide Pub, and some small ıe Civic Centre, designed by the ty Architect George Kenyon, hich was completed in 1968. It s an ellipitical Council Chamber d the focal point is the façade on e North Road. The tower is owned with a lantern and a acon, designed to mirror the own of the cathedral, and ntains a carillion of twenty-five lls which play a selection of cal tunes.

shops. The new Eldon Gardens have been built on, and over, Percy Street - entailing the demolition of the Edwardian Handyside Arcade (home of the legendary sixties Club-a-Go-Go which saw the likes of the Rolling Stones, the Animals and Jimi Hendrix in their heydays) as well as surrounding buildings. The pedestrian footbridge over Blackett Street has also been enlarged to incorporate a new store.

Further shopping facilities have been provided by the Queens Shopping Arcade, on the site of the Queens Cinema. Up-market flats have been built at Leazes Square. New multistorey car parks, adding hundreds of spaces, have been built at John Dobson Street and Eldon Gardens - whilst the University have created a few dozen parking spaces of their own by demolishing the Haymarket Cinema and Tavern.

The Suburbs.

Council house building in post-war Tyneside has undergone several phases. After the initial slum clearances of the late 1950's the council has adopted several different plans. During the 1960's several areas, such as Scotswood and Shieldfield, received their now much maligned high rise flats.

During the 1970's a different approach was used - the building of low rise, high density flats and houses and the improvement of older properties. Care was taken to ensure a pleasant landscaped environment. Within the new council estates pedestrian walkways were given priority, and where possible cars were kept to side streets. More emphasis was placed on involving the community during planning and rebuilding, none more so than with the most controversial scheme, the Byker Wall.

The Wall's architect, Ralph Erskine, had noted that previous housing schemes adopted by the council frequently split up close knit communities. He stringently avoided making the same mistakes. The result of this work is a wall of houses nearly a mile long, varying between five and nine stories in height. The north wall was designed to act as a wind break and noise barrier against a proposed new motorway. Inside there are traffic free walkways and gardens.

Polls carried out have shown a favourable response from the residents, perhaps the best assessment of one of the most radical housing schemes in Europe - *"Possibly the most brilliant solution to the problem of modern urban mass housing"*.

The Byker Wall.

Private house building has dramatically increased the size of Newcastle's suburbs since the war, with home ownership and commuting becoming more common. This has also encouraged out of town commercial developments such as at Kingston Park and the Regent Centre. More recently there has been a turn around with people moving back towards the centre, a trend which is becoming more popular. The Quayside, Jesmond and Sandyford are becoming fashionable areas to live in and for the first time in hundreds of years, professionals are living near to or in the city centre.

Transport.

From Tram to Metro

Great changes in Newcastle's public transport network have come about during the twentieth century. Electric trams continued in use until 1950 but were phased out in preference to the trolley bus. These first appeared on Tyneside in 1935, covering the route between Wallsend and Denton Square in the city's West End. The buses had the same impact on the city's residents as electric trams had thirty years earlier, and the main routes were always crowded. The network covered twenty-one miles by the outbreak of the Second World War, although only a limited service operated during the war years. After 1945 the trolley buses faced increasing competition from the much more flexible omnibus. These had been introduced before World War One but until the 1940's had operated mainly in the city's more remote suburbs.

By the 1960's it was clear that the days of the trolley bus were numbered. The rolling stock was old and maintenance costs soared. They were to be last seen on Newcastle's streets in 1966. That decade also saw the demise of the electric train on the coast route. Many of the trains dated back to the turn of the century and could not compete with the motor car. By the time of their withdrawal from service the line was costing British Rail £300,000 a year. They were replaced by diesel units which continued to operate on the route until the introduction of the Metro in 1980.

The Metro is one of the world's most modern public transit systems. It follows the route of the old railway, with a spur going to Bankfoot, and soon on towards Newcastle Airport. The service began in June 1980, albeit on a limited scale. At present there are forty-two stations on the system, focused on the Monument in the city centre, with Palmersville, on the northern route, being the most recent addition.

A unique feature of the system was the way in which Metro services were fully integrated with the bus routes. One effect of this was to cut down the number of buses within the city centre. Unfortunately the Government's controversial de-regulation of public transport in 1987 has lead to a great increase in bus traffic as rival companies compete with each other, much to the detriment of the city as a whole.

The Queen Elizabeth II Bridge was built as a crossing for the Metro, linking Central Station with Gateshead Interchange. It was designed by W.A. Fairhurst and Partners (Northern) and built by the Cleveland Bridge and Engineering Company. Construction was started in 1976 and completed on August 1st 1978. It was opened by the Queen on November 6th 1981.

The face of modern Tyneside. A Metro hurries across the Queen Elizabeth II Bridge.

End of an Era.

Throughout the early seventies the number of jobs in manufacturing fell continually, as they did throughout the country. This trend was slowed down by the policy of opening branch plants. By 1978 almost a third of the area's jobs were in manufacturing, whilst four and a half per cent were in mining. Unemployment was still a problem as the service sectors did not replace the kind of jobs that were being lost. Male employment has been particularly hard hit.

From 1978 to 1986 there was a dramatic change in the whole economy. Total employment fell drastically and once again it was heavy industry that suffered the most. The situation intensified as many branch plants, which had been actively encouraged in the previous decade, began closing down. The vast majority of companies have their bases outside the region. With no real affiliation to the North East it is not surprising that they began to pull out when the going got tough.

Closures and rationalisation led to sixty-one thousand job losses between 1976 and 1981. NEI, for instance, shed some seven thousand employees and shifted towards overseas investment. Vickers reorganised production, closing the old Elswick and Scotswood works and building a new tank factory at Scotswood within the Enterprise Zone. Another ten thousand jobs went from the shipyards, with the government closing down shipbuilding on the Wear completely. There is a rolling coal closure programme, and the steel yards at Consett have shut down losing three and a half thousand jobs.

By March 1986 unemployment in the region was at nineteen per cent (compared to thirteen and a half per cent nationally). With a growing number of those classed as 'employed' working on government schemes, even this figure does not reflect the true impact of unemployment. Many of the individual communities which fuelled industry on the Tyne have become wasted themselves. In July 1985 unemployment in Elswick Park was forty-six per cent.

With the demise of heavy industry, the area's lifeblood for so many centuries, the city and people of Newcastle faced a challenge. Forward thinking in the 1950's and 60's helped ease the blow. Whatever people may think of their architectural qualities, the transition from industrial giant to service sector city would have been difficult without the likes of Swan House, Eldon Square, The Polytechnic or the Central Library. Almost three-quarters of the working population are now employed in shops, offices and with the council. The DHSS at Longbenton is the biggest office complex in Europe and houses the largest concentration of public workers outside the Pentagon.

Unfortunately for many of those directly involved nothing can replace the living to be had from digging coal or building ships. While the city itself apparently thrives, poverty still persists - especially in the old industrial areas such as Scotswood and Elswick. The gulf between rich and poor is perhaps as wide as it ever was.

Newcastle in the 1990's.

Newcastle Now

Despite continuing poverty in some areas, Newcastle has the appearance of a prosperous city. One look at Northumberland Street or Eldon Square on a Saturday afternoon is enough to dispel any notion that the North East is an area of depression and misery. Shoppers throng the streets, accompanied on almost every corner by street entertainers.

If anything the city centre gets even busier at night. Drinking is still as popular a pastime as it ever was, although the traditional public house is virtually extinct in the centre, having been replaced by image conscious bars, complete with flashing lights, high prices, doormen - and queues to get in!

Live music of all types, from piano sing alongs to wild accordionists, can be found most nights at various venues throughout the city.

Newcastle is justifiably recognised as being a hotbed of popular music. The area has already produced many world famous musicians, from Hank Marvin and the Animals through to Lindisfarne and on to the likes of Sting and Mark Knoplfer. It has a thriving music culture with as great a potential to change the city's image as that accomplished by Liverpool during the Beatles' era. Riverside Entertainments in Melbourne Street is now nationally recognised as one of the country's leading music venues. A prime example of young local people doing things for themselves and for the benefit of the community.

The tradition of live theatre, started in the Middle Ages with the Corpus Christi plays, carries on in the recently renovated Theatre Royal - surely one of the best venues in the country. Together with the New Tyne Theatre, it ensures major touring companies are attracted to the city - including the eagerly awaited annual visit of the Royal Shakespeare Company. The city also has its small independently run playhouses, such as the University's Gulbenkien and Playhouse;

The *Light Programme* jazz group, often seen at the Monument.

Chapter 10

the People's Theatre in Heaton; and the Live Theatre on Broad Chare.

Trips to the 'flicks' are becoming more popular, witnessed by the decision to build a multi-screen complex at Manors. There is also the independent Tyneside Cinema; supported by Northern Arts, the British Film Institute, and the Council, showing the more exotic and unusual movies, and host to the annual Tyneside Film Festival.

Sport is as popular as ever. Skulling and bear baiting have been replaced by athletics and football. The International Stadium at Gateshead regularly hosts major athletics meetings. The Great North Run, part of the Great North Festival, is Europe's biggest road race. Thirty thousand people attempt the thirteen miles between Newcastle and South Shields. The event is always well supported, thousands of people lining the route to cheer on the competitors - many of whom run to raise money for charity. The race is destined to become as much a part of Geordie folklore as the Blaydon Races.

One sport above all others dominates the North East - football. Since the turn of the century thousands have taken part in the ritual of making their way to St. James Park to watch ninety minutes of sporting action.

Newcastle United

The roots of Newcastle United Football Club go back over a hundred years when two local cricket clubs, in need of some close season action, decided to branch out into football. They formed what were to become Newcastle East End and Newcastle West End respectively. Up until 1888 West End, who played at St. James Park, had been the premier club. Then, following the defection of their influential manager Tom Watson, the Westerners found themselves forced to join up with the East.

Playing in the Northern League the newly strengthened East End club suffered poor attendances and general apathy from the public. In 1892 they hit upon the masterstroke of renaming the club 'Newcastle United' and the following year earned their first point in the Football League (Division Two) when the team, wearing the now famous black and white stripes for the first time, drew 2-2 at Woolwich Arsenal. Two thousand people turned up for the return match, which Newcastle won 6-0, signalling the start of Tyneside's long and frustrating love affair with the 'mighty' Magpies.

St. James Park under construction.

Match fever reached a peak eight years later when seventy thousand people watched a home game against Sunderland - despite the fact that the ground only held thirty thousand. The match was called off due to the ensuing riot.

By the end of the 1911/12 season 'The Toon' had been in five FA Cup finals and won the League Championship three times - winning their first double in 1904/05 when one hundred and one thousand people watched them beat Aston Villa in the Cup Final.

In the years that followed the club suffered mixed fortunes. They won the FA Cup twice more and added another First Division championship to their tally. They were also demoted for the first time, in 1933/34, and very nearly sank to the Third Division - only

Michael O'Neill takes on Chris Hughes of Spurs.

Local hero Kevin Keegan, with Chris Waddle at Kenny Wharton's testimonial in 1989.

being saved by their superior goal average (one tenth of a goal).

In the 1950's United began their second Golden Era. Having clambered back into the First Division the team won three famous FA Cup victories - led by Tyneside hero Jackie Milburn. In the 1955 final Wor Jackie scored the fastest ever goal at Wembley (forty-five seconds), in what was to be the club's last major domestic title to date.

Recent successes have been few and far between. Surprising, considering the team's unrivalled support, and the North East provides more first class footballers per head than any other region. There must be few local youngsters who have not at one time or another dreamt of pulling on a black (or red) and white shirt.

The club's last major trophy was in 1968 when, during their first campaign in Europe, they won the inter-cities Fairs Cup - beating Ujpest 6-2 on aggregate. Since then the club has struggled to regain past glories. The most notable achievement in recent years has been the 1984/85 campaign when one million people watched the Kevin Keegan inspired Magpies, complete with future England players Chris Waddle, Paul Gascoigne and Peter Beardsley, climb out of the Second Division.

After failing to build on the foundations left by the Keegan era the Club is now back in the doldrums. The 1988/89 season has to go down as the saddest on record - both on and off the park. Jackie Milburn died in October 1988 and the centre of Newcastle ground to a halt as thousands lined the streets to pay their last respects. There can be few cities where a retired sportsman can generate such warmth and affection amongst its people. Later in the year two more members of the legendary 1950's team died, Joe Harvey, another who had always remained close to the club, and George Robledo. On the field the team managed to string together its worst ever set of results, finishing bottom of the Division for the first time.

What the future holds for Newcastle United is entirely in the hands of to its current Board of Directors, whose record speaks for itself. The club can, and should, play a major part in the coming regeneration of the area. It is clear that when United are playing well the whole city has an aura of optimism. It is surely time that the club which has at one time or another boasted the highest league attendance; the most FA Cup Final appearances; the fastest Wembley Cup Final goal; the first Brazilian in the Football League; the unofficial fastest goal of all time (Malcom Macdonald: four seconds from a kick off); and the tallest floodlights, took its rightful place amongst the country's leading teams.

United playing spot the ball, something they became very good at during the 1988/89 season.

Regeneration.

Today, Newcastle looks forward to a bright future as the region embarks on a phase of unprecedented rebuilding and regeneration. Derelict and run down land is being brought back into use. Areas of neglect within the city centre are being improved. New life and new civilisation is being brought to places which had been left to decay with the decline of heavy industry. Swan Hunters, NEI and Vickers are all that remain, as testimony to the world's mightiest industrial region. Most of the shipyards and docks, however, have gone, to be replaced by modern factory units, offices and leisure facilities.

The Tyne, for so long the artery which supplied the world with coal, ships and arms, is now becoming a place for leisure and recreation - indeed, the once *"coaly coaly Tyne"* is now claimed to be one of the best salmon rivers in the country.

Where once stood the fetid grime and filth of the old chares, there now stand up-market flats and houses. Hotels, shops, restaurants and bars are sprouting up along the waterfront.

Large areas of the city centre have also been earmarked for improvement. This has not meant wholesale demolitions and the loss of parts of the city's heritage as would have been the case in the past. Buildings that are under-used or unsuitable for today's needs are being modernised, in some cases almost completely rebuilt - without the loss of their impressive façades. Streets are being tidied, buildings cleaned and new pedestrianisation plans put into effect.

Much of the initial regeneration has been charged to the Tyne and Wear Development Corporation, set up by the Government in 1987. The whole TWDC development area covers almost two and a half thousand hectares of prime inner urban sites along both the Tyne and the Wear. The first stage is to reclaim and prepare these sites, including improving access, ready for development. This is expected to cost some £94 million. The TWDC will then be able to use its £28 million budget to support both local and incoming business. At the same time part of the TWDC's philosophy is to improve the environment that people live and work in, by providing good quality housing and social facilities.

By 1995 twenty-five acres of derelict land on the East Quayside, from the Milk Market to Ouseburn, will have been transformed into the *"Jewel in the Crown"* of the city wide schemes Specialist shopping, cafés, offices,

Assembling a generator at the Heaton Works of NEI Parsons Ltd, Newcastle upon Tyne.

a five-star hotel, an exhibition centre and new homes will be housed in an ambitious series of buildings along the waterfront.

At the eastern end of this development will be the new Ouseburn Village - built around the mouth of a cleaned up Ouseburn and stretching as far upstream as the historic Glasshouse Bridge.

Westwards, the central Quayside is also being improved. The imposing new multi-million pound courthouse stands on Broad Chare. Properties such as the Exchange Buildings, Baltic Chambers and those at the lower end of Dean Street and on Sandhill are being upgraded as office accommodation and luxury flats. A new hotel is being built on the Close, complete with leisure and conference facilities.

New industrial and business parks are also being established. The sixty acre Newcastle Business Park is taking shape on the old shipyard site at Elswick. It will provide low density units for offices or 'high-tech' businesses, as well as 'service units' for shops and pubs. This one park alone is expected to provide one and a half thousand jobs.

A new science park is being built at Manors. Businesses based here will be able to capitalise on the nearby University and Polytechnic, providing invaluable research facilities. The Science Park should prove an ideal springboard for industries of the future - biotechnology, electronics, materials technology and advanced manufacturing systems - whose establishment here is vital if the city and the region is to remain a dynamic manufacturing centre.

This type of initiative will build upon the success of the many high technology companies already in the region, such as MARI - a computer research group established only ten years ago. There are also smaller companies, such as Public Access Terminals in the St. Thomas Street Stables - who are leaders in computer technology and export throughout the world. The Stables are a prime example of local industry supporting small business initiatives in the city.

Vast areas of riverside, right down to the coast, have been pencilled in for redevelopment. Executives will be able to live at the new St. Peter's Basin riverside village - complete with a marina (*"if a purchaser has a boat, he will be able to moor it practically at the front door"*). There is to be an Offshore Technology Park near Walker, the Albert Edward Dock and surrounding land owned by the Port of Tyne is being prepared for redevelopment, and there are similar plans for the Tyne Dock and other areas on the south bank.

Away from the river, the Newcastle Initiative is assisting regeneration along Grey Street and Westgate Road. This campaign, centred around the Grey Street and Theatre Village Initiatives, was established by the CBI and is championed by leading figures in the life of the city.

The Grey Street Initiative aims to capitalise on the prestige of one of Europe's finest streets to draw in new office based businesses. In recent years the magnificent buildings have been underleased. There is now a boom in the office-market and there is a high demand for space, and listed buildings like those on Grey and Dean Streets are seen as prime sites.

The one hundred and fifty year old buildings are not always ideal for a modern office environment and drastic renovations are often needed. In some cases this means rebuilding all but the façade, such as at the Lloyds Bank building at the top of Grey Street. By carrying out such work the area not only retains its unique heritage but the buildings become a valuable resource contributing to the local economy, which is, after all, what they were designed for in the first place.

Further office space is to be made available following work around the Lying-in Hospital, resulting in the demolition of the last known city centre pub with an outside toilet.

The whole city wide programme is epitomised by the Theatre Village project and Westgate Road improvements. This is an ambitious scheme to bring together arts, leisure and housing into a single community. It is centred around the New Tyne Theatre - one of the few Victorian opera houses left in the country. The village aims to be able to combine live entertainment with training facilities in all aspects of theatre, both on and off the stage. The whole atmosphere of the village, with its street cafés and buskers, is expected to make it *"One of the most desired inner city residential locations in Britain"*.

Unfortunately, the village idyll is somewhat shattered by the decision to build a dual carriageway right through its centre. The city has 'needed' a new through town route for a number of years. It will run from the Redheugh Bridge to Percy Street, via Blenheim Street and Gallowgate, and will entail the demolition of a number of properties along its route. To lessen its impact, the road will be built as a *"continental boulevard"*, with a landscaped central reservation and wide pavements that will be *"attractive to the eye"*. How they intend to disguise the traffic is a different matter.

The ultimate aim of all these developments is to reconstruct the local economy. Investment has been put at £300 million, providing around six thousand jobs in construction, services and industry, and attracting tourism and business.

It is interesting to compare the rhetoric surrounding the new schemes with that of 1960's and early 70's, when the talk was of building a city of the future. There are similarities. The underlying aims are the same, bringing the city back to life, encouraging investment, and improving both the environment and the quality of life. Then, as now, it was the aim of the planners and developers to choose the best in contemporary design and materials. It is, however, surely inconceivable that today's architects will repeat the mistakes of their predecessors. It remains to be seen whether they will manage to cross the more difficult hurdles of producing striking, original designs which will, at the same time, harmonise with the unique cityscape that is Newcastle.

A more controversial aspect of the redevelopments is the slashing of red tape in order to speed up the rebuilding process. Some have seen this as a blow to local democracy. Land or building owners who have ideas which are not entirely compatible with the planner's thinking are quite likely to be persuaded otherwise - in the last resort, via the threat of a compulsory purchase order. Developers with good ideas will find the path laden with incentives to go ahead with their own particular schemes.

The foundations for the future have already been laid, ensuring that Newcastle has a head start in the regeneration game. The city has unrivalled retail facilities in Eldon Square, not to mention the nearby Metro Centre. There are excellent educational opportunities, some thirty thousand students study at the University, the Polytechnic - with its nationally renowned Fashion Design Centre - and the College of Art and Technology. The area also has outstanding transport facilities with the Metro and Newcastle International Airport, as well as steadily improving road links and the rapidly approaching East Coast Rail electrification.

Another major advantage is Newcastle's position at the centre of a region that is already attracting new investment, spearheaded by the proliferation of Japanese industrial interests such as Nissan and Komatsu. With the number of initiatives going on around the city it seems that Newcastle is destined to have a bright future.

Visitors to Newcastle are often surprised by what they see. Stereotypes are difficult to dispel. Perhaps in the future that surprise will not be quite so marked. People should arrive with high expectations - of a historic city proud of its heritage and yet thoroughly modern. They will certainly leave with those expectations fulfilled.

Further Reading.

Any new history is indebted to the works of the historians that preceded it. William Gray wrote the first history of the town, the *Chorographia or Survey of Newcastle upon Tyne*, published in 1649. It was recently reprinted and still provides a fascinating insight into the town's early history. This was followed by Henry Bourne's 1736 history and the 1789 history by John Brand. Brand's two volumes are the best of the early accounts of the town's development. The nineteenth century saw Eneas Mackenzie's useful guide in 1827 and R. J. Charleton's history of 1882. The most recent comprehensive history, Sidney Middlebrook's *Newcastle upon Tyne: its growth and achievement*, was first published in 1950. This is the best of the histories on the later development of the town.

These books are ideal sources for the local historian to start plotting the history of Newcastle. Other useful sources include P. M. Horsley's *Eighteenth Century Newcastle* (1971) and R. Welford's *History of Newcastle and Gateshead* (1884-1887). Professor Howell has done a great deal of work on the Civil War, much of which can be found in Archaeoligia Aeliana (AA) or in *Newcastle upon Tyne and the Puritan Revolution* (1967).

For readers seeking an overall survey of northern archaeology N.J. Higham's *The Northern Counties to AD 1000* (1986) is a recent boon. Newcastle's archaeological past is best covered by R. B. Harbottle and P. A. G. Clack's *Newcastle upon Tyne: Archaeology and Development* in *Archaeology in the North* (1976).

Newcastle's Roman remains are best discussed in J Collingwood Bruce's *Handbook to the Roman Wall*, edited by C. M. Daniels, 1978. The Wall's context in the history of the Roman frontier is covered by D. J. Breeze and B. Dobson in *Hadrian's Wall* (1976).

For the early medieval period R. Cramp's *Anglo-Saxon settlement* in Chapman and Mytum's *Settlement in North Britain, 1000BC - AD1000* is a good survey to supplement Higham. W. E. Kapelle's *The Norman Conquest of the North.* (1979) provides a detailed discussion on the hard fought struggle to integrate the North East into the English Kingdom. The general background to medieval towns is splendidly covered by Colin Platt's *The English Medieval Town* (1976).

The important early work on the the medieval buildings of Newcastle was undertaken by W. H. Knowles and published in various volumes of AA from 1880 to 1926. Work on the medieval archaeology of Newcastle since 1960 is covered in successive volumes of AA, with articles by a variety of archaeologists. The first stage on the important work on the Quayside is covered by Colm O'Brian et al in *The Origins of the Newcastle Quayside*, (1988).

It is probably best to cover industrialism on Tyneside through histories of the individual industries. Try David Dougan's *History of North East Shipbuilding* (1968); R. Colls' *Pitmen of the North Coalfield; Work, Culture and Protest 1790-1850* (1978); Michael Flinn's *The History of the British Coal Industry* (1984); and K. Hoole's *A Regional History of the Railways of Great Britain. Volume Four - The North East* (1965). James Rush's *A Beilby Odyssey* (1987) covers the glass industry, and the work of the Beilbys and Thomas Bewick.

It is harder to find texts on the city's social history. There are valuable sections in the *Historical Atlas of Newcastle upon Tyne* (1980), edited by John Buswell and Mike Barke. This was written by Geography lecturers from Newcastle Polytechnic for the 'Newcastle 900' celebrations. Recent history has been covered in *Post Industrial Tyneside. An economic and social survey of Tyneside in the 1980's (1988)*, edited by F. Robinson. This studies the effects of the region's industrial decline and switch to a 'service sector' city.

Nicholaus Pevsner is the most invaluable source on the city's buildings, (*The Buildings of England: Northumberland* (1957), N Pevsner and Ian Richmond). Since then the Department of Environment has produced *A List of buildings of special architectural or historic interest. The City and County of Newcastle upon Tyne* (1974). The 1830's improvements have received wide attention, the best are *John Dobson: Newcastle architect* (1987) by A. Greg and T. Faulkner: and L. Wilkes and G. Dodds', *Tyneside Classical.* (1964). This traces the careers of the Triumverate - Dobson, Grainger and Clayton - and the events leading to the building of Classical Newcastle. The City Guides published by the Council, which are readily available from the Library or the city's Tourist Information Centres, provide short histories on a whole range of the city's buildings.

Index.